A Gospel Contrary!

A GOSPEL CONTRARY!

A Study of Roman Catholic Abuse
of History and Scripture
to Propagate Error

FIRST EDITION

Kauffman & Zins

Table of Contents

About the Authors

Timothy F. Kauffman, author of *Quite Contrary: A Biblical Reconsideration of the Apparitions of Mary* and *Graven Bread: The Papacy, the Apparitions of Mary, and the Worship of the Bread of the Altar*, lives in Starkville, MS and is married to Jennifer with whom he has four children. Kauffman is a regular contributor to ThornCrown Ministries (thorncrownministries.com), producing *The Diving Board* and *The Danielic Imperative* podcasts. He also writes regularly at his blog, Out of His Mouth at whitehorseblog.com and is a contributor to *The Trinity Review*.

Robert M. Zins, author of *Romanism: The Relentless Roman Catholic Assault on the Gospel of Jesus Christ!* and *On the Edge of Apostasy: The Evangelical Romance with Rome* is the director of *A Christian Witness to Roman Catholicism* and holds a Master of Theology degree from Dallas Theological Seminary, a Master of Education degree from Springfield College, and a Bachelor of Arts degree in Political Science from Alma College. Zins has written extensively and has produced over 50 videos for *Christian Answers* in Austin, Texas. He has produced a number of booklets, videos, pamphlets on the Roman Catholic religious system. His website, CWRC, may be visited at CWRC-RZ.Org where materials are available.

Commendations for
A Gospel Contrary!

"This work by Kauffman and Zins answers one of Rome's most prominent apologists with Scripture and plain reason. Reminiscent of Luther's *Bondage of the Will*, their bold, exhaustive polemic pulls no punches when dismantling Patrick Madrid's lofty claims and the zeitgeist of false ecumenism. As a former Romanist, I would've benefited from this book then, though I'm blessed by it now, and hope to share it with our church and with those still ensnared by Romish devices."

> —Carlos E. Montijo
> ThornCrown Ministries, El Paso, TX
> ThornCrownMinistries.com

"With a culture that has turned its back on the word of God, it is no wonder that false gospels, such as Rome's gospel of justification by faith and works, continue to flourish. By many accounts, it appears that we are returning to pre-reformation darkness, which is why this book is a must-have for those who will stand for truth. *A Gospel Contrary!* is a brilliant and devastating response to the world's foremost Roman Catholic apologist Patrick Madrid. Kauffman and Zins leave no stone unturned in their examination and refutation of Madrid's Romanist teachings."

> —Tim Shaughnessy
> ThornCrown Ministries, El Paso, TX
> ThornCrownMinistries.com

"We live in an age when many professing Christians are too lazy to use the 'plumb line' of God's only infallible word, the Bible, as a standard to examine what people say and write. This is especially true when it comes to the history and teachings of Roman Catholicism. Over 500 years ago, spiritually-enlightened men of God exposed just how non-Christian Roman Catholicism truly is. Their Spirit-given wisdom is in short supply in much of professing Christendom today. *A Gospel Contrary!* is a worthy effort by Kauffman and Zins to rekindle the flames of the true, Reformation Gospel."

> —Cecil Andrews
> Take Heed Ministries, Ballynahinch, Northern Ireland
> www.takeheed.info

"According to Barna and other polls 87% of Evangelical Christians do not know what the Biblical gospel is or what justification by faith alone is. Thus Satan's masterpiece of Roman Catholicism is in a perfect position for complete deception with its false gospel in this sad spiritual environment. Christian theologians and authors Timothy Kauffman and Rob Zins with their decades of experience have brought forth their latest work, *A Gospel Contrary!,* which is an excellent resource for true Christians wishing to reach Catholics with the truth of the gospel of the Scriptures instead of fabricated traditions of men."

> —Larry Wessels
> Director, Christian Answers, Austin, TX (YouTube channel
> https://www.youtube.com/user/CAnswersTV)

"Kauffman and Zins do a masterful job of dismantling the arguments of Roman Catholic apologist, Patrick Madrid as found in his popular book *Answer Me This!* Madrid's claims appear solid when not examined closely, but they hold little water when analyzed by those who have done serious research into church history and do careful biblical exegesis. In addition, in refuting Madrid's theology, *A Gospel Contrary!* exposes numerous false teachings propagated by Catholicism. It serves as a valuable reference work for those wanting a reliable resource for understanding the heretical doctrines of Rome."

—Gary Gilley
Pastor, Southern View Chapel, Springfield, IL
Director, Think on These Things Ministries
SvChapel.org

"To Protestants: Are we still protesting the false religion of Roman Catholicism? Timothy Kauffman and Rob Zins certainly are, as evidenced by this book, *A Gospel Contrary!* They thoroughly and scholarly dissect, expose and rebuke Patrick Madrid's blatant attempt to misrepresent and twist the Scriptures, the church fathers, and then impose other inventions of this false religion. It is an encouragement and reaffirmation of grace-loving Christians to know that we have a sovereign, efficacious grace as opposed to Rome's sacramental, conditional and uncertain grace."

—Clyde Hargrove
Hargrove Real Estate, Red Oak, TX

Preface

It is quite clear that the worst kinds of sins associated with the ruination of the ancient Israelites were all related to the worship of false gods. A cursory reading of the history of Israel yields the conclusion that Israel gets in trouble when she forsakes the Law of God and panders after foreign religions. The nation pays the ultimate price in the North and the South when, under the wrath of YHWH, Israel and Judah are taken off into captivity by foreign powers.

The New Testament reminds us of Israel's failures. In recounting the history of Israel, the New Testament writers use the background of Israel as a model for what could go wrong within New Testament assemblies. The apostle Paul reminds us that "these things happened as examples for us, that we should not crave evil things, as they also craved" (1 Corinthians 10:6). Paul mentions that one of the evil things done in Israel was idolatry. All the mistakes of Israel are of benefit to the Body of Christ in that they act as instructions to Christians. Paul says they were "written for our instruction, upon whom the ends of the ages have come" (1 Corinthians 10:11).

We can glean a lot of information about the spiritual conditions that prevailed in some of the New Testament churches through a reading of Paul's two letters to the church at Corinth. The mistakes and progress (or lack thereof) of the Corinthian Christians are detailed for us in Paul's letters. In what has come to be known as 2 Corinthians (which probably is his third letter), the apostle Paul makes one of his strongest appeals. Paul understands the dangers of opening a crack of passage to the forbidden lands of unbelief. Keeping in mind the utter ruination of his forefathers due to their idolatry, the apostle warns and admonishes the Corinthians in no uncertain terms:

> Do not be unequally yoked together with unbelievers.
> For what fellowship has righteousness with lawlessness?
> And what communion has light with darkness? And what
> accord has Christ with Belial? Or what part has a believer
> with an unbeliever? And what agreement has the temple of
> God with idols? For you are the temple of the living God. As
> God has said: "I will dwell in them and walk among them.
> I will be their God, and they shall be My people." Therefore
> "Come out from among them and be separate, says the
> Lord. Do not touch what is unclean, and I will receive
> you." I will be a Father to you, and you shall be My sons
> and daughters, says the LORD Almighty. (2 Corinthians
> 6:14-7:1)

There may be many shades of practical application when it comes to the words "bound together" or "unequally yoked." But for certain all dealings between Christians and non-Christians have to be brought to the bar of Paul's injunction for scrutiny. The question of "What has a believer in common with an unbeliever?" is not a request for an itemized list of shared experiences and tastes. It is a formal declaration that those in Christ have not one thing in common, in the spiritual realm, with an unbeliever.

Given this background, what are we to make of the persistent efforts among professing evangelicals and Roman Catholics to bring Christians and Roman Catholics under the same umbrella? If Roman Catholics are Christians of a different stripe, then all is well. But if Roman Catholicism is a religion unto itself with no common bond of unity with Christianity, then all is not well. In fact, all is amiss. In fact, it would be idolatry of the worst sort to bring the belief system of the Roman Catholic into the house of the Living God. If Roman Catholicism is another one of the modern Belials, then what harmony has Christ with Rome? If Roman Catholicism is another modern temple of idols, then what agreement has the temple of God with idols? If those whose faith is in the Roman Catholic religion are not Christians, then what has a believer in common with an unbeliever?

In our day there are many evangelicals who have raised their voices in favor of complete harmony with Rome. Some say the Protestant Reformation was a mistake. Others say Rome has changed and the issues of the sixteenth century are no longer relevant today. Others say Rome is close enough and must be considered Christian, albeit they have some strange and serious errors. Some throw up their hands and simply reduce Christianity to belief in some kind of Jesus with some kind of way to heaven and this is good enough.

On Rome's side the drumbeat since Vatican II has been consistent. Most Roman Catholic writers now accept their counterparts in Protestantism as "separated brethren." Most Roman Catholic writers are willing to say that Protestant Christians are OK with them. The entire idea behind modern Rome is to get Christians to agree that Rome is OK since Rome has already agreed that Protestants (and all that word entails) are OK.

But is this "I'm OK and you're OK" business OK with the revelation of God? Or is this simply another way for Rome to seduce Christians to come home to Rome? Or, worse yet, is all this an example of a modern apostasy from the truth of the gospel in hopes of shaping a new gospel that ultimately is no gospel at all?

In the following pages we will let Rome speak in her own defense. In so doing we will encourage the readers to decide for themselves. What will it be: the Christian gospel or Roman Catholicism? We are convinced that there is no middle ground. We maintain that a fair analysis of Roman Catholicism yields only one possible conclusion. Someone is right and someone is wrong. Rome does attempt to defend her belief system with Scripture. But is this defense credible? Is the net result of Rome's use of Scripture Christian? We say no. There is a myth of the middle ground promoted by many on both sides. But in our examination, there is no middle ground. One is either a Roman Catholic or a Christian. One cannot be both Christian and Roman Catholic.

We do not use the term "Christian" lightly or haphazardly. We encourage all professing Christians to take stock of what they believe, bring their faith to the table, and compare it with what Rome has to offer. Like all adverse religions, Rome forces us to know our Bibles well. And as with all adverse religions, our witness to Rome is their only hope of salvation. May the Lord give ears to hear and eyes to see, and may all Christians understand their obligation to come out from the midst of idols. All idols are for destruction, even if they lodge only in our minds. For in the mind is where they grow and bear fruit as tools for the obliteration of true Christianity.

Introduction

The purpose of this book is to answer the Roman Catholic claim that the religion of Rome is based upon good solid biblical exegesis and sound hermeneutics (an interpretation of the Bible that can be justified). There are any number of Roman Catholic authors writing to convince us that Roman Catholicism can be biblically justified in Her dogma and doctrine. Timothy F. Kauffman and Robert M. Zins have selected one author with whom to interact because of the boldness of his book and the trendy way in which he writes. By his own reckoning Patrick Madrid writes for the common man. His book titled *Answer Me This!* has been widely distributed throughout the Roman Catholic community. We read this introduction of Patrick Madrid taken from the end of *Answer Me This!*

> Patrick Madrid is an author, public speaker, television host, and publisher of the award-winning *Envoy* magazine, a journal of Catholic apologetics and evangelization. Its Web site is www.envoymagazine.com.
>
> He is the author of several best-selling books, including *Pope Fiction, Where Is That In the Bible? Why Is That In Tradition? Search and Rescue, Any Friend of God is a Friend of Mine*, and he is the editor and contributor of the acclaimed *Surprised by Truth* series of books (with more than four hundred thousand combined copies in print). He is also host of three popular EWTN television series: *Pope Fiction, The Truth About Scripture and Tradition, and Search and Rescue*. He has conducted hundreds of apologetics and

evangelization conferences in English and Spanish across the U.S., as well as throughout Europe, Asia, and Latin America. He is a veteran of numerous formal public debates with Protestant ministers, Mormon leaders, and other non-Catholic spokesmen.

We of course do not believe that the Roman Catholic religion can be proven or defended from the Bible. It is not the religion of the Bible. If it were, we would urge all to become Roman Catholic. That said, it is important to place all the cards on the table. Mr. Kauffman and Mr. Zins take turns in alternate chapters addressing Mr. Madrid topic by topic, point by point. Someone is right and someone is unquestionably wrong. It is illogical and completely untenable to take the position that everyone is right even though we believe contradictory things. We have titled our response to Madrid *A Gospel Contrary!*, taken from the admonition of the apostle Paul in the first chapter of Galatians, wherein he admonishes the Galatian Christians to not receive "A Gospel Contrary" to the one he first delivered to them.

In today's wacky world of ecumenical madness and the overwhelming flood of sentiment that somehow hopes for a happy blending of truth and error, we recoil and find the entire idea absurd. We are not Roman Catholic for all the right reasons found in a careful study of the revelation of God in His Word. We have looked hard into the Bible and cannot find Roman Catholicism. We do not believe it is there. We also believe that no one else can find it unless they first put it in the Bible.

Patrick Madrid tries in vain to put Roman Catholicism in the Bible. But it does not fit. It never will fit. The Bible is clear, and all the wordsmithing and tortuous twisting of Scripture will not alter its cherished message of God's salvation to a broken and lost world.

Making every attempt to be upright and transparent, we have followed the table of contents from Madrid's book. The format of his book is to answer questions posed to him taken from his radio broadcasts. Hence, we present Madrid's answers to these questions followed by our rebuttal.

Where is the wise man? Where is the scholar? Where is the philosopher of this age? Has not God made foolish the wisdom of the world? For since in the wisdom of God the world through its wisdom did not know him, God was pleased through the foolishness of what was preached to save those who believe. Jews demand miraculous signs and Greeks look for wisdom, but we preach Christ crucified: a stumbling block to Jews and foolishness to Gentiles, but to those whom God has called, both Jews and Greeks, Christ the power of God and the wisdom of God. For the foolishness of God is wiser than man's wisdom, and the weakness of God is stronger than man's strength. (1 Corinthians 1:20-25, NIV)

Catholicism

———————— (Kauffman) ————————

T he format of Patrick Madrid's book, *Answer Me This!,* is to put
forth a typical Protestant or Orthodox objection to Roman
Catholicism and use it as a conversation point. His initial volley is
to raise, and to answer, the typical objection, "Why are Catholics so
hung up on rules and regulations?"

A Religion of Rules

He responds that Catholics are only "hung up" on rules and regulations because God is "hung up" on them, and therefore "how we
follow rules" determines "how happy or unhappy" our relationship
with Him will be. Jesus and His apostles of course had a lot to say
about rules, and Madrid cites several examples: "And why call ye
me, Lord, Lord, and do not the things which I say?" (Luke 6:46) and
"And he that keepeth His commandments dwelleth in Him, and He
in him" (1 John 3:24).[1] No Christian would deny that good works
are produced by the Holy Spirit in the person who is in Christ, and
the life of the Christian is in fact a life of good works, "For every tree
is known by his own fruit" (Luke 6:44).[2] But the Christian is not

---

1   Unless otherwise noted, Mr. Kauffman cites the *King James Version* throughout.
2   Madrid, p. 25

"hung up" on rules and regulations because he knows not only that his good works cannot gain salvation (Romans 4:5), but also that his bad works cannot lose it (John 10:28-29). Rather, he has "an inheritance *incorruptible*, and *undefiled*, and *that fadeth not away*, *reserved* in heaven" (1 Peter 1:4).

The Roman Catholic, on the other hand, is taught that while works done before baptism are not meritorious, *after baptism* Christ "continually infuses his virtue" into him, and by obedience the Catholic fully satisfies "the divine law" and has "truly merited eternal life ... through the observance of the commandments."[3] Thus obedience to the commandments becomes meritorious as soon as one is in a relationship with Christ, resulting in an increase in righteousness unto justification and eternal life by those good works.

Perhaps the best way to say it is that for the Christian, "Christ *is* the *end* of the law for righteousness to every one that believeth" (Romans 10:4), but for the Roman Catholic, Christ is the *beginning* of the law for righteousness. And that is the real reason Roman Catholicism is so "hung up" on good works: each individual's eternal destiny is determined by his own personal obedience *after* entering into a "relationship" with Christ. For a Christian, the motive toward obedience is much different: Each individual's eternal destiny is determined by the obedience of Christ *before* entering into a relationship with Him by faith. This is why Paul says,

> For by grace are ye saved through faith; and that not of yourselves: it is the gift of God: Not of works, lest any man should boast. For we are his workmanship, created in Christ Jesus unto good works, which God hath before ordained that we should walk in them. (Ephesians 2:8-10)

For this reason, Peter says we "are kept by the power of God through faith unto salvation" (1 Peter 1:5).

---

3   Council of Trent, First Decree on Justification, ch. 16 (January 13, 1547).

The Definition of "Catholicism"

Madrid's next volley is to discuss the origin of the word "Catholicism." He correctly observes that the term "catholic," meaning "universal," did not originate in the Scriptures, but was used commonly in a secular sense to refer to that which is universal, global or pervasive. It began to be used very early in the history of church when the ancient writers adopted the term to describe the widespread presence of the church.

When approaching the term "catholic," it is important first to understand whence it came, and second where the Roman Catholic apologist would like to take it if left to his own devices. Catholic means "general," or "worldwide" or "universal." It comes from the Greek word καθόλου, *catholou*, a term encompassing "all" or "every." With the suffix -ικος (-ikos), the term becomes an adjective describing something universal, global, far-reaching or broad in scope. Ignatius of Antioch (107 AD) referred to the catholicity of the church—"wherever Jesus Christ is, there is the Catholic Church."[4] Justin Martyr (c. 150 AD) used the term to refer to the general or "catholic" (καθολικήν) resurrection, including both the elect and the damned,[5] and Irenæus (189 AD) used the term to refer to the four principal or "catholic" (καθολικά) winds.[6] Thus, even Christians freely acknowledge that they are members of the "catholic" church. Of course they are. Christ's special people represent every tribe, tongue and nation on earth. But Madrid would arrive at a much different application of "catholic."

Having identified its ancient usage, Madrid alleges that the term was used as a way to discern truth from falsehood, then asserts that Jesus Christ established a Catholic church through which men may discern the truth necessary for salvation, and finally that the Catholic Church is the means God has established for men to be reconciled to Himself by the truth. Madrid will thus use "catholic" as a substitute for the Gospel, and "Catholic Church" as a substitute for Christ, essentially alienating Jesus from the people He came to save. We will show, however, that the ancient

---

4   Ignatius of Antioch, *To the Smyrnæans*, paragraph 8.
5   Justin Martyr, *Dialogue with Trypho*, 81 (Migne, P.G. VI, 669).
6   Irenæus, *Against Heresies*, Book III, chapter 11, paragraph 8 (Migne, P.G. VII, 885).

Catholic Church of the post-apostolic era was certainly no ancient "Roman Catholic Church" as Madrid imagines, and certainly did not see the church as the means of reconciliation between a Holy God and His fallen creation.

Catholicism is Alleged to be the Source of Truth...

Patrick Madrid's first step is to present the word "Catholic" as a shibboleth of truth. Because different factions arose early in the church, Madrid says, "it became difficult for the faithful to discern" between truth and error, so the term Catholic "arose very early to serve that need."[7] But was "Catholic" really used to discern between truth and falsehood? We certainly do not find that in Ignatius of Antioch, for he simply says that the believers of Smyrna ought to honor the officers of the church—the bishops, the presbyters and the deacons—"as being the institution of God" because "wherever Jesus Christ is, there is the Catholic Church."[8] At the time, a heretical document, *The Apocalypse of Peter*, had been circulating throughout Asia Minor, instructing the sheep to cast off their bishops and deacons who think "they have received their authority from God." Ignatius corrected that error with a Scriptural precept — for the apostles certainly *had* established church officers — and then reasoned to the particular from the general, saying wherever the bishop is, the people ought to be, "even as, wherever Jesus Christ is, there is the Catholic Church." Jesus shepherds His catholic church and the bishop, with the deacons and presbyters, legitimately shepherds his local congregation. Ignatius had merely affirmed the Church's catholicity, but had not used "catholic" as the measure of its legitimacy.

Ignatius' use of "catholic" is thus a far cry from Madrid's. In the early centuries of the church, the bishop was the shepherd of the local congregation, and was himself shepherded by Christ. All the individually shepherded churches comprised the Catholic Church, of which Jesus was Himself the Chief. There was no intermediate

---

7   Madrid, p. 28
8   Ignatius, *To the Smyrnæans*, 8.

chief shepherding bishop on earth, and therefore nothing "Roman" about the early Catholic Church. Even in his letter *To the Romans*, when Ignatius, bishop of Antioch, was on his way to be martyred, he asked the Romans to pray for "the Church in Syria, which now has God for its shepherd, instead of me. Jesus Christ alone will oversee it…"[9] Lacking a local shepherd, Christ would shepherd the church in Syria. In another letter, Ignatius addressed Polycarp as "Bishop of the Church of the Smyrnæans, or rather, who has, as his own bishop, God the Father, and the Lord Jesus Christ."[10] Another second century document, *The Martyrdom of Polycarp*, refers simultaneously to Polycarp, "bishop of the Catholic Church which is in Smyrna"[11] and to Jesus Christ, "the Shepherd of the Catholic Church throughout the world."[12] Clearly, there was no common or widespread belief that the Catholic Church was shepherded from Rome. That the early writers used "catholic" to refer to the whole church vis-à-vis the local church, and that Justin and Irenæus in the same century were using the term to refer to the "general" resurrection and the "principal" winds, suggests that "catholic" still was not being used as the shibboleth of truth even at the turn of the third century. Rather, it was still being used to describe something broad and expansive, as Jesus' church certainly was.

…but Truth is Actually the Source of Catholicism

In reality, even as "catholicity" was being used to describe the worldwide community of locally shepherded churches, *the shibboleth of truth was still the Scriptures*. Ignatius applauded the Ephesians not because they were "catholic" but because they "have always been of the same mind with the apostles."[13] He did not exhort the Magnesians to be catholic, but rather to "[s]tudy … to be established in the doctrines of the Lord and the apostles."[14] The Trallians were not encouraged to be catholic, but rather to

---

9   Ignatius, *To the Romans*, 9.
10   Ignatius, *To Polycarp*, greeting.
11   *The Martyrdom of Polycarp*, 16.
12   *The Martyrdom of Polycarp*, 19.
13   Ignatius, *To the Ephesians*, 11.
14   Ignatius, *To the Magnesians*, 13.

"continue in intimate union with Jesus Christ our God, and the bishop, and the enactments of the apostles."[15] He did not encourage the Philadelphians to be catholic, but rather instructed them that "the doctrine of Christ" may be found "in the ancient Scriptures," for "[i]t is written."[16] In his letter to the Philippians (c. 130 AD), Polycarp did not encourage the faithful to be "catholic," but rather admonished them to be "joined together in the truth," for "I trust that you are well versed in the Sacred Scriptures, and that nothing is hid from you."[17] A half century later, Irenæus did not insist that truth was to be found in catholicity, but rather that we must "revert to the Scriptural proof furnished by [the] apostles" if we are to understand "the doctrine regarding God."[18] Even in the third century, Dionysius of Alexandria criticized the bishop of Rome for claiming falsely to possess an apostolic tradition *for which no authentic written evidence could be found.* If a "custom took its beginning … from the apostles," Dionysius wrote, it is compulsory, but "as to things which were written afterwards … they are ignored by us … no matter what they are."[19] Our point here is simply that two centuries after the establishment of the church, *catholicity* was still not a tool for discerning between truth and falsehood. The *Scriptures* served that purpose. Catholicity flowed from fidelity to the Scriptures. Fidelity to the Scriptures did not flow from Catholicity. It is important to establish that because from his initial formulation on the purpose of Catholicity, Madrid attempts to make *Catholicity* the driving factor in doctrinal uniformity:

> The truth is, even though the early Church progressed from referring to itself in the more generic form of "Christian" to the more specific "Catholic," it remained one and the same Church *with all the same teachings, Traditions, Scriptures and ministry.*[20]

---

15   Ignatius, *To the Trallians*, 7.
16   Ignatius, *To the Philadelphians*, 8.
17   Polycarp, *To the Philippians*, 10, 12.
18   Irenæus, *Against Heresies*, Book III, chapter 5, paragraph 1.
19   Dionysius, to Stephen of Rome.
20   Madrid, p. 30

To the degree that various churches were faithful to the Scriptures, the churches throughout the world enjoyed communion and fellowship with each other, and therefore *catholicity*, "with all the same teachings, Traditions, Scriptures and ministry." But "catholicity" was the effect, not the cause, of that communion. We do not deny that the term *eventually* came to be used the way Madrid describes, but that use came too late to be considered anything but a novelty. Madrid's claim that it "arose very early to serve that need" is misleading. For several centuries after the apostles, the term was still not being used the way Madrid alleges, and therefore not so "very early" as he has imagined.

The Gospel, not the Church, is the Means of Reconciliation

Madrid's next step, having attempted to establish "catholicity" as the shibboleth of truth, is to show that God chose to reconcile all men to Himself *through the Catholic Church*. But God reconciles men to Himself through the cross, which is not the same thing. The church, or ἐκκλησία (*ekklesia*), as it is used in the Scriptures, comes from a word meaning the "called out ones," or literally, the assembly, as in "the general assembly and church" (Hebrews 12:23). It will be well for the Christian to understand that the church includes preachers and teachers and evangelists, and that God has been pleased to reconcile Himself to His creation through the foolishness of preaching and teaching (Colossians 1:28; 1 Corinthians 1:21) and through the ministry of evangelism and reconciliation (2 Corinthians 5:18-20). It is through the "foolishness of preaching" and the "ministry of reconciliation" that God reconciles "all things unto himself," "having made peace through the blood of his cross" (Colossians 1:20). The Scriptures teach that men are added to the church when they are saved, and they are saved through belief in the Gospel (1 Thessalonians 2:13-14; Acts 2:47; Ephesians 1:13). It is important to establish those biblical facts because Madrid so quickly diverges from them. The Scriptures teach that we are reconciled to God through Christ's death, that we hear this good news through the preaching of the Gospel and believing the Gospel, we are added to the church.

Madrid, on the other hand, would have us reconciled to God through the church, something the Scriptures do not teach. In Ephesians 3:8-10, Paul says he was commissioned to preach "the unsearchable riches of Christ" to the Gentiles so that they might be saved, and thereby that "the manifold wisdom of God" might be made known to "the principalities and powers in the heavenly places" *through the church*. Because of Madrid's misuse of it, the reader is invited to ponder what that verse does and does not say. It says the wisdom of God was made known to principalities and powers *through the church* because the Gospel was made known to the Gentiles *through preaching*. It does not say that the Gentiles had been reconciled to God *through the church*. Yet that is precisely how Madrid understands the passage.

Madrid camps on Ephesians 3:8-10, and particularly on that phrase *through the church* (Madrid's emphasis), to claim that God uses the church as the means of reconciliation between Himself and man: "in and through this one Church," Madrid says, Jesus "wants all men to be reconciled to the Father through himself."[21] Thus Madrid concludes that "it is completely alien to the Scriptures, indeed to the Gospel message itself, to attempt to separate the Church and the Gospel." We will remind the reader that nobody actually wants to separate the church from the Gospel. We merely want to distinguish between them: the church is not the Gospel, but the church must preach the Gospel. What is utterly alien to the Scriptures, and indeed alien to the Gospel, is to place the church between Jesus and the people He came to save.

Madrid provides three passages of Scripture to prove that men are reconciled to God through the church: Matthew 16:18, Matthew 18:15-18 and Acts 9:31. Yet none of the verses support his claim. Matthew 16:18 says "upon this rock I will build my church," but does not say "through this church I will reconcile all men to the Father." Matthew 18:15-18 addresses the church's role in disciplinary matters to maintain peace within and keep the

---

unrepentant without, but does not say "through this church I will reconcile all men to the Father." Acts 9:31 says the church walked "in the fear of the Lord, and in the comfort of the Holy Ghost" but does not say "through this church I will reconcile all men to the Father."

Madrid would substitute the Catholic Church for Christ

Here we arrive at the ultimate end of Madrid's focus on the term "catholic." Catholicity is proposed by Madrid as the means by which truth, unity and uniformity are established and maintained, arguing that men are reconciled to God through the church, and finally, that there is only one Catholic Church through which men are to be reconciled to God. He suggests that the reference to a singular church, ἐκκλησία (ekklesia), in Acts 9:31 indicates the particularity of the Catholic Church:

> Notice the singular 'church,' not 'churches,' which points to the singular quality of the *ekklesia* the Lord had established. He did not come to initiate 'Christianity,' per se, an amorphous collection of like-minded believers who were not united. No. He established a particular Church that was (and is) His Body, one, holy, Catholic and apostolic.[22]

It is plainly an invalid conclusion from an invalid premise, but we must nevertheless point out the error. Madrid first takes the singular ἐκκλησία of Acts 9:31, then loads it with his own perception of "catholicity," and finally concludes that Jesus had come to establish the Roman Catholic Church. Madrid presents his readers with a false dilemma, forcing a choice between "an amorphous collection of like-minded believers who were *not united*" and the ostensible unity of the One, Holy, Apostolic, Roman Catholic Church. To the credit of the early Christians, they knew quite well that there was a third option: an amorphous collection of like-minded believers who *were united*. That is exactly how the early church

---

22   Madrid, p. 32

expressed itself. Alexander of Alexandria (c. 320 AD), predecessor and mentor of Athanasius, expressed the unity of the Catholic Church in precisely that way when he wrote to the churches to address the heresy of Arius:

> Since the body of the Catholic Church is one, and it is commanded in Holy Scripture that we should keep the bond of unanimity and peace, it follows that we should write and signify to one another the things which are done by each of us; that whether one member suffer or rejoice we may all either suffer or rejoice with one another.[23]

Alexander continued his letter, explaining that the bishops of Egypt and Libya had declared Arius and his followers "to be aliens from the Catholic Church and faith," not because they had spoken contrary to *Catholicism*, but rather because they had "spoken contrary to the mind of *Scripture*."[24] In Alexander's letter we see the true expression of the ancient catholicity and unity of the Christian Church. Congregations throughout the world were unified in their adherence to the Scriptures—geographically separated, individually and particularly shepherded, locally unique, but nevertheless globally "catholic" in the sense that they were everywhere unified in the faith under their Chief Shepherd, Jesus Christ. We can imagine no better way to describe the true Scriptural "catholicism" of geographically scattered congregations than the way Peter did:

> …to the strangers scattered throughout Pontus, Galatia, Cappadocia, Asia, and Bithynia … ye were as sheep going astray; now returned unto the Shepherd and Bishop of your souls. (1 Peter 1:1, 2:25)

> The elders which are among you I exhort … Feed the flock of God which is among you, taking the oversight thereof …

---

23   Alexander of Alexandria, *Deposition of Arius.*
24   Alexander of Alexandria, *Deposition of Arius*, chapter 2.

And when the chief Shepherd shall appear, ye shall receive
a crown of glory that fadeth not away. (1 Peter 5:1-4)

Under the inspiration of the Spirit, the New Testament writers
repeatedly referred to the plurality of churches throughout the
world, Christ Himself instructing John to write "unto the seven
churches (ἐκκλησίαις, ekklesiais) which are in Asia" (Revelation
1:11). We understand from the Scriptures, as did the early writers,
that Christians were to be locally shepherded under their bishops,
elders and presbyters, under the infallible guidance of the Chief
Shepherd, Jesus Christ through His Spirit.

Jesus, not Roman Catholicism, is "the Gate"

On the other hand, what Madrid means to suggest in his chapter
on Catholicism is that there is but one Christian *denomination*
(Roman Catholicism) and that God has ordained that all men are
to be reconciled to Himself through *that denomination*. By such
means, Madrid makes a subtle but deadly shift away from the
Scriptural teaching that men are reconciled to God through Christ
and attempts to make the Scriptures say that men are reconciled to
God *through the church*. This has the effect of erecting the church
as a gate between Jesus and the people He came to save, rather than
Jesus alone being the gate (John 10:9). Like the Pharisees, however,
Madrid and his kind, by setting up Roman Catholicism as the gate,
rather "shut up the kingdom of heaven against men: for ye neither
go in *yourselves*, neither suffer ye them that are entering to go in"
(Matthew 23:13).

Rather, we are "reconciled to God by the death of his Son"
(Romans 5:10) and, having been saved, become members of the
church (Acts 2:47). Paul makes exactly this distinction when he
writes,

And all things are of God, who *hath reconciled us to himself*
by Jesus Christ, and hath given to us *the ministry of reconciliation*; To wit, that God was in Christ, reconciling the
world unto himself, not imputing their trespasses unto

them; and hath committed unto us *the word of reconcilia-tion.* (2 Corinthians 5:18-19)

The sinner is not reconciled to God *through the Catholic Church,* as Madrid alleged. And thus we come to the fruition of Madrid's analysis of the word "catholic." That word, he says, came to be the way to discern truth from falsehood. Catholicity, he says, establishes uniformity of doctrine. The catholicity of the church thereby becomes the means by which God reconciles a fallen world to Himself. Yet none of it is true. The church did not teach true doctrine of the Scriptures because it was "catholic." It was "catholic" because it taught the truth of the Scriptures. And it was truth, not catholicity, that set men free and reconciled them to God; and when men are reconciled to God *by the truth,* the manifold wisdom of God is made manifest to the principalities and powers of the heavens *through the church.* But men are not reconciled to God *through the church.*

Roman Catholicism does not live up to the "hype"

Having acknowledged that Roman Catholics are "hung up" on rules because their *obedience to the rules* determines how "happy and harmonious" their relationship is with God, and having attempted to show that Catholics are to be reconciled to God *through the Catholic Church,* which is ostensibly both Holy and Roman, Madrid is now faced with the accurate perception that his Holy Roman Catholic Church has a problem following the very rules upon which it is "hung up." As a blemished "bride," she must struggle to maintain a "happy and harmonious" relationship with her Spouse. In his response, Madrid concedes that many of the Roman Catholic Church's "unworthy popes, bishops, priests, Religious, and lay people" who know the truth but do not live accordingly, therefore "fall by the way." None of this matters, Madrid says, because "[i]f the sinful behavior of the members of his Church" could thwart the Lord's purposes, "then Christ was either a liar or a fool for saying in Matthew 16:18-19 that He would build His Church upon a rock

and that nothing, *not even the gates of hell,* could overcome it."[25]
But here Madrid has merely assumed what it was his duty to prove.
The public, glaring reprobation and moral rot that emanates from
within the Roman religion cannot be used as evidence against
her, he says, because that would mean Christ was "a liar or a fool"
to promise that the gates of hell would not overcome it. In other
words, the Roman Catholic religion cannot *not* be the church of
Christ because that would mean it was *not* the church of Christ,
which, in his mind, it is. Such is the comical circularity of Madrid's
reasoning.

On the contrary, it is evident that the gates of hell have
prevailed against the Roman Catholic religion from ages past,
demonstrating that she cannot possibly be Christ's Church.
Pædophile priests, bishops, archbishops and cardinals, the Arch-
diocese of Detroit's gay Polish pipeline through which Polish
seminarians are groomed as gay partners for homosexual priests,
financial scandals at the Vatican bank, Pope Francis installing
the idol of the Pachamama goddess at the Vatican, the Vatican's
Secretariat of State investing in the gay pornographic Elton John
biopic, *Rocketman*—all show that the Roman Catholic fish rots from
its Roman head. "Ye are of your father the devil, and the lusts of
your father ye will do," Jesus said (John 8:44). Madrid's attempt to
sweep Rome's diabolical and injurious offenses against God and
men under the rug of "a divine institution comprised of human
members" is a pathetic half-truth. That it is made up of human
members, we do not deny, but that it is a "divine institution" *is the
very point in contention.* Madrid has simply assumed Roman Catholicism's divine origins as proof of its divine origins, which is to
beg the question. Until Madrid can prove otherwise (as he attempts
to do later in his book), we are satisfied to let Rome's diabolical rap
sheet serve as evidence of the Devil's paternal relationship with
her.

---

25   Madrid, p. 36

The Word of God

(Kauffman)

Protestants have historically understood that the Bible alone is the Word of God *and is therefore the whole corpus of divine revelation available to us today*. We call this *Sola Scriptura*, or *Scripture Alone*. Roman Catholics, on the other hand, have historically held that the totality of the Word of God is passed on not only in written form but is also conveyed orally as Tradition. Pope Paul VI with the assembled bishops at the Second Vatican Council affirmed that "Sacred tradition and Sacred Scripture form one sacred deposit of the word of God."[26] We call this *Sola Verbum Dei*, or *the Word of God Alone*.

Thus, while Roman Catholics and Protestants agree in principle that "the Word of God" is the sole rule of faith, they disagree on what "the Word of God" is. It is therefore inappropriate merely to compare the Roman Catholic view of *Scripture* with the Protestant view of *Scripture*, as Madrid does, and then to address separately the alleged need for Tradition and a Magisterium. Such an approach contrasts what Protestants believe is *the totality of special revelation* with what Catholics believe is *only a portion of it*, which is hardly a valid comparison. The apologist must instead compare

---

26 Second Vatican Council, *Dei Verbum*, ii.9-10 (November 18, 1965).

the Roman Catholic view of *the Word of God* with the Protestant view of *the Word of God*, something Madrid has managed to avoid by addressing Scripture, Tradition and the Magisterium in three separate chapters: "Scripture Alone?", "Sacred Tradition" and "The Magisterium."

By taking that approach, Madrid allows himself the luxury of addressing two different views of *Scripture*—the Protestant view and the Catholic view—while avoiding the epistemological difficulties of addressing the two different views of *"the Word of God."* Those two paradigms ought to be compared side by side. Thus, while the bulk of our response to Madrid will answer him chapter by chapter, question by question, claim by claim, we make an exception here by aggregating Madrid's chapters on Scripture, Tradition and the Magisterium so that we may properly address "the Word of God" under a single heading.

Madrid's aim is to showcase the superiority of Roman Catholicism over Protestantism in three ways in three separate chapters: first, by alleging that *Sola Scriptura* "is nothing more than a self-refuting proposition" and that Paul wanted Timothy to hold onto not only the Scriptures "but also the oral teaching he delivered"[27] (see his chapter "Scripture Alone?"); second, by claiming that because the Bible has "no inspired table of contents," Protestants implicitly embrace a tradition "that comes down to us entirely outside of the Bible"[28] (see "Sacred Tradition"); and third, that the diversity of Protestant interpretations of Scripture "demonstrates the need for an authoritative teaching church"[29] (see "The Magisterium"). Madrid's solution to these problems is an ostensibly unified theory of "the Word of God," including both Scripture and Tradition, faithfully and infallibly interpreted by the Magisterium of the Roman Catholic religion. By Madrid's reckoning, if the reader will simply defer to the Magisterium to interpret Scripture and Tradition, all these "Protestant" problems will go away.

The flaw in Madrid's reasoning is easily confuted when it is demonstrated how thoroughly he ensnares himself in his own

---

27   Madrid, p. 38, 42
28   Madrid, p. 127
29   Madrid, p. 174

argument. Before one can receive both Scripture and Tradition, one must first discern which books are included in the Bible and which Traditions are included within "the Word of God." In Roman Catholicism, "the Word of God" includes "[t]he words of the holy fathers,"[30] the canons of church councils, and the *ex cathedra* proclamations of the Pope, "preserved by an unending succession of preachers until the end of time."[31] While Rome claims to have determined the canon of Scripture through the church councils, there is no formal "canon of Tradition" by which a Roman Catholic may understand with certainty which "words of the holy fathers" are true, which church councils are to be embraced, and which papal teachings are infallible. And to discover *that* one must ultimately rely on information that exists nowhere within *Scripture and Tradition*, which is to say, nowhere within "the Word of God."

The predictable and expansive diversity of opinions within Roman Catholicism about what qualifies as "the Word of God" shows that, despite an allegedly "authoritative teaching church" that can "demonstrate that its interpretation of the Bible is consistent with how the early Christians interpreted the Bible"[32] (as Madrid claims), the hapless Roman Catholic is still left to his own devices to determine what his "authoritative teaching church" has taught him. The end result is precisely what Patrick Madrid thinks he had avoided: innumerable opinions, divisions, disagreements and theories *within Roman Catholicism* on the very issue of what "the Word of God" says and means. Paul VI boasted that Roman Catholicism enjoys "certainty about everything which has been revealed,"[33] but "certainty" is the very thing that is missing from Madrid's epistemology.

---

30 *Dei Verbum*, ii.8.
31 *Dei Verbum*, ii.8.
32 Madrid, p. 174
33 Second Vatican Council, *Dei Verbum*, ii.9-10 (November 18, 1965).

Scripture Alone

The Bible Does not Teach *Sola Scriptura*

Madrid's opening volley on *Sola Scriptura* is that the Bible does not teach it, but instead teaches the importance of oral traditions:

> The theological principle of going by the Bible alone is itself taught nowhere in the Bible. And this is the fatal flaw of this Protestant theory. … The fact is, the notion of the Bible being the sole, sufficient rule of faith is nowhere present in the Bible, either implicitly or explicitly.… But guess what *is* in the Bible: the teaching that we are to embrace Tradition, those Traditions that come from God himself.[34]

Madrid concludes that *Sola Scriptura* is not only a "self-refuting proposition" (because it is not taught in the Bible), but also that *Sola Scriptura* is itself a "tradition of men that 'voids the Word of God'" (because it ignores non-scriptural Traditions). On its face, the argument seems plausible enough, but it fails upon even a cursory examination.

First, *Sola Scriptura* does not deny the validity of oral teachings. The Father Himself spoke orally from heaven (Matthew 3:17), Jesus was charged to preach His Father's Words orally (John 12:49), and the disciples were commissioned to preach Jesus' Words orally (Luke 10:16). We are quite aware that the Word of God has in times past been delivered orally. *Sola Scriptura* by no means claims that the Word of God has never existed in oral form, but claims rather that the Word of God exists only in written form *today*.

Second, the Scriptures warn against oral traditions. Not only must we avoid, and repent of, oral traditions that nullify the Word of God (Mark 7:9), but we are also warned how easy it is for oral teachings to be or become corrupted. Jesus' admonition to Peter (John 21:22) was immediately and incorrectly propagated *orally* "among the brethren" (John 21:23). As John's response illustrates,

---

34   Madrid, p. 38

corrupted oral tradition is not corrected with more unwritten tradition but with Scripture.

Third, the Scriptures caution us not only that the recipients of the apostles' own oral teachings quickly abandoned them and began to propagate their own errors *orally* (1 Timothy 1:20; 2 Timothy 2:15-18), but also that false apostles went about claiming *oral* teaching authority, and that Christians were taught to reject them (2 Corinthians 11:13, Revelation 2:2).

We do therefore maintain not only that God's Word was once delivered orally, as the Scriptures plainly testify, but also that even true oral apostolic traditions are easily corrupted through oral transmission and extrascriptural writing, as the Scriptures also testify (2 Thessalonians 2:2). Any claim of an authoritative oral apostolic teaching must itself be supported by a reliable source of apostolic teaching, of which none exist today save the Scriptures. Thus, while Madrid has attempted to ensnare the Protestant by posing a false dilemma—namely, that for *Sola Scriptura* to be true, the Scriptures must teach *Sola Scriptura*—the Protestant need not be drawn into such a snare. All that is required for *Sola Scriptura* to be true is that the oral Traditions to which the Scriptures refer are no longer available outside of the Scriptures, a considerably lighter burden than that which bears down upon the proponent of *Sola Verbum Dei*.

Based on Madrid's belief that Roman Catholicism is the curator of oral apostolic Tradition, we may well wonder where those true oral teachings of the apostles may be discovered. Certainly not in the early church fathers, as they themselves were susceptible to error and argued with each other about whether their own traditions were binding or even apostolic.[35] Hilary of Poitiers lamented, "there are as many creeds as opinions among men, as many doctrines as inclinations, and as many sources of blasphemy as

---

35   See Polycarp's argument with Anicetus on the celebration of the Eucharist: "For neither could Anicetus persuade Polycarp not to observe what he had always observed with John the disciple of our Lord, and the other apostles with whom he had associated; neither could Polycarp persuade Anicetus to observe it as he said that he ought to follow the customs of the presbyters that had preceded him" (Eusebius, *Church History*, V.24.16).

there are faults among us."[36] Certainly not in the church councils where writers learned early and often that they could not trust their own judgment: "We make creeds arbitrarily, and explain them as arbitrarily. The *Homoousion* is rejected and received and explained away by successive synods. ... Every year, nay, every moon, we make new creeds to describe invisible mysteries."[37] Certainly not in the "unending succession of bishops" who were known to argue amongst themselves "even unto blood" from ancient days.[38] Certainly not in the bishops of Rome who were known to sow error, heresy and division in the early church.[39] Certainly not in the Roman religion where even Scriptural traditions are nullified and replaced with abominable error. Where then can these oral traditions be found? Madrid believes we must turn to Roman Catholicism to discover the oral traditions of the apostles, yet Rome has shown herself manifestly unable to produce them, and always eager to invent them!

"Hold the traditions"

Madrid's first proof text for the absolute necessity of oral tradition is 2 Thessalonians 2:15, in which Paul commands the believers in Thessalonica to "hold the traditions which ye have been taught, whether by word, or our epistle." In light of this, Madrid elsewhere says, "every Catholic can and should say with humble confidence, 'By God's grace, for the last two thousand years, we have stood firm and held fast to the written and unwritten Traditions that were taught to us, we hold fast to them now, and we always will.'"[40] In his own words, the deposit of faith "proclaimed and defended" by Roman Catholicism "is incomplete if it is missing the oral Traditions that are part of it."[41]

Very well! We wonder, then, who is the restrainer that "withholdeth" until the Son of Perdition, the Wicked One, be revealed, an

---

36   Hilary of Poitiers, *ad Constant.* ii. 4, 5 (see also Eusebius, *Church History*, Book V.24.12-16.
37   Hilary of Poitiers, *ad Constant.* ii. 4, 5.
38   Cyril of Jerusalem, *Catechetical Lectures*, 15: 7.
39   Hippolytus, Firmilian, Cyprian, Tertullian.
40   Madrid, *Why is* That *in Tradition?* (208).
41   Madrid, *Why is* That *in Tradition?* (Huntington, IN: Our Sunday Visitor, 2000), 18.

oral instruction to which Paul referred in the second chapter of 2
Thessalonians:

> Remember ye not, that, when I was yet with you, I told you
> these things? *And now ye know* what withholdeth that he
> might be revealed in his time. (2 Thessalonians 2:5-6)

The Thessalonians were plainly instructed to hold fast to *that particular oral tradition*. Surely Madrid can identify the restrainer for
us because Roman Catholicism is alleged to hold fast to unwritten
apostolic traditions. Yet an inspection of the early writers reveals
that nobody seems to know what that Pauline tradition was. Athanasius (370) believed Satan was the restrainer.[42] Chrysostom (389
AD) reported, "Some indeed say, the grace of the Spirit, but others
the Roman empire," and felt that the latter was more likely.[43]
Severian of Gabala (389 AD), Theodore of Antioch (c. 400 AD) and
Theodoret of Cyrus (c. 425 AD) assumed it is the Holy Spirit who
withholdeth.[44] Augustine threw up his hands in despair: "I frankly
confess I do not know what [Paul] means."[45] Lacking any certain
knowledge of the oral apostolic Tradition of the identity of the
restrainer, the *Catholic Encyclopedia* demurs: "We can here only
enumerate the principal opinions as to the meaning of this clause,
without discussing their value."[46] If Rome cannot even produce
the unexpounded oral traditions of which the Scriptures plainly
testify, how on earth can she produce those which the Scriptures
do not even mention? And how can she claim to "hold fast" to
unwritten apostolic traditions that she has *never possessed* and
cannot identify?

---

42   Athanasius *Expositiones Psalmos* 56, Migne P.G., XXVII, 257.
43   Chrysostom, *Homily 4 on 2 Thessalonians*.
44   Severian of Gabala, 2 Thessalonians 2:6-8; Theodore of Mopsuestia, *In Epistolorum Pos-
teriorem Pauli ad Thessalonicenses Commentari Fragmenta* 2:6-7 (*Migne P.G.*, LXVI, 936); Theodoret Cyrensis, *Interpretatio Epistolae ad II Thessalonicense* 2:6-7 (*Migne P.G. LXXXII.665*)
45   Augustine of Hippo, *City of God*, XX.19.
46   Catholic Encyclopedia.

"Maintain the traditions"

Under this same heading, Madrid mentions the oral tradition to which Paul refers in 1 Corinthians 11:1-2, and elsewhere appeals to the passage to justify the church's role in preserving oral apostolic tradition. He writes, "Now let's turn to St. Paul and see how he approaches the subject of Tradition," for it is in this passage that Paul instructs the Corinthians to "maintain the traditions even as I have delivered them to you."[47] Very well! If Paul's oral instructions to the Corinthians are not to be found in the Scriptures, we desire to know from Madrid the nature of those traditions. Chrysostom is among the few ancient writers to consider what tradition Paul might have had in mind, observing, "It appears then that he used at that time to deliver many things also not in writing." His best guess is that Paul must be referring to those traditions he explains in writing in the rest of the chapter.[48] Perhaps Madrid will enlighten us? Nay, rather Madrid too, adopts the Protestant position here, and is only willing to identify those oral traditions *that Paul committed to writing*. Of the traditions in 1 Corinthians 11:2, Madrid says, "later in that chapter, he explains in more detail one of those Traditions he handed on," but offers no other insight than that.[49]

The Apostles Taught Tradition Orally

Madrid's next proof is Paul's charge to Timothy: "And the things that thou hast heard of me among many witnesses, the same commit thou to faithful men, who shall be able to teach others also" (2 Timothy 2:2). This, Madrid says, is evidence that the Word of God is passed on in both written and oral form.[50]

Ironically, an inspection of the early writers reveals that they did not believe Paul's instructions to Timothy here were actually *oral traditions*! Clement of Alexandria (c. 215 AD) understood that the "many witnesses" that attested to Paul's instructions were *the Scriptures*: "the law and the prophets. For these the apostle made

---

47   Madrid, *Why is That in Tradition?* 26.
48   Chrysostom, Homilies on 1 Corinthians, *Homily 26.*
49   Madrid, *Why is That in Tradition?* 26.
50   Madrid, p. 42

witnesses of his own preaching."[51] Tertullian (235 AD) rejected any attempt to find in this passage evidence of an oral tradition, "[f]or, when he says 'these things,' *he refers to the things of which he is writing at the moment.*"[52] Chrysostom (390 AD) understood "the things that thou hast heard of me" to refer to what Paul had only just written in the previous chapter, namely, that he had been "a prisoner, and afflicted, yet is not impatient, nor discontented upon the desertion of his friends. … it was for this reason he mentioned his trials and afflictions."[53] Many other early writers refer to "the things that thou hast heard of me," and yet none attempt to identify the contents of that oral tradition *apart from what can be discerned from the Scriptures.* It is indeed a supreme irony that Madrid's *personal belief* that 2 Timothy 2:2 refers to *oral traditions,* is itself a tradition *the early church did not "maintain"*!

Madrid's "apostolic tradition" Problem

We dwell so long on the identity of the restrainer of 2 Thessalonians 2:6, Paul's admonition in 1 Corinthians 11:2 and his instructions in 2 Timothy 2:2 because they all clearly refer to *apostolic traditions.* Yet for well over three centuries after the apostles, the early writers evince no ancient knowledge of *those apostolic traditions* apart from what may be discerned from the Scriptures. Neither can Roman Catholicism produce them, protest though she may to be their sole custodian. Even Madrid, who appeals to these very passages to prove the indispensability of nonscriptural oral tradition, *will not even dare to guess what they may be unless the Scriptures attest to them!* A Protestant could not ask for a better opponent, so haplessly does Madrid make our argument for us.

As Protestants we do not deny that the Word of God has at various times been delivered orally. Nor do we deny that the Word of God delivered orally was God-breathed and binding

---

51   Clement of Alexandria, *Fragments from the Hypotyposes* (Schaff, ANF02, 579). His *Hypotyposes* are controverted, but notable, if valid, for rendering "in front of many witnesses" as "by many witnesses," referring to the Scriptures bearing witness to Paul's instruction.
52   Tertullian, *Prescription Against Heretics*, 25.
53   Chrysostom, Homilies on 2 Timothy, *Homily IV.*

upon those who heard it and remembered it accurately. Only a fool would suggest otherwise. *But only a fool would claim to possess those same oral teachings today outside of the Scriptures.* Roman Catholicism certainly does not have them! Because oral traditions can easily be corrupted in their transmission (John 21:22-23), false apostles can easily come claiming to possess them (2 Corinthians 11:13; Revelation 2:2), false teachers can "bring in damnable heresies" (2 Peter 2:1), evil seducers can come, "deceiving, and being deceived" (2 Timothy 3:13) and the apostles' own disciples quickly corrupted their oral teachings (1 Timothy 1:20; 1 Timothy 2:15-18), we might well wonder where we, *today*, may turn to find the truth. We need not wonder long, for the apostles remind us repeatedly that it is the Scriptures to which we must turn if we would be sure.

The Scriptures are the Antidote

Peter personally recalled the oral instruction of God from heaven (2 Peter 1:17), and yet even with a personal recollection of that theophany, he nevertheless insisted that he must commit his instructions to writing "that ye may be able after my decease to have these things always in remembrance" (2 Peter 1:15). The words of the prophets and the commandments of the apostles were committed to writing for this very purpose:

> This second epistle, beloved, I now write unto you; in both which I stir up your pure minds by way of remembrance: That ye may be mindful of the words which were spoken before by the holy prophets, and of the commandment of us the apostles of the Lord and Saviour. (2 Peter 3:1-2)

Paul commended Timothy to study the Scriptures because of their value "for doctrine, for reproof, for correction, for instruction in righteousness" (1 Timothy 3:15-16), and then commands him to "preach the word" to "reprove, rebuke, exhort with all longsuffering and doctrine" (2 Timothy 4:2), clearly referring to the preaching of the Scriptures. Why the urgency? "For I am now

ready to be offered, and the time of my departure is at hand"
(2 Timothy 4:6).

Committing their teachings to *writing* was imperative because
"there shall be false teachers among you … with feigned words"
delivered orally (2 Peter 2:1-3) and "there shall come in the last
days scoffers … saying" falsehoods orally (2 Peter 3:3-4). Paul,
too, when instructing Timothy to "continue thou in the things
which thou hast learned and hast been assured of" from "the holy
scriptures" (2 Timothy 3:14-15), did so that he might be guarded
against the deceiving seducers (2 Timothy 3:13) and those who
"will not endure sound doctrine" but will instead prefer false oral
teachings (2 Timothy 4:3). If the apostles themselves inscripturated truths as a defense *against the oral teachings of deceivers and
seducers*, why indeed should we now turn to Rome, who has proven
herself for 1600 years to be one of the deceiving seducers of which
the apostles warned us? The Scriptures are the only refuge for
those who would know the truth, and we remain shameless in our
allegiance to *Sola Scriptura*. If Madrid disagrees, let him produce the
identity of the restrainer in 2 Thessalonians 2 and "the traditions"
of 1 Corinthians 11:1-2 and "the things that thou hast heard" in 2
Timothy 2:2. We shan't hold our breath.

Sacred Tradition

The Canon of Scripture is an extrascriptural "Tradition"

Madrid's next volley is to allege that *Sola Scriptura* is self-defeating
because to subscribe to it, one must first embrace the canon of the
Scriptures, which itself is outside of Scripture:

> There is no 'inspired table of contents' anywhere in the
> Bible that will tell you which books belong in the Bible.
> Think about it: You must rely on that Tradition to know
> what the New Testament itself is, and you do accept it,
> by virtue of the fact that you have a Bible. Without that
> Tradition of the canon, you simply can't know which books

make up the New Testament. ... As soon as Protestants begin to appeal to the canons drawn up by this or that Church Father, or this or that council, they immediately concede defeat, since they are forced to appeal to the very 'testimony of man and Church' that they claim not to need.[54]

Madrid's solution to the Protestant dilemma is Scripture *plus Tradition*, which together comprise "the Word of God." Believing the canon is revealed to him through Tradition, Madrid thinks he has defeated *Sola Scriptura*. Unlike the Protestant, he does not have to rely on something outside of *the Word of God* to know *the books of the Bible.*

It is an interesting argument as far as it goes, but it contains a subtle categorical error that we must not overlook. Both parties—Protestant and Roman Catholic—affirm what they believe to be "the Word of God." For Protestants it is *Scripture.* For Roman Catholics it is *Scripture* and *Tradition.* To prove the superiority of *Sola Verbum Dei*, therefore, the Roman Catholic cannot merely show that *the canon of Scripture* is contained within *Tradition.* Rather, he must prove that he can do what the Protestant cannot: identify the Word of God *without appealing to something outside the Word of God.* As we shall demonstrate, Madrid is manifestly unable to do so and suffers from the very problem that he thinks is exclusively Protestant. In fact, *Sola Verbum Dei* fails to meet the very standard by which Madrid condemns *Sola Scriptura.*

The "Canon of Scripture" from the Fathers and Councils

Madrid acknowledges that the Roman Catholic religion did not "formally" declare the canon of the Bible until 1546 at the allegedly ecumenical Council of Trent, but assures his reader that there were many "authoritative" lists of the canon of Scripture in the early church, including from the synod of Laodicæa (363 AD), the Synod of Rome (382 AD), and the regional councils of Hippo (393 AD) and

---

54   Madrid, p. 127

Carthage (397 AD).[55] Madrid's curious choice of words — "formal" to describe the canon of Trent and "authoritative" to describe the others — is quite revealing in itself as it is calculated to deceive. Church councils fall into two categories: ecumenical (assemblies in which the Pope and "all the bishops of the world" are represented) and national, provincial or regional (in which only a portion of the world's bishops are represented). By Rome's definition, provincial councils are not infallible, while ecumenical councils are infallible insofar as they receive "papal approbation ... subsequent to conciliar action."[56] What Madrid knows, but attempts to obscure, is the fact that his "authoritative" councils of Laodicæa, Rome, Hippo and Carthage were not *ecumenical* and therefore did not produce "formal" infallible declarations of the canon. In fact, they provided contradictory and inconsistent lists. Similarly, while Pope Paul VI claimed that "[t]he words of the holy fathers witness to ... the Church's full canon of the sacred books,"[57] they, too, provided contradictory and inconsistent lists.

A brief survey of patristic and conciliar attempts at establishing a canon of Scripture will reveal how misleading it is to say that the words of the holy fathers "witness to" the full canon and that the ancient provincial councils provided "authoritative" lists. None did. Nor did the councils, until the ostensibly ecumenical councils of Florence and Trent.

Yet even those ecumenical councils cannot rescue Madrid from the "Protestant problem." As we shall demonstrate, before one can appeal to a list of books provided by an ecumenical council, one must first know which councils were ecumenical, and there exists no infallible list of ecumenical councils within what Madrid calls "Tradition."[58] Madrid cannot therefore claim to stand on the Word of God — Scripture and Tradition — alone without first appealing to a canon of ecumenical councils that exists outside of Scripture

---

55   Madrid, p. 175
56   *Catholic Encyclopedia*, "Infallibility."
57   *Dei Verbum* ii.8.
58   Roman Catholicism distinguishes between "Tradition" (apostolic teachings allegedly preserved by the church's Magisterium through the centuries), and "tradition" (informal practices and disciplines manifesting throughout history that do not claim apostolicity). We will maintain that distinction here by referring to "Tradition" and "tradition."

and Tradition. To put it more bluntly, Madrid fails his own test, and "immediately concedes defeat" (his own words), because he cannot "know" the contents of "the Word of God" without appealing to something that exists outside of "the Word of God."

The Words of the Holy Fathers on the Canon of Scripture

As we will note in a later chapter, the "holy fathers" provide the Roman Catholic no help at all. Their opinions offer only contradictory testimony as to the "full canon of the sacred books," some accepting as canonical what others regarded as apocryphal, and rejecting as apocryphal books that others regarded as Scripture. A cursory review of just a few church fathers from the early centuries reveals at least ten different lists of "the sacred books," none of which can possibly claim to have passed on to us "the Church's full canon of the sacred books."

The *Muratorian Fragment* (170 AD) includes the book of Wisdom in the Old Testament but omits 3 John from the New, and appears to include the Epistle to the Laodicæans.[59] Bishop Melito of Sardis (170 AD) omitted Esther from the Old Testament as well as the seven additional apocryphal books of the Roman Catholic Bible: Sirach, Tobit, Wisdom, Judith, 1 and 2 Maccabees, and Baruch.[60] Irenæus of Lyons (289 AD) appears to have included the Shepherd of Hermas in the Scriptures.[61] Cyril of Jerusalem (350 AD) omitted Esther from the Old Testament, as well as the seven apocryphal books.[62] Hilary of Poitiers (360 AD) omitted the apocryphal books from the Old Testament, but allowed that "some add Tobit and Judith."[63] Athanasius (367 AD) omitted Esther from the Old Testament, as well as the other books of the apocrypha saying, "these [are] not indeed included in the Canon."[64] Epiphanius of Salamis (375 AD) omitted the apocrypha from his list but allowed that the Jews "have two more books of disputed canonicity, the Wisdom of Sirach and the Wisdom of

---

59　Muratorian Canon.
60　Melito of Sardis, Letter to Onesimus (Eusebius, *Ecclesiastical History* iv. 26).
61　Irenæus of Lyons, *Against Heresies*, IV.20.2.
62　Cyril of Jerusalem *Catechetical Lectures*, iv. 33-37.
63　Hilary of Portiers, *Expositions of the Psalms*, 15.
64　Athanasius, *Festal Letter 39.7*.

Solomon, apart from certain other apocrypha."[65] The *Apostolic Constitutions* (380 AD) included 1, 2 and 3 Maccabees in the Old Testament, but omitted Sirach, and included 1 and 2 Clement in the New Testament while omitting Revelation. Gregory Nazianzus (389 AD) omitted Esther from the Old Testament and Revelation from the New.[66] Jerome (391 AD), when creating a new Latin translation of the Bible for Pope Damasus, claimed that "we may be assured" that Wisdom, Sirach, Judith, Tobias and the Shepherd of Hermas "are not in the canon."[67] Pope Gregory the Great himself also acknowledged that the books of the Maccabees were "not Canonical."[68] Thus, the holy fathers most certainly do not, as Pope Paul VI claimed, "witness to … the Church's full canon of the sacred books."[69] The Roman Catholic must therefore look elsewhere to determine the canon of Scripture.

Provincial Councils on the Canon of Scripture

The early provincial councils also provided inconsistent and contradictory testimony. Canon 59 of the Synod of Laodicæa (363 AD) refers to "canonical" and "uncanonical" books, prohibiting the reading of "uncanonical" books in church. Canon 60 provided the list, including Esther but omitting the apocrypha from the Old Testament and Revelation from the New.[70] The Synod of Rome (382 AD) provided a list of the Old Testament and New Testament books, including most of the apocryphal books of the Old except

---

65   Epiphanius, *Panarion* viii. 6.
66   Gregory Nazianzus, *Carmina Dogmatica, Book I, Section I, Carmen XII.*
67   Jerome, "Helmeted Preface" to the books of Samuel and Kings (Schaff, NPNF-06, 489). Some Roman Catholics claim that Jerome eventually came around and accepted the apocrypha in his *Apology Against Rufinus* (402 AD), but that *Apology* merely contained a defense of the apocryphal sections of Daniel. It did not reverse his previous sentiment. Jerome appears to have maintained (403 AD) his original conviction that the apocryphal books were not canonical, as evidenced by this apparent reference to Maccabees and others the next year: "Let her avoid all apocryphal writings, and if she is led to read such not by the truth of the doctrines which they contain but out of respect for the miracles contained in them; let her understand that they are not really written by those to whom they are ascribed, that many faulty elements have been introduced into them, and that it requires infinite discretion to look for gold in the midst of dirt" (Jerome, Epistle 107.12 *to Læta* (403 AD)).
68   Gregory, *Moralia on Job*, Volume II, Book XIX, chapter 34.
69   *Dei Verbum* ii.8.
70   Karl Joseph von Hefele - *A History of the Christian Councils: from the original documents.* (While Canon 60 of Laodicæa is controverted, highly esteemed Roman Catholic bishop and church historian Karl Joseph von Hefele considered it legitimate.)

Baruch.[71] Canon 36 of the Synod of Hippo (393 AD) listed the Old and New Testament canons, reflecting the complete 27 book New Testament, omitting Baruch, and adding 2 Ezra. The 3rd Synod of Carthage (397 AD) reaffirmed the canonical list from Hippo.

The Council in Trullo (692 AD), so-called because it was held in the dome (*trullus*) of the palace at Constantinople, did not provide an explicit list of the canon. However, the 215 assembled bishops at Constantinople affirmed the canons of Laodicæa and Carthage as well as the canons of Athanasius of Alexandria and Gregory Nazianzus of Constantinople, unwittingly embracing *four different canonical lists*.[72] As noted above, Laodicæa included Esther and omitted the apocrypha and Revelation, while Carthage included the apocrypha plus 2 Ezra, less Baruch. Athanasius omitted the Apocrypha and Esther, while Gregory Nazianzus omitted the Apocrypha, Esther and Revelation. None of these matches the current Roman Catholic canon, and what will become momentarily quite relevant, Madrid does not personally consider the Council of Trullo to be ecumenical, *but other Roman Catholics do*.[73]

The Ecumenical Councils on the Canon of Scripture

"The infallibility promised to the Church is also present," the *Catholic Catechism* claims, "above all in an Ecumenical Council."[74] As Roman Catholic theologian and conciliar historian Heinrich Joseph Denzinger reminds us, "General [ecumenical] councils represent the universal Church and demand absolute obedience."[75]

---

71   We allow that various canonists believe some of the ancients subsumed Lamentations, Baruch and "the epistle of Jeremiah" under the single heading of "Jeremiah", while others listed them individually. The same may be said of any number of combinations of 1st, 2nd, 3rd & 4th Ezra. The matter can hardly be considered resolved by the scholars, except by hopeful gloss, as there can be no incontrovertible proof, say, that Gregary Nazianzus—"Jeremiah"; Jerome—"Jeremiah with Lamentations"; Hilary—"Jeremiah with Lamentations and the Epistle"; and Athanasius—"Jeremiah with Baruch, Lamentations, and the epistle"; were all referring to the very same text! It is indicative, rather, that there was no central unifying authority in the early Church to declare the Canon "authoritatively."
72   Council in Trullo, Canon 2.
73   Hadrian I, letter to Tenasius of Constantinople. His letter affirms all the ecumenical councils, and he refers in his statement to "a Lamb being pointed to by the Precursor as being found in certain of the venerable images," a plain reference to the 82nd canon of Trullo.
74   *Catechism of the Catholic Church*, 891.
75   Denzinger, *Enchiridion symbolorum et definitionum quae de rebus fidei et morum a conciliis oecumenicis* et summis pontificibus emanarunt (Wirceburgi: Sumptibus Stahelianis,1856) 461, "*Concilium generale representat ecclesiam universalem, eique absolute obediendum.*"

But how can one obey an "ecumenical" council absolutely, without knowing which councils are "ecumenical"? Or in Madrid's case, how can he know that the canon of Scripture was "formally" declared at the ecumenical Council of Trent in 1546, without first having access to an infallible list of councils that qualify as "ecumenical"? The problem for Roman Catholics in general, and for Madrid in particular, is that he can have no such knowledge for the simple reason that there exists nowhere within Scripture or Tradition an "authoritative" or "formal" list of "Ecumenical" Councils.

The attentive reader will immediately recognize Madrid's dilemma. Professor of Canon Law, Fr. George Nedungatt, Ph.D., observed in 2010 that there have been 21 ecumenical councils in the history of the church, but "no authoritative church magisterium established this canon."[76] To put a fine point on it, because "Sacred tradition and Sacred Scripture form one sacred deposit of the word of God,"[77] and neither Scripture nor "Sacred tradition" contain a list of ecumenical councils, Madrid must appeal to something outside of them in order to claim he knows the canon of Scripture from an ecumenical council.

What compounds Madrid's dilemma is that even among church fathers, Roman Catholic historians, and modern clergy, there exists no consensus on a formal, infallible list. As Dr. Nedungatt emphasizes, the traditional list of 21 ecumenical councils "is not an official list or canon fixed by any ecumenical council or papal definition or decree."[78] One such list is as follows:

1. Nicaea I (325 AD)
2. Constantinople I (381 AD)
3. Ephesus (431 AD)
4. Chalcedon (451 AD)
5. Constantinople II (553 AD)
6. Constantinople III (680 AD)
7. Nicaea II (787 AD)

---

76   Nedungatt, George, S.J. "The Council in Trullo Revisited: Ecumenism and the Canon of the Councils." *Journal of Theological Studies*, vol. 71, no. 3, 2010, 658.
77   *Dei Verbum*, 10.
78   Nedungatt, 657.

8. Constantinople IV (869 AD)
9. Lateran I (1123 AD)
10. Lateran II (1139 AD)
11. Lateran III (1179 AD)
12. Lateran IV (1215 AD)
13. Lyons I (1245 AD)
14. Lyons II (1274 AD)
15. Vienne (1311 - 1313 AD)
16. Constance (1414 - 1418 AD)
17. Basle (AD 1431), continued at Ferrara and concluded at Florence (1438 - 1439 AD)
18. Lateran V (1512 - 1517 AD)
19. Trent (1545 -1563 AD)
20. Vatican I (1869 - 1870 AD)
21. Vatican II (1962 - 1965 AD)

Other such lists could be and have been compiled, none are authoritative, and even the above list could be loaded with asterisks, caveats, conditions and exceptions, as clergy and theologians of Rome even today argue amongst themselves about which councils, and which sessions of those councils, and which decrees and paragraphs produced in those sessions, were truly ecumenical and must be obeyed.[79] The list itself is subject to continuing reinterpretation, as councils previously believed to be provincial are considered by some to be ecumenical even as modern scholars debate whether councils previously believed to be ecumenical are really worthy of the title. In 2020, Bishop Athanasius Schneider expressed hope that "a future Pope or Ecumenical Council will correct the erroneous statement made" at Vatican II, after the example of Pope Pius XII, who had ostensibly corrected in 1947 an error committed by the ecumenical Council of Florence in 1439.[80] Theologian Ron Conte was quick to correct him with his own opinion: "Bishop Athanasius Schneider errs gravely

---

79   See Hefele, vii (Of the Council of Constance, Pope Martin V "did not choose to express himself more clearly," but "[h]is successor, Eugenius iv., declared himself with greater distinctness.").
80   Schneider, Athanasius. "There Is No Divine Positive Will or Natural Right to the Diversity of Religions." *Gloria Dei*, 15 Jun. 2020, https://www.gloriadei.io/there-is-no-divine-positive-will-or-natural-right-to-the-diversity-of-religions/.

when he claims that Pope Pius XII corrected an error in a prior Ecumenical Council."[81] Thus, neither the "words of the holy fathers," nor the opinions of scholars and clergy, nor even the Magisterium itself, are able to compile a list of ecumenical councils. There is therefore no official "Traditional" canon of ecumenical councils, as we will show, forcing Madrid to appeal to something that exists outside the *Verbum Dei* in order to arrive at the Canon of Scriptures.

The Opinions of the Holy Fathers on Ecumenical Councils

As noted above, Pope Paul VI believed erroneously that "[t]he words of the holy fathers witness to" the canon of Scripture,[82] and those "holy fathers" are also unable to provide a reliable list of ecumenical councils. For example, Augustine believed the Council of Arles (314 AD) to be ecumenical,[83] and Pope Hadrian I believed Trullo[84] to be ecumenical.[85] Pope Innocent I (401 – 417 AD) apparently believed there had been another ecumenical council of the apostles in Antioch, in addition to the council in Jerusalem recorded in Acts 15, making mention of a "conventum Apostolorum" in his letter to Alexander of Antioch.[86] Further, as observed in Percival's history of the first seven ecumenical councils, the canons of Sardica "were received by the Greeks as of Ecumenical authority by the Council in Trullo."[87] Yet neither the Apostolic Council of Antioch, nor Arles,

---

81   Conte, Ron. "Correcting Bishop Athanasius Schneider on Traditio Instrumentorum." *The Reproach of Christ*, 26 June 2020, https://ronconte.com/2020/06/26/correcting-bishop-athanasius-schneider-on-traditio-instrumentorum/.

82   *Dei Verbum* ii.8.

83   Augustine, Epistle 43.19 (Migne, P.L. 33, 169, "plenarium Ecclesiæ universæ concilium"). Hefele attempts to diminish the significance of such terminology by claiming that regional or national councils "frequently received the name of universal or plenary (*universale* or *plenarium*)" (Hefele, vol. 1). But Augustine does not dither so, using both "plenary" and "universal" to describe the church council. The Synodal Letter from the Council of Arles affirms as much. The bishops acknowledged "the countries from which we come are different," attesting to the fact that it was no merely national or regional synod, and further that their decrees had been made "in the presence of the Holy Spirit and His Angels," and that their decrees "should be brought to the knowledge of all." (Optatus, *Against the Donatists* (1917) Appendix IV).

84   Also called the Quinisext (Fifth-Sixth) Council, because it attempted to compile a list of disciplinary canons from the 2nd and 3rd councils of Constantinople, the fifth and sixth ecumenical councils, respectively.

85   Hadrian I, letter to Tenasius of Constantinople. He refers in his statement to "a Lamb being pointed to by the Precursor as being found in certain of the venerable images," a plain reference to the 82nd canon of Trullo.

86   Innocent I, Epistle XXIV, 1. Migne, P.L, volume 20, 548.

87   *Nicene and Post-Nicene Fathers*, Second Series NPNF-02 volume 14. Henry R. Percival, editor (NY: Charles Scribner's Sons, 1900), 414.

nor Trullo nor Sardica are currently included in the above canon of
Ecumenical councils.

The Opinions of Roman Catholic Historians on Ecumenical Councils

Roman Catholic historians also struggle blindly to compile an
authoritative list of ecumenical councils. Nineteenth century
conciliar historian, Karl Josef von Hefele, while subscribing to all
the ecumenical councils through Trent, acknowledged that the
5th Lateran Council (1512 - 1517 AD) was "doubted by many" and
that other historians "have also raised doubts" about Vienne (1311
AD).[88] Additionally, while Hefele denied that the Council of Pisa
(1511 AD) was ecumenical and the papal legate of Pope Benedict
XII "called it an heretical and diabolical assembly,"[89] fourteenth
century French scholar Johannes Gerson, together with "almost
all the Gallicans," believed Pisa to be ecumenical.[90] Robert Bellarmine, for his part, calls Pisa a "general council" that was "neither
approved nor disapproved,"[91] and omits Constance from his list.[92]
As for the Council of Basle, Hefele records that "Richer and the
advanced Gallicans" held Basle as ecumenical, while Bellarmine, Roncaglia, and Holstenius did not.[93] Obviously there is no
agreement to be found among them, and various scholars hold to
different lists.

The Opinions of the Clergy on Ecumenical Councils

To make matters even more confusing to the Roman Catholic, the
"progress of scholarship in the study of the church councils" is still
underway,[94] resulting in contradictory versions of history being
published simultaneously from ostensibly authoritative Roman
Catholic sources. In 1962, *Les canons des conciles oecuméniques*,
including the "ecumenical" Council of Trullo, was published with

---

88   Hefele, Vol. I, 52-54.
89   Hefele, Vol. I, 54.
90   Hefele, Vol. I, 54-55.
91   Bellarminus, Robertus (1605). Chapter 8, Controversies of the Christian Faith, Volume II.
Ingolstadt: Sartorius. pp. 45–46 *"[Concilium] Generale nec approbatum nee reprobatum."*
92   Bellarminus.
93   Hefele, Vol. I, 56.
94   Nedungatt, 660.

the blessing of Cardinal Peter-Gregory Agagianian. The same year, "[t]he most widely used modern Catholic collection of the decrees of ecumenical councils, *Conciliorum oecumenicorum decretal*" was published without Trullo. Of this embarrassing debacle a Roman Catholic expert in canon law observes: "it was curious and even symptomatic that two Catholic editions of the ecumenical councils appeared simultaneously in 1962 .... The former included the Council in Trullo; the latter did not."[95]

Symptomatic, indeed! Simultaneously publishing contradictory lists of "the canon of Ecumenical councils" remains a symptom of the fact that the canon of ecumenical councils has never been, and never will be, authoritatively canonized as Tradition. It therefore will never be found within what Madrid claims to be "the Word of God." Clergy and theologians of Rome even today are still arguing. In 2020, Bishop Athanasius Schneider expressed hope that a future pope or council will correct Vatican II,[96] but others think Schneider needs correcting.[97] Dr. Nedungatt is not ashamed to admit that the list of ecumenical councils is still subject to change: "And what may seem to many Catholics a surprising novelty ... Trullo is increasingly being recognized as belonging among the ecumenical councils."[98] Even as Nedungatt talks of adding Trullo to the list, Archbishop Carlo Maria Viganò advocates for the removal of Vatican II: "And it will also have to be determined whether an anomalous and disastrous event such as Vatican II can still merit the title of Ecumenical Council, once its heterogeneity compared to previous councils is universally recognized."[99] Fifty "priests, scholars, journalists, and other persons of prominence" joined with Viganò to implore

---

95   Ibid.
96   Schneider, Athanasius. "There Is No Divine Positive Will or Natural Right to the Diversity of Religions." *Gloria Dei*, 15 Jun. 2020, https://www.gloriadei.io/there-is-no-divine-positive-will-or-natural-right-to-the-diversity-of-religions/.
97   Conte, Ron. "Correcting Bishop Athanasius Schneider on Traditio Instrumentorum." *The Reproach of Christ*, 26 June 2020, https://ronconte.com/2020/06/26/correcting-bishop-athanasius-schneider-on-traditio-instrumentorum/.
98   Nedungatt, 652.
99   Archbishop Carlo Maria Viganò September 21, 2020 6 Comments. "Archbishop Viganò: Is Vatican II 'Untouchable'?" *OnePeterFive*, Crisis Publications, 28 Sept. 2020, https://onepeterfive.com/archbishop-vigano-is-vatican-ii-untouchable/.

the church to debate "[w]hether or not Vatican II can be reconciled with Tradition."[100]

Lacking any formal, infallible canon of Ecumenical councils, the dubious Roman Catholic and the curious Protestant are equally justified in asking: If the councils of Arles, Sardica, Trullo and Pisa can be *added* to the "canon of Ecumenical Councils," and Constance, Basle, Lateran V and Vatican II can be *removed*, what prevents Florence and Trent from being debated as well? As the Roman religion has never "formally" defined the canon of ecumenical councils, how can one know with certainty *which ecumenical council* has "formally" approved the canon of Scripture? One cannot be certain at all for the simple reason that the evasive "canon of Ecumenical councils" exists outside "the Word of God," and therefore outside the realm of "certainty about everything which has been revealed." And thus Madrid must rely on a fallible, and apparently disputed, "table of contents" *of ecumenical councils* in order to arrive at his own fallible, personal opinion about the "table of contents" *of Scripture*. But that is just the beginning of his problems.

The Magisterium

According to the *Catholic Encyclopedia* the Magisterium is "an official organ" by which Sacred Tradition is transmitted.[101] And according to the *Catholic Catechism*, "It is this Magisterium's task to preserve God's people from deviations and defections and to guarantee them the objective possibility of professing the true faith without error."[102] Yet the Magisterium has demonstrated time and time again that it is manifestly unable to "preserve" Roman Catholics from confusion, deviations and defections, leaving them to their own devices to determine what the Magisterium has taught them. Thus, contrary to Madrid's claims, rather than

---

100 Hickson, Maike. "50 Priests, Scholars, Journalists Thank Viganò, Schneider for Raising Vatican II Questions." *LifeSite News*, 15 July 2020, https://www.lifesitenews.com/blogs/50-priests-scholars-journalists-thank-vigano-schneider-for-raising-vatican-ii-questions/. ("Open Letter to Archbishop Carlo Maria Viganò and Bishop Athanasius Schneider" (July 9, 2020)).
101 *Catholic Encyclopedia*, Tradition and Living Magisterium.
102 Catechism, 890.

helping him, the Magisterium only continues to exacerbate his epistemological problem.

One of Madrid's favorite ways to illustrate the need for a Magisterium is to write a six-word sentence on a piece of paper and ask someone to interpret it: "*I never said you stole money.*" As simple as the sentence is on paper, it takes on different nuances when spoken out loud, as can be demonstrated by changing the emphasis on each word: "I never said you *stole* money" has a slightly different meaning than "I never said you stole *money*," and so on. Madrid then poses the question: "Which is more likely to be open to a misunderstanding of its meaning: this six-word sentence, or the holy Bible comprised of all these different scriptures written by different people at different times for different purposes in different languages?" From this, Madrid concludes that while everyone has his own personal interpretation of the Bible, only Roman Catholics "have access to how the earliest Christians understood these doctrines" through the Magisterium.[103] What Madrid does not appear to understand is how fatal that six-word illustration is to his own argument. This will become clear as we respond to Madrid's arguments for the Magisterium.

The Need for Teachers

Madrid's first foray into the topic of the Magisterium is simply to contextualize John's admonition, "ye need not that any man teach you" (1 John 2:27), a verse occasionally used by Protestants to discount the need for a teaching Magisterium. Madrid responds, "[I]f Christians don't need teachers, then why did the Lord establish in the Church the office of teacher?"[104] We will not begrudge Mr. Madrid the opportunity to correct the misperception, and we agree with him at least in one limited sense: The apostle's admonition does not mean the church has no need of teachers. John wrote it in the context of the growing Gnostic assault on the incarnation. In its original context it means rather that his audience is sufficiently

---

103 Coming Home Network. "The Fathers Know Best: Scripture and Tradition in the Early Church - Patrick Madrid." *YouTube*, 16 June 2016, https://www.youtube.com/watch?v=elIN-GUpOcTo.
104 Madrid, p. 169

equipped to stave off the decidedly unapostolic overtures of the Gnostics, who denied the incarnation and were notorious for "boasting themselves as improvers of the apostles"[105] and for claiming that "the truth was not delivered by means of written documents."[106] As John acknowledges in the previous verse, "I write these things to you about those who are trying to deceive you" (1 John 2:26). John had already instructed the flock as to the reality of the incarnation and the truth of the bodily resurrection (1 John 1:1), but his congregation certainly had more than personal recollections of his oral instructions to guide them. Not only did they have access to a written copy of his Gospel and epistles, but they also could read other epistles in circulation, just as other congregations did (Colossians 4:16, 1 Thessalonians 5:27). Late first and second century writers also attest to the common availability of the Scriptures to the many Christian congregations. Clement of Rome (first century) indicated that the Corinthians had immediate access to the Scriptures, citing the gospels of Matthew and Luke[107] and instructing them to "[l]ook carefully into the Scriptures" and to read 1 Corinthians.[108] Ignatius of Antioch (107 AD) implies not only that the Law, the Prophets, the Pauline Epistles and the Gospels were in circulation in Asia Minor in his day (d. 107 AD) but also that the Gnostics could read them but did not believe them: "These persons neither have the prophets persuaded, nor the law of Moses, nor the Gospel."[109] Thus, John's admonition simply means that his flock did not need the "additional revelation" the Gnostics were purveying orally. Well-equipped saints have no need of additional "teaching" from heretics.

Just me and my Bible

Madrid's next argument for the Magisterium is narrowly targeted at the nondenominational Evangelical Christian who says, "I have the Bible, and that's all I need." Here Madrid returns to his

---

105 Irenæus, *Against Heresies*, 3.3.1.
106 Irenæus, *Against Heresies*, 3.3.2.
107 Clement, *To the Corinthians*, 27 & 24.
108 Clement, *To the Corinthians*, 46 & 47.
109 Ignatius, *To the Smyrnæans*, 5, 7; *To the Ephesians*, 12.

arguments against *Sola Scriptura*, pointing out that it is inconsistent to go only by the teachings found in the Bible, if the Bible does not contain *that particular teaching*.[110] We suspect here that Madrid has rather missed the point because the "Evangelical Christian" who prefers the Bible to the Roman Magisterium has very sound Biblical reasons for his preference.

The Bible certainly indicates that Christians need to fellowship together and encourage and teach one another (Acts 8:31, 18:25-26; Hebrews 3:13, 10:25). As Madrid correctly observes, Jesus gave apostles, prophets, evangelists, shepherds and teachers, "to equip the saints" (Ephesians 4:11-12).[111] We hasten, however, to add the apostolic warning that even within the church "there shall be false teachers among you" who arise "from among your own selves" (Acts 20:29-30, 2 Timothy 4:3, 2 Peter 2:1), for which reason the apostles inscripturated their admonitions (1 Timothy 6:2, 2 Peter 3:2, 1 John 2:26), "that ye may be able after my decease to have these things always in remembrance" (2 Peter 1:15), for "after my departing shall grievous wolves enter in among you" (Acts 20:29). Though the Spirit provided teachers, the apostles did not instruct their flocks to place their unwavering trust in a succession of bishops in "Pontus, Galatia, Cappadocia, Asia, and Bithyniam" (1 Peter 1:1), Colossae, Thessalonica, Corinth, Ephesus, Philippi, and certainly not in Rome. Rather, they documented their teachings as a defense against the orally transmitted errors that were sure to follow. As the Roman Magisterium has shown itself unable to recall the actual oral traditions of the apostles, but very zealous to transmit error under the guise of apostolicity, the Evangelical Christian who appeals to the Scriptures alone certainly stands closer to the apostles than the Roman apologist does. As we will demonstrate later, Madrid's arguments in support of the papacy, the sacrifice of the transubstantiated Eucharist and the veneration of Mary are distant departures from the Scriptures and the expressed beliefs of the apostolic and subapostolic church. He claims to "have access to how the earliest Christians understood

---

110 Madrid, p. 170
111 Ibid.

these doctrines,"[112] and yet each argument he makes is easily falsified when we find that the early church did not believe in the primacy of Rome, or the sacrifice of Jesus' body and blood in the Eucharist, or the sinlessness of Mary.

Upon the Rock

Madrid continues his criticism of the "nondenominational" Christian by observing that Jesus founded only one denomination, the Catholic Church: "Christ said, 'On this rock I will build my church,' ... He did not say, 'On this rock I will build a network of loosely affiliated nondenominational fellowships.'"[113] Madrid's objection is easily refuted if it can be shown that the church Jesus founded really was "a network of loosely affiliated nondenominational fellowships," and indeed it was! This is evident not only from the Biblical record but from the historical record of the subapostolic church. The earliest congregations were scattered throughout the known world with nothing to hold them together but the ministry of the Holy Spirit and the teachings of the Law, the Prophets and the Apostles, as is plainly evident from the *Book of Acts, 1 & 2 Peter* and the first three chapters of *Revelation*. When Paul left the Ephesian elders at Miletus, he commended them not to a monolithic denomination headquartered in Rome, but rather "to God, and to the word of his grace" (Acts 20:32). When Peter was approaching death, he commended his flocks not to his alleged successor in Rome, but to the local shepherds, to "the God of all grace" (1 Peter 5:1-11) and to the words of the prophets, Jesus and the apostles (2 Peter 3:2). Jesus commanded John to write directly to "the seven churches" of Asia Minor, not to the infallible papal Magisterium in Rome (Revelation 1-3). In addition to the Biblical account of the early church, the subapostolic writers described the scattered and diverse congregations in much the same way, different in their ecclesiology and liturgy, but unified in their profession of faith, held together by an invisible power that administered the church from heaven rather than from Rome.

---

112 Coming Home Network
113 Madrid, p. 171

As we have elsewhere observed, the early congregations believed they were shepherded by a local pastor who was himself shepherded by Christ, not by a Roman pope. One first century writer believed it was "Michael" who invisibly administered the scattered congregations throughout the world,[114] and Mathetes (second century) observed that the scattered congregations did not "inhabit cities of their own"[115] and though unified, the source of their unity "remains invisible."[116] When Victor of Rome attempted to establish a carnal uniformity of the celebration of the Lord's Passion and Resurrection, Irenæus (c. 189 AD) rebuked him, describing precisely the "loosely affiliated nondenominational fellowships" Madrid claims did not exist in the early church:

> For the controversy is not only concerning the day, but also concerning the very manner of the fast. For some think that they should fast one day, others two, yet others more; some, moreover, count their day as consisting of forty hours day and night. And this variety in its observance has not originated in our time; but long before in that of our ancestors. It is likely that they did not hold to strict accuracy, and thus formed a custom for their posterity according to their own simplicity and peculiar mode. Yet all of these lived nonetheless in peace, and we also live in peace with one another; and the disagreement in regard to the fast confirms the agreement in the faith.[117]

Keep in mind, the "controversy" to which Irenæus refers was about how to celebrate "the eucharist," which in Madrid's religion is "the source and summit" of the faith. And yet, in the early church, there was no mechanism for establishing uniformity of the eucharistic liturgy, try though Victor may to establish it by coercion. As Irenæus illustrated, when Polycarp of Smyrna visited Anicetus of Rome (c. 160 AD), *neither could persuade the other to change his*

---

114 *The Shepherd of Hermas*, Book III, Similitude 8, chapter 3.
115 *The Epistle of Mathetes to Diognetus*, chapter 5.
116 *The Epistle of Mathetes to Diognetus*, chapter 6.
117 Eusebius, *Church History*, V.24.12-13.

traditional mode of celebrating the Supper.[118] At the dawn of the Nicæan era, Alexander of Alexandria, in his letters to all the congregations of the world, observed that while the individual congregations were widely scattered and distant, nevertheless, "it is commanded in Holy Scripture that we should keep the bond of unanimity and peace." By what means that unanimity, and by what mechanism that peace? Perhaps by deferring to a chief shepherd in Rome, or possibly to the papal Magisterium there presiding as supreme interpreter of Sacred Tradition? Nay, none of these: "it follows that we should write and signify to one another the things which are done by each of us; that whether one member suffer or rejoice we may all either suffer or rejoice with one another."[119] Indeed, the church scattered throughout the world with a *heavenly* metropolis—the very church Jesus founded "upon this rock," bound loosely together by their common fellowship in Christ by the Word and through the Spirit—was the very religion of "loosely affiliated nondenominational fellowships" Madrid now rejects in favor of his carnal uniformity, centrally administered from an *earthly* metropolis. We do not deny that the Roman episcopate eventually came to ecclesial and civil power to establish a carnal, earthly unity by force, but *that* is not the church Jesus founded "upon this rock." Nor, as we shall see, has Madrid's Magisterium brought about the unity he claims.

Madrid's *Anarchy* Problem

In Madrid's mind, *Sola Scriptura* is a recipe for anarchy. To summarize his claim, he cites his own article, "A Blueprint for Anarchy":

> Protestantism is so divided over central doctrinal issues (e.g., infant baptism, baptismal regeneration, the nature of justification, salvation, divorce and remarriage, etc.) …. All Protestants believe they have embraced the 'correct' interpretation of Scripture, but doing so includes the implicit

---

118 Eusebius, *Church History*, V.24.16.
119 Alexander of Alexandria, Catholic Epistle.

assertion that all the other denominations don't have the correct interpretation on all things. If they did, why the need for denominations?[120]

That "anarchy," of course, would go away, Madrid says, if the Protestant would simply repent of *Sola Scriptura* and submit to the Magisterial interpretation of Sacred Tradition. Before the Protestant accepts such an invitation, he would do well to write down these six words on a piece of paper and ask Madrid what they mean: "That all doubt may be removed." As it turns out, that is a very, very complicated phrase, and even the Magisterium of the Catholic Church is unable to decode its meaning.

The Puzzle of ex cathedra *Papal Statements*
Included within the construct of the Magisterium are the infallible teachings of the pope. According to the *Catholic Catechism*, the Pope teaches infallibly "when, as supreme pastor and teacher of all the faithful … he proclaims by a definitive act a doctrine pertaining to faith or morals."[121] The technical term for such a proclamation is *ex cathedra*—a Latin phrase meaning "from the chair," i.e., the chair of St. Peter. Roman Catholics are bound to adhere to such proclamations "with the obedience of faith."[122] It is important to understand that the pope does not possess this infallibility simply by opening his mouth and speaking. His casual comments are not "infallible." He is only alleged to exercise the charism of infallibility when he proclaims a doctrine "by a definitive act." The problem is that Roman Catholics are on their own to determine which acts are "definitive" and thus must be received "with the obedience of faith." Madrid personally believes he can know when a pope has spoken infallibly,[123] but if that were true, Roman Catholics everywhere would know with confidence and agree with each other about what has been taught "from the chair." But they do not.

---

120 Madrid, pp. 45-48
121 *Catechism of the Catholic Church*, 891.
122 Ibid.
123 Patrick Madrid Show, June 14, 2019 https://relevantradio.com/2019/06/the-patrick-madrid-show-june-14-2019-hour-2/

Gary Wills, in his book, *Why I am a Catholic*, believes *ex cathedra* infallibility "has been used only once": in 1950 to declare Mary's assumption into heaven.[124] But Kevin Considine, writing for *US Catholic*, says "there are only two" *ex cathedra* statements in history: Pope Pius IX's 1854 proclamation on the Immaculate Conception of Mary, and Pope Pius XII's 1950 proclamation on Mary's Assumption.[125] But according to Klaus Schatz, there have been seven such proclamations,[126] and even then, he believes there are yet three more pronouncements by John Paul II— *Veritatis Splendor* (1993), *Ordinatio Sacerdotalis* (1994) and *Evangelium Vitae* (1995)—that "would be 'ex cathedra definitions' in the sense of Vatican I," but are not considered *ex cathedra* by the Magisterium, creating "an unclear situation as regards the teaching office."[127] According to Adam Miller's 1997 reckoning, there have been eleven such statements,[128] and according to Fr. Leslie Rumble, there have been eighteen, but he is not entirely sure; two of those eighteen, he believes, are "very probably" *ex cathedra*, but two others on that list may "fall short" of the bar.[129]

Where does Patrick Madrid plant his stake? "I tend to hold the view," he says, that the 1854 and 1950 proclamations were *ex cathedra*, but "beyond that, it is somewhat of an open question."[130] Open question, indeed! And to our point, Madrid's official list of *ex cathedra* statements is an informal "tradition," but is not an apostolic "Tradition," because, as Kevin Considine acknowledged, "There is no set list of *ex cathedra* teachings."[131] And thus, to hold to *Sola Verbum Dei*, Madrid must not only rely upon a fallible, and

---

124 Wills, Gary *Why I am a Catholic* (Houghton Mifflin Company, 2002), xiii.
125 Considine, K. P. (2011, May 18). *Is there a list of infallible teachings?* U.S. Catholic. Retrieved November 18, 2021, from https://uscatholic.org/articles/201105/is-there-a-list-of-infallible-teachings/.
126 Sullivan, F. A. *Creative Fidelity: Weighing and Interpreting Documents of the Magisterium* (Wipf & Stock Publishers, 2003), 86.
127 Schatz, Klaus, S.J. *Papal Primacy: From its origins to the present* Otto, John A, Maloney, Linda M. *trans.* (Collegeville, MN: The Liturgical Press, 1996), 173.
128 Miller, Adam *The Final Word* (Gaithersburg, MD: Tower of David Publications, 1997).
129 Rumble et al., *That Catholic Church: A Radio Analysis,* (St. Paul, MN, Radio Replies Press, 1954), 80-81.
130 Patrick Madrid Show, November 10, 2021 https://relevantradio-od.streamguys1.com/madrid/PM20211110b.mp3.
131 Considine, Kevin. "Is There a List of Infallible Teachings?" *U.S. Catholic*, 18 May 2011, https://uscatholic.org/articles/201105/is-there-a-list-of-infallible-teachings/.

apparently disputed, canon of Ecumenical Councils, he must also rely upon a fallible, disputed, canon of *ex cathedra* proclamations that, like the canon of councils, does not exist within the *Verbum Dei* and has come down to him entirely outside of "the Word of God."

The Puzzle of Ordinatio Sacerdotalis

As we have noted, a formal declaration by an ecumenical council or a "definitive" *ex cathedra* proclamation by a pope is ostensibly infallible. Such a teaching is an exercise of the *extraordinary* Magisterium. On the other hand, according to Vatican II, individual bishops also exercise infallibility when they "proclaim Christ's doctrine" unanimously in communion with the pope.[132] Such is an exercise of the *ordinary* Magisterium. The Roman Catholic is obligated to believe the infallible teachings of the Magisterium as a condition of salvation. According to Canon Law, "No doctrine is understood as defined infallibly unless this is manifestly evident,"[133] so the Roman Catholic does not have to receive a teaching as infallible unless its infallibility is manifestly evident to him.

Of course, not everything taught by a pope is *ex cathedra*, nor is everything proclaimed by bishops in union with the pope infallible.[134] As Ludwig Ott observed in his *Fundamentals of Catholic Dogma*, "not all the assertions of the Teaching Authority of the Church on questions of Faith and morals are infallible," and though the Roman Catholic is obligated to accept all such teachings "with an inner assent," the "obligation of inner agreement may cease" if a fallible teaching has been found, upon "renewed scientific investigation" by a "competent expert" to be in error. [135] Thus, the Roman Catholic is only

---

132 Vatican II, Dogmatic Constitution *Lumen Gentium*, 3.25.
133 *Code of Canon Law*, Canon 749.3.
134 Shaw, Russell "Understanding the Infallibility Teaching." December 17, 1995, *Our Sunday Visitor*.
135 Ludwig Ott, *Fundamentals of Catholic Dogma*, ed. James Canon Bastible, translated by Patrick Lynch, Rockford, Illinois: TAN Books and Publishers, 1974; orig. 1952 in German, 4-5, 9-10.

obligated to believe fallible teachings unless and until they are proven to be wrong.

The challenge facing the Roman Catholic therefore is to know when it is manifestly evident that the Magisterium is teaching infallibly, and to know when it is not teaching infallibly, and further to know when an "expert" is sufficiently competent, or a "renewed investigation" is sufficiently scientific, to determine that a fallible teaching is in fact wrong. And yet, despite these ostensibly clear guidelines, a great deal of confusion—or rather, *anarchy*—remains for Roman Catholics, because each is left to his own devices to determine what has been taught, whether it is infallible, who is an expert, what might be wrong and what must be believed.[136] John Paul II himself expressed this very concern in his 1995 address to the *Congregation for the Doctrine of the Faith*, lamenting the "widespread misunderstanding of the meaning and role of the Church's Magisterium" and its "various degrees of teaching":

> That this authority includes various degrees of teaching ... does not entitle one to hold that the pronouncements and doctrinal decisions of the Magisterium call for irrevocable assent only when it states them in a solemn judgment or definitive act... .[137]

Clearly, it had come to the attention of the Supreme Pontiff that his sheep did not know, understand or believe what it is that they were to know, understand and believe. In other words, the whole purpose of papal and magisterial infallibility (according to *Madrid*)

---

136 Roman Catholic philosopher, Timothy Gordon, laments this state of affairs explicitly: "It's asinine, that it's this unclear. ... It's asinine that someone has to go do a doctoral dissertation in the third Christian millennium on whether or not the magisterium can err in thus and such proclamation in an encyclical or an exhortation. It's asinine that this is not more constitutionally laid out, procedurally" (*No More Latin Mass? YouTube*, Rules for Retrogrades, 26 May 2021, www.youtube.com/watch?app=desktop&v=RNkJ1sQmadI). "The dumbest part about being Catholic ... is that it takes a dissertation ... to figure out what the metamagisterium is. ... We need a Vatican III to explain Vatican I and to explain Vatican II" (*A Word of Encouragement YouTube*, Rules for Retrogrades, 29 July 2021, https://www.youtube.com/watch?v=9r_EVx-0qe4Q).
137 John Paul II, *Address to Congregation for the Doctrine of the Faith*, paragraphs 5-6 (November 24, 1995).

was lost on the general Roman Catholic population. The reason this was of particular concern to John Paul II was the confusion resulting from his 1994 Apostolic Letter, *Ordinatio Sacerdotalis*, a letter that he wrote "that all doubt may be removed" and which he personally believed was a teaching of the *ordinary* Magisterium. While it did not contain "a solemn judgment or definitive act," it was nevertheless a restatement of "the unanimous teaching of the Pastors."[138]

By Madrid's reasoning, such a teaching by the pope—ordinary or extraordinary—should have removed all doubt and prevented the resulting anarchy. But John Paul II's Letter had the opposite effect, raising the question as to whether it was an *infallible* teaching of the extraordinary Magisterium, or a *fallible* teaching of the ordinary Magisterium but worthy of irrevocable assent, or a fallible teaching that might later be overturned by a "competent expert" after thorough scientific investigation. Apparently, the words "that all doubt may be removed" mean different things to different Roman Catholics, and even the Magisterium itself does not know. A historical survey of the changing and varied inter-pretations of *Ordinatio Sacerdotalis* demonstrates that Madrid's religion suffers from the very anarchy that he thinks he has avoided.

John Paul II published *Ordinatio Sacerdotalis* on May 22, 1994, proclaiming "definitively" that women may not be ordained to the priesthood:

> Wherefore, in order that all doubt may be removed regarding a matter of great importance, a matter which pertains to the Church's divine constitution itself, in virtue of my ministry of confirming the brethren (cf. Lk 22:32), I declare that the Church has no authority what-soever to confer priestly ordination on women and that this judgment is to be definitively held by all the Church's faithful.[139]

---

138 John Paul II, *Address to Congregation for the Doctrine of the Faith*, paragraph 6 (November 24, 1995).
139 John Paul II, *Ordinatio Sacerdotalis*, 4.

Because he appeared to "declare" something "definitively," faithful Roman Catholics, using the guidelines from Vatican I, immediately concluded "that John Paul II was exercising his prerogative of infallibility when he issued it," and had been speaking *ex cathedra.*[140] It appeared to have been an infallible exercise of the *extraordinary* Magisterium. By October 28 the next year, then Cardinal Ratzinger, Prefect of the Sacred Congregation for the Doctrine of the Faith, issued a clarification, noting that *Ordinatio Sacerdotalis* "has been set forth infallibly by the *ordinary* and universal Magisterium,"[141] but was "in itself not infallible."[142] However, some clergy dismissed Ratzinger's attempted clarification because "the decisions of the Roman Congregations," like Ratzinger's Congregation for the Doctrine of the Faith, "are not infallible"[143]:

> With all due respect to Cardinal Ratzinger, ... the Holy Father's statement *Ordinatio Sacerdotalis* is an infallible exercise of the *extraordinary* papal magisterium.[144]

But in 1998 the Congregation for the Doctrine of the Faith, under Cardinal Ratzinger, continued to dismiss such objections and insisted that John Paul II had not wished to issue "a dogmatic definition," and further that the church had not yet progressed *"to the point where this teaching could be defined as a doctrine to be believed as divinely revealed."*[145] But

---

140 Mirus, Jeff. "Ordinatio Sacerdotalis: Exercise in Infallibility" EWTN Global Catholic Television Network, 4 June 1994, https://www.ewtn.com/catholicism/library/ordinatio-sacerdotalis-exercise-in-infallibility-11028.

141 Congregation for the Doctrine of the Faith, Joseph Cardinal Ratzinger, Prefect "Responsum ad Dubium, Concerning the Teaching contained in *Ordinatio Sacerdotalis*" (October 28, 1995). Emphasis added.

142 Joseph Cardinal Ratzinger, Concerning the Reply of the Congregation for the Doctrine of the Faith on the Teaching Contained in the Apostolic Letter *Ordinatio Sacerdotalis* (October 28, 1995).

143 Ott, 9-10.

144 Pilsner, Fr. Peter. "Is *Ordinatio Sacerdotalis* an Infallible Exercise of the Extraordinary Papal Magisterium?: EWTN." EWTN Global Catholic Television Network, https://www.ewtn.com/catholicism/library/is-ordinatio-sacerdotalis-an-infallible-exercise-of-the-extraordinary-papal-magisterium-11032. Emphasis added.

145 Cardinal Ratzinger, *A Doctrinal Commentary on the Concluding Formula of the Professio Fidei*, 11 (June 29, 1998) https://www.vatican.va/roman_curia/congregations/cfaith/documents/rc_con_cfaith_doc_1998_professio-fidei_en.html.

staunch Roman Catholics continued to disagree with him. In 2001, Roman Catholic layperson, E. Lane Core Jr., published a rigorous analysis of John Paul's II statement, concluding that it had indeed been an infallible exercise of the *extraordinary* Magisterium:

> Objections to the contrary notwithstanding, the teaching in *Ordinatio Sacerdotalis* is infallible because it fulfills the only requirements that must be fulfilled: those specified in *Pastor Aeternus* [Vatican I] and repeated in *Lumen Gentium* [Vatican II].[146]

But in November 2002, another layperson, Eric Stoutz of *Catholics United for the Faith*, insisted that while *Ordinatio Sacerdotalis* was infallible, it had only been an exercise of the *ordinary* Magisterium.[147] But in May 2003, a self-professed "progressive" Roman Catholic layperson disagreed with Core and Stoutz, concluding from his own studies that John Paul II had not made it "manifestly evident" that he intended to speak infallibly.[148] But in 2005, another layperson, recognizing the "confusion under which we labor," analyzed the history of the proclamation and the commentaries related to it, concluding that John Paul II had made it manifestly evident that *Ordinatio Sacerdotalis* was infallible, and in fact was "also *ex cathedra*."[149] But James Akin, Senior Apologist at *Catholic Answers*, a Roman Catholic apologetics ministry, weary of people attempting to prove that the Pope's statement had been *ex cathedra*, objected:

---

146 Core, E. Lane. "Ordinatio Sacerdotalis: Infallible Teaching?" *Ordinatio Sacerdotalis: Infallible Teaching? @ ELCore.Net*, 5 Dec. 2001, http://catholicity.elcore.net/CoreOnOrdinatioSacerdotalis.html.

147 Catholics United for the Faith, Faith Facts: *The Infallibility of the Magisterium of the Catholic Church* (November 2002). http://www.cuf.org/2002/11/pillar-and-bulwark-of-the-truth-the-infallibility-magisterium-of-the-catholic- church/ (retrieved July 5 2015).

148 Cecil, J. *Is Ordinatio Sacerdotalis Infallible?*, 10 May 2003, http://isosinfallible.blogspot.com/.

149 Howard, Peter *Here's why no women priests is infallible teaching and closed* (January 1, 2005). (http://www.ewtn.com/vexperts/showresult.asp?RecNum=423666&Forums=0&Experts=0&Days=2002&Author=&Keyword=&pgnu=4&groupnum=193&record_bookmark=48448) (Retrieved July 5, 2015).

The pope simply *didn't* use the word that he normally used
in making definitions and he *didn't* use other language
making it 'manifestly evident' that this is what he was
doing. Therefore, he didn't do it. [150]

Akin's readers were unconvinced, choosing instead to believe
that John Paul II had indeed been speaking *ex cathedra*: "I am
not that all convinced yet that [*Ordinatio Sacerdotalis* was]
an ordinary teaching."[151] Others complained that Akin was
"parsing the doctrine of infallibility so finely that it loses any
real meaning."[152] By 2008 another Roman Catholic apologist,
Robert Sungenis, was insisting that *Ordinatio Sacerdotalis* was
"non-infallible," because "the language John Paul II used in the
decree gave some doubt as to whether he was making it infallible."[153] But in 2009, another lay apologist published a book
defending *Ordinatio Sacerdotalis* as an *ex cathedra* pronounce-
ment of the extraordinary Magisterium, because John Paul II
clearly intended to remove all doubt.[154] But Bishop William M.
Morris in Australia was not so sure. In December of 2009, he
thought that the ordination of women priests was still an open
question, and proposed that ordaining women might solve the
priest shortage.[155] Such a suggestion earned a stern rebuke from
former Cardinal Ratzinger, later elevated to Pope Benedict XVI.
Gone was the language of Ratzinger *the Cardinal*, who had said
that *Ordinatio Sacerdotalis* was "in itself not infallible." Now
Ratzinger *the Pope* insisted that "the late Pope John Paul II has
decided infallibly and irrevocably that the Church has not the
right to ordain women to the priesthood."[156] But Pope Benedict's

---

150 Akin, Jimmy. "Saddle up!" *Jimmy Akin*, 26 May 2005, http://jimmyakin.com/2005/05/
saddle_up-2.html. Emphasis in original.
151 Akin, http://jimmyakin.com/2005/05/saddle_up-2.html#comments.
152 Ibid.
153 Sungenis, Robert *Catholic Apologetics International*, August 5, 2008 (retrieved July 5,
2015 from the world wide web at http://catholicintl.com/question-85-july-2008).
154 Trudeau-LeBlanc, Roger *Ordinatio Sacerdotalis On the Ordination of Men Alone: A case for
its Infallibility* (USA: Roger LeBlanc, 2009).
155 Morris, William M. *Benedict, Me, and the Cardinals Three* (Australian Theological Forum
Press, 2014).
156 Benedict XVI, Letter to William Morris, Bishop of Toowoomba, December 22, 2009 (see
Appendix 16 of Morris).

own Cardinals were not so sure. In a May 2011 interview with the Portuguese Bar Association, Cardinal Policarpo expressed his belief that *Ordinatio Sacerdotalis* was simply a fallible tradition.[157] Only a few weeks later the editorial staff at the *National Catholic Reporter* agreed, arguing that John Paul II had not made it "manifestly evident" that he intended to speak infallibly, and further, while the Congregation for the Doctrine of the Faith had alleged the teaching to be infallible, it was nevertheless "beyond [the doctrinal congregation's] authority to determine which church teachings are infallible and which are not."[158] In the meantime, a month later, Cardinal Policarpo was "forced … to accept the Magisterium of the Holy Father," and thus to issue a "humbling clarification" that the matter was indeed an infallible tradition, not a fallible one.[159] But in 2016, *America Magazine* quoted Pope Francis I as saying during a press conference that the church's teaching on the matter was either "never likely to change," or was "unlikely to ever change," depending on how the Pope's words were translated into English, seeming to leave open the possibility that the church's position *could* change in the future.[160] Because doubts apparently still remained in 2018, the prefect of the Congregation for the Doctrine of the Faith was compelled once again to issue a statement on the matter because "doubts raised about the definitive nature of *Ordinatio sacerdotalis* also have grave consequences for the manner of understanding the Magisterium of the Church."[161] And yet, in March of 2019, some Roman Catholic clergy were still calling for the

157 Cabo, Ana Isabel *OA Boletim da Ordem dos Avogados*, Mensal No. 78, Maio 2011, 34-41 (English translation available here: https://rorate-caeli.blogspot.com/2011/06/mediocre-leader-of-most-mediocre.html).

158 NCR Editorial Staff, NCR Editorial Staff. "Ordination Ban Not Infallibly Taught." *National Catholic Reporter*, 23 May 2011, https://www.ncronline.org/news/ordination-ban-not-infallibly-taught.

159 Policarpo, D. José. "Esclarecimento Do Cardeal-Patriarca De Lisboa." *Patriarcado*, 6 July 2011, https://www.patriarcado-lisboa.pt/site/index.php?id=904. (English translation here: https://rorate-caeli.blogspot.com/2011/07/humbling-clarification.html#more).

160 Davis, Zac, and Sawyer, Sam, S.J. "Explainer: Why Pope Francis' Comments on Women's Ordination Are Both Business as Usual and a Big Deal." *America Magazine*, 3 Nov. 2016, https://www.americamagazine.org/faith/2016/11/03/explainer-why-pope-francis-comments-womens-ordination-are-both-business-usual-and.

161 Congregation for the Doctrine of the Faith, Cardinal Luis F. Ladaria, S.I., Prefect "In Response To Certain Doubts Regarding The Definitive Character Of The Doctrine Of *Ordinatio Sacerdotalis*" (May 29, 2018).

ordination of women,[162] and in 2020, German Archbishop Stefan Hesse "called for an open debate on the ordination of women in the Catholic Church." Though John Paul II's 1994 letter was written "in order that all doubt may be removed," Hesse nevertheless believed that "new arguments had emerged in the conversation around women's ordination that needed to be addressed."[163] At this writing, nearly forty years after *Ordinatio sacerdotalis* was promulgated, Roman Catholics are still awaiting the outcome of "renewed scientific investigation" by "competent experts" so they may finally know what their Magisterium had taught them. Thus, it seems that even the Magisterium is not quite sure what John Paul II meant by the six words, "that all doubt may be removed." This is only one example, of which there are myriad.

This state of affairs casts an ironic glare on Madrid rejection of *Sola Scriptura* because "Protestantism is so divided," he says, "over central doctrinal issues," even as Roman Catholicism, with its "infallible" Magisterium, clearly suffers similar divisions over central issues. In addition to the meaning of *Ordinatio sacerdotalis*, Roman Catholics today debate whether Pope Francis has the power to abrogate the Traditional Latin Mass, dividing into different camps with names suited to their political and ecclesial allegiance: Trads (traditionalists), Radtrads (radical traditionalists), Normies (middle-of-the-road Roman Catholics), LeftCaths (politically left-leaning Catholics), Beneplenists (who believed Benedict XVI was the true pope even after Francis was elected), Popesplainers (who believe Francis is the true pope, but feel compelled to justify his public statements), Sedevacantists (who believe the chair of Peter has been vacant since Pius XII), Sedeprivationists (who believe the chair of Peter is occupied but without authority or power), Lefebverites (who believe Marcel Lefebvre was not validly excommunicated), and with the passing of Pope Benedict, Benevacantists (a derogatory term for

162 Pongratz-Lippitt, Christa, "Leading Benedictine Nun in Germany Calls for Women Priests." *International.la*, 17 Mar. 2019, https://international.la-croix.com/news/religion/leading-benedictine-nun-in-germany-calls-for-women-priests/9694.
163 Dulle, Colleen. "German Archbishop Calls for Open Debate about Women Priests in the Catholic Church." *America Magazine*, 20 Aug. 2020, https://www.americamagazine.org/faith/2020/08/20/german-archbishop-debate-women-priests-deacons-catholic.

Beneplenists, implying that they must now be Sedevacantists as their beloved Benedict no longer occupies Peter's chair).

In India, the Roman Catholic Church is divided between those who have accepted the "Hindu rite," and those who reject it. In South America, there is a contentious faction practicing the "Amazonian rite," and in Mexico, a new division has arisen between tradition-alists and those who prefer the new "Mayan rite." In China the Roman Catholic religion is divided between the church endorsed by Pope Francis and sanctioned by the Chinese Communist Party, and an underground Chinese Catholic Church that claims to be truly Catholic but is not endorsed by Francis. All of these have different and varying views on the "real presence" of Christ in the Eucharist, the ordination of women, which councils are ecumenical and which papal statements are *ex cathedra*. The list could go on and on, and with each variant belief comes a whole new "denomination" within Roman Catholicism, resulting in thousands of divergent belief systems within what is alleged to be a single religion. In desperation as their religion moves into heterodoxy, Marxism and heresy under Francis, conservative leaning Roman Catholics are imploring the various factions to "unite the clans" against the errors of the Magis-terium—an ironic situation considering that Madrid identified *Sola Scriptura* as the cause of doctrinal anarchy. He asked, if Protestants have found the truth, "why the need for denominations," implying the necessity of submitting to Magisterial interpretation of Sacred Tradition. Yet we would ask him: If Rome is unified, why the need for "clans" and why the need to "unite" them? Despite his "infallible" Magisterium, the anarchy remains. Clearly, the "anarchy" is not a result of *Sola Scriptura*, for even Madrid's own Magisterium suffers from it, as do the innumerable denominations within the realm of Roman Catholicism.

The Puzzle of Scripture

A similar problem is faced by the Roman Catholic who desires to understand his religion's official interpretation of Scripture. Madrid asked what was more likely to be misunderstood: the six-word sentence "I never said you stole money," or the vast compendium of Scriptures "written by different people at different times for different purposes in different languages?"[164] By his question we might suppose that the Roman Catholic religion had interpreted the Scriptures, removing all doubt from the minds of the faithful. Unfortunately, there is no official list of official interpretations of Scripture, and in fact there are many diverse and conflicting opinions within "tradition" on the meaning of the text of Holy Writ. See, for example, our previous discussion on the identity of the "restrainer" in 2 Thessalonians 2.

Or consider the Roman Catholic translation of Genesis 3:15, which has the woman crushing the head of the serpent: "she shall crush thy head" (Genesis 3:15, *Douay Rheims*). Popes Pius IX,[165] Pius X,[166] Leo XIII[167] and Pius XII[168] all interpreted the passage to refer to Mary crushing the head of the serpent. But Pope John Paul II corrected that long-held traditional interpretation in a General Audience in 1996:

> Exegetes now agree in recognizing that the text of Genesis, according to the original Hebrew, does not attribute action against the serpent directly to the woman, but to her offspring. ... in fact the one who defeats the serpent will be her offspring.[169]

Remarkable as it may be that the Magisterium took so long to decide what Genesis 3:15 actually means (if indeed it has decided at all, for John Paul was not speaking *ex cathedra*), it is far less remarkable than the fact that Roman Catholics face exactly this issue on every single verse of Scripture that the Roman Catholic Magisterium has ever claimed to interpret. A verse that meant one thing throughout their childhood, or since the Council of Trent, can now mean something entirely different. And that fact in turn is even

164 Coming Home Network.
165 Apostolic Constitution *Ineffabilis Deus* (December 8, 1854).
166 Encyclical *Ad Diem Illum Laetissium* (February 2, 1904).
167 Prayer of St. Michael (1886).
168 Apostolic Constitution *Munificentissimus Deus* (November 1, 1950).
169 John Paul II, General Audience, "Victory Over Sin Comes Through a Woman" (January 24, 1996).

less remarkable than the Roman Catholic's challenge of interpreting for himself the thousands of Bible verses that the Magisterium still has not yet interpreted!

In a letter to the US Conference of Catholic Bishops (USCCB), an inquirer desired to know how many Bible verses the Roman Catholic religion had officially interpreted. The Executive Director of the USCCB responded candidly that "a case could be made that the Church has defined something about the correct interpretation of … seven passages," including Genesis 3:15. And even then, he continued, "It is difficult, also, to say exactly what was defined … and that this is the only meaning of the text."[170] Such is the poverty of the Roman Catholic who would rely on the Magisterium to interpret the Bible for him. Fewer than ten Bible verses have been interpreted, and of those, it is difficult to determine what the actual interpretation is. As for the other more than 30,000 verses, there exists no official Roman Catholic interpretation of them. For this reason, Madrid's illustration of the need to have a Magisterium to interpret the Scriptures rings quite hollow. After allegedly 2,000 years, the Roman Catholic Magisterium has only provided *possible* interpretations of seven verses!

The Puzzle of the Catechisms

A similar problem exists for anyone who would turn to the various catechisms of the Catholic Church in order to be taught by the Magisterium. In his 1846 Catechism, Stephen Keenen responded with abject indignation to the proposition that Catholics must believe the pope to be infallible:

> This is a Protestant invention: it is no article of the Catholic faith: no decision of his can oblige under pain of heresy, unless it be received and enforced by the teaching body, that is, by the bishops of the Church.[171]

---

170 deNoia, O.P., J. Augustine, Executive Director, Secretariat for Doctrine and Pastoral Practices, National (US) Conference of Catholic Bishops, letter to Ronald C. Loeffler (August 4, 2000).
171 Keenan, Stephen *Controversial Catechism, or Protestantism Refuted and Catholicism Established* (Edinburgh: James Marshall, 1846), 117.

However, infallibility was proclaimed as a doctrine of the faith in 1870 at Vatican I, so in his 1876 Catechism, "revised and corrected, conformably to the decrees of the [first]council of the Vatican," Keenan updated the question on infallibility to indicate that Catholics must believe, and have always believed the pope to be infallible, "according to the promise made to Peter, and in him, to his successors."[172] Such are the changes that occur to the catechisms within a few decades. Even the modern 1994 *Catechism of the Catholic Church* offers no comfort to the ignorant, riddled as it is with a growing list of errors continually being discovered and corrected. Not all of the errors are trivial, as evidenced by paragraph 1481. In its original version, that paragraph accidentally implied that it was not the Publican but *the Pharisee* who had gone home justified in Luke 18:14.[173] Likewise, as acknowledged by Roman Catholic *Crisis Magazine*, even the *Catechism of the Council of Trent* had to be corrected by a later pope because it incorrectly described the requirements for the valid ordination of a priest.[174]

Apart from the shifting doctrinal and liturgical sands and errors of transposition, there remain for the Roman Catholic the perils of papal whim and pontifical fancy that can change Rome's teachings by fiat. By way of example, the *Roman Catechism*, originally published at the order of Pius V after the Council of Trent, plainly taught that "lawful slaying" to "punish the guilty and protect the innocent … is an act of paramount obedience" to God by the civil power.[175] In 2018, Pope Francis updated the *Catechism of the Catholic Church* to declare that the church now teaches that "the death penalty is inadmissible" in light of the Gospel.[176]

Such is the perilous condition of the Roman Catholic who can go to bed each night compelled by the Magisterium to believe one

---

172　Keenan, Stephan, *A Doctrinal Catechism; Wherein Divers Points Of Catholic Faith And Practice Assailed By Modern Heretics* (New York: P. J. Kennedy and Sons, 1876), 171.
173　*Catechism of the Catholic Church* (Paulist Press, 1994), 1481 (p. 372).
174　Coulombe, Charles. "Can the Catechism Get It Wrong?" *Crisis Magazine*, 29 Nov. 2019, https://www.crisismagazine.com/2019/can-the-catechism-get-it-wrong.
175　*The Catechism of the Council of Trent for Parish Priests, Issued by Order of Pope Pius V.* Translated by McHugh JA, Callan CJ. (New York: Joseph F. Wagner, Inc., 1923), 421.
176　Congregation for the Doctrine of the Faith, *Letter to the Bishops regarding the new revision of number 2267 of the Catechism of the Catholic Church on the death penalty* (February 8, 2018).

thing, and then wake up the next morning, commanded by that same Magisterium to believe another on pain of excommunication.

The Puzzle of the Apparitions

Compounding Madrid's difficulties are the visions, or apparitions, that have appeared throughout the world for centuries, including Guadalupe, Mexico (1531), La Laus, France (1664), Paris, France (1831), Lourdes, France (1858) and Fatima, Portugal (1917). Those visions claimed to be Mary, the Mother of Jesus, and were frequently accompanied by messages for the visionaries, the popes and the world. The *Catholic Catechism* insists that such private revelations are not compulsory and do not contribute to the deposit of faith once received.[177] Yet the scholars are not so sure. Pope Pius XXIII insisted that it was his duty, and the duty of popes before him, "to recommend to the attention of the faithful" the "always valid warnings of the Mother of God" at Lourdes (1858), and "forcibly" convey it "to all those who run the serious risk of … losing the real sense of religious values."[178] Such forcible recommendations, Marian scholars observed, "gave the feeling that this was neither a simple permission nor an act of faith, but a positive encouragement, to which it was difficult not to adhere without contempt for the magisterium." For this reason several speakers at the Mariological Congress of Lourdes that year insisted that the revelations from the apparitions "have the character of a dogmatic fact" and are "a matter of Ecclesial faith," requiring "filial obedience" possessing the character "of moral certitude."[179] Fr. William Most believed the same of the apparitions of Mary at Fatima (1917), complaining that the term "private revelation" was inappropriate for the visions at Fatima because they were not private but were "addressed to the whole world."[180] How then to navigate the delicate boundary between private and general revelation, when the apparitions of

177 Catechism of the Catholic Church, 67.
178 *The Catholic Standard and Times*, Volume 64, Number 22, 20 February 1959, "Pontiff Closes Lourdes Centennial Year With World Appeal for Humility, Prayer," p. 5.
179 Laurentin René, and Bertrand A Buby. "Marian Apparitions: Facts and Theological Meaning." *Mary in Faith and Life in the New Age of the Church: Marian Seminar 1980*, Kenya (Nairobi), Zambia (Monze, Ndola), Franciscan Mission Press, Ndola, Zambia, 1983, pp. 353–486.
180 Fr. William Most Collection, "The Brown Scapular," https://www.catholicculture.org/culture/library/most/getwork.cfm?worknum=170.

Mary seem to straddle it? This is what Fr. Bertrand Buby called "The Boundary Problem of Apparitions," and he had little to offer except that "the boundary is less clear than it appears" and "[w]e are very poorly equipped to judge such matters."[181]

Madrid, for his part, can offer nothing more definite than to say that unlike "Divine Revelation," the church does not require people to believe in "Private Revelation," but in the case of the apparitions of Mary, "the church also says it is kind of foolish not to."[182] Thus are Roman Catholics left with an empty ambiguity in which the popes consider it their duty "forcibly" to pass on the "always valid warnings" of the apparitions, which, according to Madrid, one would be foolish to reject — but leave each individual Catholic to determine for himself whether an apparition's teachings fall into the category of "dogmatic fact" and "moral certitude." This from the religion that claims to possess "certainty about everything which has been revealed"![183]

The *Sola Verbum Dei* Fallacy

As we noted in the introduction to this chapter, Madrid attempted to demonstrate the pitfalls of *Sola Scriptura*. In his opinion it "is nothing more than a self-refuting proposition" that requires the Protestant to embrace a tradition "that comes down to us entirely outside of the Bible," resulting in anarchy that "demonstrates the need for an authoritative teaching church." He observes, "Evangelical Lutherans, Anglicans, Church of Christ, Southern Baptists, Orthodox Presbyterians, Methodists, Reformed Baptists, and other more conservative Bible-only groups" all disagree with each other about one thing or another, and yet "[e]ach of these groups claims to go by the Bible alone."[184] *Sola Verbum Dei* is alleged to be the solution. Yet when *Sola Verbum Dei* is measured by Madrid's own standard, it fails for exactly the same reasons. We as easily observe that Normies, RadTrads, LeftCaths, Beneplenists, Sedevacantists,

---

181 Laurentin René, and Bertrand A Buby, 353–486.
182 Relevant Radio, The Patrick Madrid Show (March 16, 2022), https://relevantradio.com/2022/03/the-patrick-madrid-show-march-16-2022-hour-1/.
183 Second Vatican Council, *Dei Verbum*, ii.9-10 (November 18, 1965).
184 Madrid, pp. 171-174.

Sedeprivationists, Popesplainers, Lefebverites, Benevacantists and other Catholic groups all disagree with each other about one thing or another, and yet each of these groups claims to be an authentic representation of the Catholic religion. Oh, if only there were an infallible Magisterium to unite them!

Madrid is correct that the Protestant must appeal to something outside of Scripture to know the canon of Scripture, but so too must Madrid appeal to something outside of the *Verbum Dei* to know the canon of the *Verbum Dei*. Before he can produce a canon of Scripture with the blessing of an ecumenical council, he must first produce a list of ecumenical councils, a list that does not exist within the scope of Tradition or within the Scriptures. Each Roman Catholic is left to his own devices to arrive at his own personal list. Similarly for the canon of *ex cathedra* papal statements. Madrid has chosen his own canon of two, but beyond that it is an "open question," and each Roman Catholic must decide for himself. Madrid points out that the apostles explicitly affirmed oral traditions (2 Thessalonians 2, 2 Timothy 2 and 1 Corinthians 11), but neither he nor the Magisterium, nor the early church, can identify what those specific oral traditions were. Of those passages upon which he relies to prove that the apostles passed on oral tradition, the early church knew nothing of them, save what could be deduced from Scripture, and even Madrid himself is only willing to commit to those that were actually inscripturated. Additionally, the Magisterium is itself to blame for the fact that Roman Catholics do not know what to make of *Ordinatio Sacerdotalis,* which was intended to remove all doubt but instead created more. *A generation of Roman Catholics is still trying to determine what John Paul II meant!* Madrid claims that the ostensible Protestant "anarchy" manifests because of *Sola Scriptura*, but whence the anarchy within his own Roman religion? Surely he cannot blame *Sola Scriptura* for *that*. Madrid can only paper over it by burying his head in the shifting sands of Rome's Magisterium. The very Magisterium that is alleged to prevent "anarchy" and chaos has actually caused it by producing contradictory lists of ecumenical councils, publishing inconsistent and contradictory catechisms, failing to interpret the

Scriptures, leaving each person to decide for himself which apparitions are authentic, and even failing to interpret its own Magisterial teachings.

The Soft White Underbelly of Madrid's Epistemology

We have examined Madrid's rejection of *Sola Scriptura* first by aggregating his three separate chapters on the substance of "the Word of God"—Scripture, Tradition and the Magisterium—and then subjecting *Sola Verbum Dei* to the same scrutiny to which Madrid subjected *Sola Scriptura*. It is neither our burden nor our intent here to prove that *Sola Scriptura* is superior to *Sola Verbum Dei*, but only to prove that *it is not inferior to it.*

It is beyond the scope of this book to prove or disprove either position, as each is based upon an axiomatic proposition that is taken by faith to be true and by definition cannot be proved. The Protestant reads the Word of God (the Scripture) and trusts the Savior revealed therein to save him. The Roman Catholic reads the Word of God (Scripture and Tradition, interpreted by the Magisterium and supplemented by visions) and trusts the "church" revealed therein to save him. Whether the Scriptures have revealed the correct Savior to the Protestant or whether the Scriptures and Tradition and the apparitions of Mary have revealed the correct church to the Roman Catholic is at the core of our disagreement. But there is no getting around the fact that, epistemologically, *Sola Scriptura* and *Sola Verbum Dei* are structurally equivalent. The only difference is the starting point of each, which is to say, the object of faith upon which each proposition rests—Scriptures or the church. The Protestant, believing the Scriptures, is led ultimately to place his trust in Christ Who cannot change, while the Romanist places his trust in a church that changes with the times, and in a Magisterium that is unable even to explain what "that all doubt may be removed" might mean or whether the "always valid" teachings of the apparitions are "always valid." Nothing Madrid has said in his chapters on Scripture, Tradition and the Magisterium can persuade the

Protestant to abandon *Sola Scriptura*, but much that he has said substantiates why *Sola Scriptura* is our only option.

The Early Writers on "Scripture Alone"

As Madrid continues through his chapter on the Scriptures, he begins to interact with various ancient writers in order to show that they did not believe *Sola Scriptura*. We conclude our chapter on "The Word of God" by interacting with Madrid on the three Church Fathers he selected to prove his point: Basil of Cæsarea, Athanasius of Alexandria and Cyril of Jerusalem.

Basil of Cæsarea

By way of example some Protestants note that Basil, in his letter to Eustathius, agreed to "let God-inspired Scripture decide between us."[185] Madrid correctly responds that Basil's epistemology cannot be reconstructed from a single letter.[186] In fact, Basil elsewhere bolsters Madrid's own position, deriving his beliefs and practices from Scripture and unwritten apostolic tradition together: "both of these in relation to true religion have the same force."[187] While this citation from Basil substantiates Madrid's position, it is nevertheless to Basil's detriment that he was, in his own words, "not content" with the Scriptures:

> For we are not, as is well known, content with what the apostle or the Gospel has recorded, but both in preface and conclusion we add other words as being of great importance to the validity of the ministry, and these we derive from unwritten teaching.[188]

That citation from Basil (364 AD) was in the context of "the words of the invocation" (i.e., the consecration) for the Supper, for which words Basil concedes that he relied not on the Scriptures but upon "silent and mystical tradition" and "unpublished and secret

---

185 Basil of Cæsarea, Epistle 189.3.
186 Madrid, pp. 48-52.
187 Basil of Cæsarea, *On the Holy Spirit* 27.
188 Ibid.

teaching."[189] Small wonder that men of his late fourth century ilk were stumbling into such nonsense as the liturgical offering of Christ's body and blood in the Supper, prayers to Mary, prayers for the dead, bowing to relics and venerating the alleged wood of the cross. Such practices we find neither in the Scriptures, nor in the three centuries that preceded Basil. As for Basil's rejection of *Scripture Alone* and his embrace of unwritten mystical traditions, we stand against him and with the Scripture, and no evidence from antiquity can persuade us otherwise. It is quite notable that Basil, in the same work where he expresses his discontent with Scripture, alleges that the "unwritten teachings" to which he subscribed are those same traditions to which Paul had referred in 1 Corinthians 1:1 and 2 Thessalonians 2:15[190] — a very convenient epistemology, indeed! Neither Chrysostom, nor Athanasius, nor Severian, nor Theodore, nor Theodoret, nor Augustine could venture to guess what those traditions might have been, but when Basil was pressed on his unwritten mystical traditions, he simply assumed that those Pauline epistles must have been referring to whatever his current beliefs or practices happened to be.

It is by just such a flawed epistemology as Basil's that men of old stumbled eagerly and headlong into error and sin in their discontent, so dissatisfied were they with "the scripture of truth" (Daniel 10:21). How far Basil had fallen from the days of Irenæus, who warned his friend Florinus against the wiles of the Gnostics who shared Basil's epistemology: "For [they allege] that the truth was not delivered by means of written documents, but *vivâ voce.*"[191] Quite the contrary, Irenæus warned that if the apostles had any unwritten secrets to be delivered, they would be readily apparent to all: "if the apostles had known hidden mysteries, which they were in the habit of imparting to 'the perfect' apart and privily from the rest, they would have delivered them especially to those to whom they were also committing the Churches themselves."[192]

---

189 Ibid.
190 Basil, *On the Holy Spirit* 71.
191 Irenæus, *Against Heresies* III.2.1.
192 Irenæus, *Against Heresies* III.3.1.

But Irenæus could think of no examples of such "hidden mysteries" apart from the Scriptures:

> Since, therefore, the tradition from the apostles does thus exist in the Church, and is permanent among us, let us revert to the Scriptural proof furnished by those apostles who did also write the Gospel, in which they recorded the doctrine regarding God.[193]

Athanasius of Alexandria

Madrid continues, responding to a claim that Athanasius believed in *Scripture Alone*. "And we can dispense with the myth that St. Athanasius was a *sola scriptura* man,"[194] Madrid opines, because Athanasius' letter to the African bishops attested to the sufficiency of the Council of Nicæa:

> The confession arrived at Nicæa was, we say once more, sufficient and enough by itself, for the subversion of all irreligious heresy, and for the security and furtherance of the doctrine of the Church.[195]

Madrid's vacuous observation is overturned simply by reading Athanasius' letter. Athanasius' position—citing Exodus, Hebrews, John and Colossians—was that Nicæa's response to Arianism had been derived from the Scriptures: "This enables us to see, brethren, that they of Nicæa breathe the spirit of Scripture."[196] Nicæa was "sufficient and enough by itself" *because the council's conclusions were Scriptural.*

Cyril of Jerusalem

Madrid next responds to a quote from Cyril of Jerusalem (350 AD) in which Cyril admonishes his readers to "give not absolute credence, unless thou receive the proof of the things which I

---

193 Irenæus, *Against Heresies* III.5.1.
194 Madrid, pp. 52-54.
195 Athanasius, *Ad Afros* 1.
196 Athanasius, *Ad Afros* 4.

announce from the Divine Scriptures."[197] This apparent deference
to the Scriptures as the sole rule of faith is dismissed by Madrid
who provides abundant evidence from Cyril's other *Lectures*
that appear to support Roman Catholic teachings: the teaching
authority of the Roman Catholic Church (Lecture 18.23), the Lord's
Supper as a sacrifice (Lecture 23.6-8), purgatory and prayers for the
dead (Lecture 23.10), the "real presence" of Christ in the Eucharist
(Lectures 19.7; 21.3; 22.1-9), the sacraments (Lecture 1.3), the
intercession of the saints (Lecture 23.9), an ordained priesthood
(Lecture 23.2), frequent reception of the Supper (Lecture 23.23),
and baptismal regeneration (Lectures 1.1-3, 3.10-12; 21.3-4). This
is alleged to pose quite a dilemma to the Protestant reader, ostensibly leaving him only two options: to accept either that Cyril had
found all these Roman Catholic doctrines using Scripture Alone,
or that Cyril did not really believe in *Sola Scriptura*.[198] There is of
course a third option: Like Madrid, Cyril professed faithfulness to
the Scriptures as a cloak for introducing error. A brief review of
Madrid's citations of Cyril in support of Roman Catholic doctrines
demonstrates the necessity of that third option.

While Cyril insisted to his listeners that his own teachings
must pass the test of Scripture, he was unable to answer when
they took up his challenge. In Cyril's day Veneration of the Cross,
the practice of kneeling to and kissing "the wood of the cross,"
had come into fashion.[199] Cyril claimed that the wood of the cross
that had been discovered in Jerusalem and had been "distributed
piecemeal from hence to all the world."[200] The wood of the cross
itself had power, he said, and "life comes by means of wood."[201]
His hearers cried foul, saying, "You are inventing subtleties; show
me from some prophet the Wood of the Cross; unless you give
me a testimony from a prophet, I will not be persuaded."[202] Cyril
then proceeded to cite Genesis, Deuteronomy, Jeremiah, John and

---

197 Cyril of Jerusalem, *Catechetical Lectures* 4.17.
198 Madrid, pp. 54-56.
199 See Jerome, *Epistle 108* "To Eustochium" 9 (Before the Cross she threw herself down in
adoration as though she beheld the Lord hanging upon it."
200 Cyril of Jerusalem, *Catechetical Lectures* 13.4.
201 Cyril of Jerusalem, *Catechetical Lectures* 13.20.
202 Cyril of Jerusalem, *Catechetical Lectures* 13.19.

Matthew, but could prove nothing more than that the Scriptures had foreseen Jesus' death.[203] He was unable to provide evidence from the Scripture that *the wood itself* had any power.

Similarly, when we examine Madrid's citations of Cyril's support for the infallible teaching authority of the Catholic Church (Lecture 18.23), we see that Cyril explains the meaning of the word "Catholic," but does not provide any scriptural support for Madrid's claim of infallibility. Regarding the Lord's Supper as a sacrifice (Lecture 23.6-8), Cyril again provides no Scriptural support for it. In the matter of intercession of the saints, purgatory and prayers for the dead (Lecture 23.9-10), Cyril attempts to "persuade you by an illustration," but does not attempt to persuade by the Scriptures. Where Cyril is alleged to support the power of the Sacraments at which "devils tremble" (Lecture 1.3), he offers no Scriptural support for the claim. In regard to an ordained priesthood to offer the sacrifice of the mass (Lecture 23.2), Cyril justifies "the washing of hands" as part of the Supper by citing Psalms 26:6: "I will wash mine hands in innocency: so will I compass thine altar, O LORD." Yet such washing is something that Jesus had not instituted during the Supper and for which the Psalm is no proof. On regular participation in communion (Lecture 23.23), Cyril cites 1 Thessalonians 5:23, but that verse says nothing of the sacraments.

In truth, Cyril had stumbled into the error of his day, embracing the heresies of the new religion of Roman Catholicism, thinking that because they were suddenly popular, they must be true, even without Scriptural proof. As such, he simply invoked a long-embraced test—proof from the Scriptures—and then proceeded to argue in favor of practices that he could not prove from the Scriptures. Therefore, we choose option three: that Cyril used his ostensible loyalty to the Scriptures as means to propagate plainly unscriptural errors. As the old saying goes, "Hypocrisy is the homage vice pays to virtue," and Cyril paid homage indeed.

---

203 Ibid.

The True Church?

 (Kauffman)

In his defense of Roman Catholicism as the "True Church," Madrid attempts to reach across denominational boundaries—both to Orthodox and to Protestants—to heal the divide and span the gulf that exists between them and Rome. Although his initial focus is on the discourse between Roman Catholic and Orthodox, he extends a similar overture to Protestants with an equally simple solution: Return to Rome. We consider the Roman Catholic-Orthodox discussion to be an intramural debate in which Protestants have no vested interest, but Madrid's overtures to the Orthodox spill over to Protestants, and we therefore address them all in that light.

Madrid's Stubbornness

With a view toward Jesus' words in John 10:16 ("there shall be one flock, one shepherd") and His prayer in John 17:21 ("that they all may be one"), and Paul's rebuke in 1 Corinthians 1:13 ("Is Christ divided?"), Madrid asks rhetorically,

Isn't it an unbiblical, even *anti*biblical, attitude to refuse to seek the unity that St. Paul commands us to seek? Or are we free to disregard St. Paul's exhortation?

To Madrid, it is "wrongheaded," "deeply contrary," and "stubborn" to refuse to resolve the Catholic-Orthodox rift,[204] and by implication, the Catholic-Protestant divide. We agree. He should repent of his schismatic ways and return to the Protestant orthodoxy of the early church that we "all may be one." All he would have to do is turn from his medieval novelties, abominable sacrifices, rampant idolatries, Roman superstitions, his stubborn and willful ignorance of church history, and return to the church Jesus founded. Of course, to Madrid, that is out of the question because of his wrongheaded, stubborn and deeply contrarian resistance to the truth of the Scriptures. But we digress.

The point we illustrate is simply that Madrid has staked out a position of moral authority, declaring that all who disagree with his fallible and defective opinions are enemies of Biblical unity, and yet finds himself chronically unable to prove that he occupies the high ground. He has simply assumed that his position is correct and expects others to fall in line and conform to his personal, private interpretation of Scripture, history, Tradition and the Magisterium. And yet his own private interpretation is all he can offer—the very error of which he accuses his opponents. After all, as we noted in the chapter on "The Word of God," Roman Catholicism has only "infallibly" interpreted six or seven Bible verses in its "two thousand year history," and lacking any teaching authority, Madrid would presume to tell us what John 10:16, John 17:21 and 1 Corinthians 1:12 *actually mean*. In truth, Madrid has only offered his best guess, and stubbornly insists that he personally knows what "Jesus Christ wants" and what "St. Paul commands." Does he? How does Madrid know? Where can we find an infallible interpretation so we may understand infallibly what the passages mean? Certainly, Madrid would not have us convert to Rome based on his

---

204 Madrid, p. 65.

own personal, private interpretation of the passages, yet neither can he provide an official infallible interpretation of them.

Madrid's Eastern Problem

Madrid appeals to the alleged ancient unity that once existed between the Roman bishop and his eastern brethren. Based on Matthew 18:17 he says that "ecclesiastical problems" should be resolved by "the church." But one must first know that he is truly in "the church," and according to Madrid, "communion with the bishop of Rome" was once the *sine qua non* of church membership in the east:

> In the early centuries of Christianity, when the people of what would today be known as the Orthodox Churches were in full communion with the Catholic Church, it was understood that to be in communion with the bishop of Rome, the pope, was the single most important criterion for claiming to be "in the Church."[205]

The facts of history tell a much different story. As we have noted previously, the early church did not see in the bishop of Rome a unifying chief shepherd. It is well documented that the early congregations believed that they had a visible *local* shepherd, and an invisible Chief Shepherd *in heaven*. Bishop Ignatius of Antioch (c. 107 AD) believed the Smyrnæan bishop had "as his own bishop God the Father and the Lord Jesus Christ,"[206] and the Magnesian "bishop that is visible" had as his bishop "Him that is invisible."[207] In Ignatius' own absence from Antioch, "the Church in Syria ... now has God for its shepherd, instead of me," for "Jesus Christ alone will oversee it."[208] Mathetes (c. 130 AD), in his letter to Diognetus, would have found Rome's later quest for supremacy and thirst for power unbecoming in a servant of Christ: "It is not by ruling over his neighbours, or by seeking to hold the supremacy ...

---

205 Madrid, pg. 65.
206 Ignatius of Antioch, *to Polycarp*, greeting.
207 Ignatius of Antioch, *to the Magnesians*, 3.
208 Ignatius of Antioch, *to the Romans*, 9.

that happiness is found; nor can any one by these things become an imitator of God."[209] When Polycarp of Smyrna (c. 160 AD) went to Rome to visit Bishop Anicetus, the Roman bishop could not persuade Polycarp to abandon the practices he had learned from "John … and the other apostles."[210] Polycrates of Ephesus (c. 190 AD) not only refused to bow to the dictates of Bishop Victor of Rome, but attested to the "great multitude" of eastern bishops who joined him in his stand.[211] John Chrysostom (386 – 397 AD) claimed that Antioch was the chief metropolis of the church and that Ignatius was Peter's immediate successor there,[212] and what is more, none of Chrysostom's writings suggest that Rome held a similar or equal prominence.[213] The record makes clear that eastern bishops believed the Roman bishop had no authority and very little influence outside his limited parochial domain in Rome and its suburbs. They certainly had no illusion that communion with the bishop of Rome was the indispensable criterion for being "in the Church."

Far from being the standard of orthodoxy, the bishop of Rome was instead often found advancing heresy and defending heretics. While eastern[214] and western[215] councils were busy condemning the Montanist heresy, the Roman episcopate under Eleutherius (174 – 189 AD) was writing letters in support of it.[216] Bishop Zephyrinus (199 – 217 AD.) of Rome, "an uninformed and shamefully corrupt man" as Hippolytus relates, "hurried headlong" into heresy, and his successor Callistus (218 – 222 AD) with him:

> The school of these heretics during the succession of such bishops continued to acquire strength and augmentation … we have frequently offered them opposition, and have refuted them, and have forced them reluctantly to acknowledge the truth. And they, abashed and constrained

209 Epistle of Mathetes to Diognetus, chapter 10.
210 Eusebius, *Church History*, Book V, chapter 24, 14-24.
211 Eusebius, *Church History*, Book V, chapter 24, paragraph 7-8.
212 John of Chrysostom, *Homily on St. Ignatius*, chapter IV.
213 Catholic Encyclopedia, volume 8:457A.
214 Eusebius, *Church History*, Book V, chapter 16, paragraph 10.
215 Eusebius, *Church History*, Book V, chapter 3, paragraph 4.
216 Tertullian, Against Praxeas 1.

by the truth, have confessed their errors for a short period, but after a little, wallow once again in the same mire.[217]

Firmilian of Cæsarea (256 AD) wrote to Cyprian of Carthage, complaining that, under Bishop Stephen, "they who are at Rome do not observe those things in all cases which are handed down from the beginning, and vainly pretend the authority of the apostles"; in fact, Stephen had "disagreed with so many bishops throughout the whole world, breaking peace with each one of them in various kinds of discord" both in the east and the south.[218] Dionysius of Alexandria (256 AD) rebuked Stephen for claiming falsely that his novelties originated with the apostles.[219] Cyprian (256 AD) would later point out "Pope" Stephen's "error in endeavouring to maintain the cause of heretics against Christians," complaining that "Pope" Stephen was "forgetful of unity," adopting "lies" and "contagion" instead. Bishop Stephen had demonstrated "obstinacy" and "presumption" by preferring "human tradition to divine ordinance," and his "blindness of soul" and "degradation of faith" had caused him "to refuse to recognize the unity." Cyprian believed things would not go well for Stephen on the Day of Judgment because he "does not hold the unity and truth that arise from the divine law, but maintains heresies against the Church."[220] These statements from multiple sources, many of them eastern, do not sound like "communion with the bishop of Rome." The widespread universal church was sufficiently versed in the Scriptures to know better than to look for doctrinal and ecclesiastical leadership from him. More often, the early church was forced into constraining and correcting the Roman bishop and cleaning up the messes he left in his arrogant wake.

So driven and tossed on the sea of sin, error and heresy was the bishop of Rome in the eyes of the surrounding churches that Polycrates in Asia Minor joined the other bishops in standing up to him, Irenæus of Lyons joined the other bishops in rebuking him,

---

217 Hippolytus, *Refutation of All Heresies*, Book IX, chapter II.
218 Firmilian, to Cyprian, Epistle 74 6.
219 Dionysius, to Stephen of Rome.
220 Cyprian, to Pompey, Epistle 73 1, 2, 3, 4, 8.

Firmilian of Cæsarea criticized him for breaking with the "eastern bishops," and Cyprian of Carthage mocked him for his schismatic behavior. Bishops on three continents dismissed the absurdity, ignorance and forgetfulness of the Roman bishop, and rejected his obstinacy, presumption and heresy. Such were the public follies of the one with whom Madrid claims the early bishops sought communion in order to remain in the church!

As the facts show, Madrid's claim that communion with the pope "was the single most important criterion" to the early eastern bishops is an ignorant and fanciful revision of history. Ignatius, Mathetes, Polycarp, Polycrates, Firmilian, Dionysius and Chrysostom—eastern bishops, all!—beg to differ. Ignatius had no conviction that any bishop had the Roman bishop over him, and Chrysostom, as the Catholic *Encyclopedia* concedes, thought so little of Roman primacy that "there is no clear and direct message in favor of the primacy of the Pope" in all of his writings!

Madrid's "Protestant" Problem

For the Orthodox (and by implication, for the Protestant) Madrid thinks he has a "silver bullet" response to all of this: If he were to join the Orthodox (or Protestants), which denomination would he join?

> To which of the many Orthodox Churches …? The Russian Orthodox? The Orthodox Church in America? The Greek Orthodox Church? What about the Armenian Orthodox or the Orthodox Church of Albania? How would you know which of them, if any, to turn to, since they're all fiercely independent of one another?[221]

He could (and often does) make a similar argument against the many Protestant denominations. He imagines the case is closed, but we would ask a similar question of him. Which "Roman Catholic" religion should we join? There are legion from which to choose.

---

221 Madrid, p. 66.

Roman apologist Matthew Leonard says he was "drop-kicked" into the Catholic Church[222] by Ignatius of Antioch, who taught that nothing should be done apart from the bishop.[223] But Roman traditionalists are bucking under the very authority Leonard is inviting Protestants to embrace. Catholic apologist John Henry Westen, frustrated with the lack of leadership from the bishops, says it is now "the time of the laity" because the laity must act *apart from the bishops*,[224] and Michael Voris of *Church Militant* says that Pope Francis, the bishop of Rome at this writing, should fire his cardinals and then resign because his whole papacy is "absolutely pathetic."[225] All these—Leonard, Westen, Voris—believe they are representing the authentic "True Church," but which "authentic" truth should we believe: Leonard's, who converted to Catholicism because nothing should be done apart from the bishop, or Westen's, who believes the laity must rise up because the bishops are not acting with sufficient alacrity or resolve, or Voris', who insists circumstances are sufficiently dire that the only way for the church to recover is if its "pathetic" Roman bishop resigns? So many choices.

Madrid thinks Vatican II was an infallible ecumenical council that binds the conscience,[226] but Archbishop Carlo Maria Viganò says that Vatican II was the "devil council,"[227] an occasion for error, and that the whole council ought to be retroactively dismissed and "fall into oblivion."[228] Both believe they are representing the truth of the "True Church." How do we know which councils to trust? Why should we trust the opinion of Madrid, a mere lay apologist,

---

222 "Matthew Leonard On St. Ignatius of Antioch." *St. Paul Center*, 16 Oct. 2012, stpaulcenter.com/matthew-leonard-on-st-ignatius-of-antioch/.
223 Ignatius of Antioch, *to the Philadelphians* 4, 7.
224 Marshall, Taylor R., director. *Is Pope Francis Driving the Agenda? w John Henry Westen (Dr Taylor Marshall #219). YouTube*, YouTube, 25 Feb. 2019, www.youtube.com/watch?v=jdn-7WK2V2Oc.
225 Marshall, Taylor R., director. *Michael Voris Interviewed by Dr Taylor Marshall. YouTube*, YouTube, 20 Dec. 2018, www.youtube.com/watch?v=s3tsOqAN3AM. Retrieved May 7, 2019 from the world wide web.
226 *More Catholic than the Pope*.
227 "conciliablo". (Viganò, Carlo Maria. "Letter #21, Monday, August 10, 2020: Again, the Council." *Inside The Vatican*, 11 Aug. 2020, insidethevatican.com/news/newsflash/letter-21-monday-august-10-2020-again-the-council/.)
228 "para deixá-lo cair no esquecimento". (Irae, Dies. "'Sois Um Povo Com Uma Grande Responsabilidade' – Monsenhor Viganò." *DIES IRÆ*, Blogger, 24 Apr. 2020, www.diesirae.pt/2020/04/sois-um-povo-com-uma-grande.html.)

over that of an archbishop who was once the Apostolic Nuncio to the United States?

Madrid criticizes "the extreme-traditionalist movement spawned by the late Archbishop Marcel Lefebvre," arguing in his book, *More Catholic than the Pope*, that Lefebvre entered into formal schism with the church in 1988, and was wrong to reject the second Vatican Council. That is Madrid's position based on his own personal interpretation of relevant canon law and the statements of the hierarchy.[229] But lay Roman Catholic apologist Chris Jackson has reviewed the same evidence and believes Lefebvre's excommunication was "based on a legal error," and was therefore invalid.[230] And while Madrid implores the followers of Lefebvre to repent of their schism and return to unity, Archbishop Viganò instead criticizes the likes of Madrid, imploring them to stop blaming Lefebvre and simply acknowledge that Vatican II is the true cause of the schism: "before assuming schisms and heresies where there are none, it would be appropriate and more useful to fight error and division where they have nested and spread for decades."[231] So many choices, and so many ways to interpret the evidence. Whom are we to believe? The traditional Lefebvrites or the modern ecumenists? Certainly not Madrid, who is neck deep in fallible opinions.

Roman Catholic philosopher Timothy Gordon and *Church Militant* broadcaster Michael Voris appeared together on theologian Taylor Marshall's podcast on December 20, 2018, united in their criticism of the Magisterium.[232] Only a few months later Marshall received communion at a Lefebvrite church for Easter, an act for which he was roundly and publicly criticized by Voris and Gordon. Gordon is absolutely convinced, based on his own reading of the evidence, that Lefebvre died separated from the church, while

229 *More Catholic than the Pope*, 9, 13.
230 Jackson, Chris. "Was Archbishop Lefebvre Really Excommunicated?" *The Remnant Newspaper*, 7 Oct. 2014, remnantnewspaper.com/web/index.php/fetzen-fliegen/item/1108-was-archbishop-lefebvre-really-excommunicated.
231 Hickson, Maike. "Abp. Viganò to Critics: Instead of 'Assuming Schisms' Where There Are None, Better to Fight Long-Lasting Errors." *Catholic Family News*, 4 Sept. 2020, catholicfamilynews.com/blog/2020/09/03/abp-vigano-to-critics-instead-of-assuming-schisms-where-there-are-none-better-to-fight-long-lasting-errors/.
232 Marshall, *Michael Voris Interviewed by Dr Taylor Marshall*, 20 Dec. 2018.

Marshall, convinced by his own different reading of the evidence, is convinced that he did not. Marshall's December 20, 2018 podcast has since been removed, and "civil war" has broken out between these traditionalist "mini-popes," according to Roman Catholic apologist Dave Armstrong.[233] This leaves observers wondering which version of Roman Catholicism we are to affirm—Marshall's ostensibly Lefebvrite Tridentine traditionalism, Gordon's and Voris' Vatican II traditionalism, or Armstrong's more pragmatic modern conservatism?

Pope Francis I, in the ecumenical spirit of the second Vatican Council and the Amazon Synod of 2019, believes it is appropriate to display images of the Inca fertility goddess Pachamama in a church in Rome. Alexander Tschugguel, on the other hand, thinks such displays are a violation of the commandments. Tschugguel removed the idols under cover of darkness and threw them reverently and ceremonially into the Tiber.[234] An indignant Pope Francis apologized to the offended parties—not, by the way, to those who were offended at the presence of an idol, but rather to those who were offended by the sacrilegious treatment of the idols themselves—reporting that the idols had been safely recovered and were undamaged.[235] To which of these versions of Roman Catholicism should we turn to find the "True Church"—Tschugguel's Mosaic traditionalism or Pope Francis' modern pantheistic ecumenism?

Roman Catholic apologist Tim Staples argues with Roman Catholic apologist Robert Sungenis on geocentrism as they dispute the degrees to which they are bound by an encyclical or an infallible papal decree.[236] Sungenis argues that Roman Catholic apologist

---

233 Armstrong, Dave. "SSPX & Taylor Marshall vs. Timothy Gordon & Michael Voris." *Biblical Evidence for Catholicism*, Patheos Explore the World's Faith through Different Perspectives on Religion and Spirituality! Patheos Has the Views of the Prevalent Religions and Spiritualities of the World., 18 Apr. 2020, www.patheos.com/blogs/davearmstrong/2020/04/sspx-taylor-marshall-vs-timothy-gordon-michael-voris.html.

234 Archbishop Vigano, Carlo Maria. "Letter #60, 2019: Viganò: 'He Is a Hero.'" *Inside The Vatican*, 5 Nov. 2019, insidethevatican.com/news/newsflash/letter-60-2019-vigano-he-is-a-hero/.

235 Editor, CNA. "Pope Francis Apologizes That Amazon Synod Pachamama Statues Were Thrown into Tiber River." *Catholic News Agency*, 25 Oct. 2019, www.catholicnewsagency.com/news/42636/pope-francis-apologizes-that-amazon-synod-pachamama-was-thrown-into-tiber-river.

236 "Question 217 - R. Sungenis Answers Tim Staples Charges." *Bellarmine Forums*, 16 Jan. 2010, bellarmineforum.xanga.com/2010/01/16/question-217-r-sungenis-answers-tim-staples-charges/.

Mark Shea may not have properly understood the nature of the Old Covenant,[237] and questions whether Roman Catholic apologist Scott Hahn is correct in his characterization of the femininity of the Holy Spirit. Hahn meanwhile tries to make the case, based on his own interpretation of "tradition," that the church has long held Mary to be the "quasi-incarnation" of the Holy Spirit.[238] Tridentine traditionalists buck against Francis' prohibition of the Latin Mass, as Vatican II traditionalists implore them to accept the Council, all while LGBTQ+, pagan Hindu, Mayan and Amazonian rites and Pachamama liturgies are allowed to prosper. German bishops approve the blessing of same sex couples and show inclinations toward ordination of women priests, and Francis' Synod on Synodality moves ever onward toward a female diaconate. The Chinese underground Catholic Church complains that it has been betrayed by Pope Francis, who is aligned with the Chinese state-sanctioned version of the Roman Church, even as the Roman Catholic news media allege that the Vatican was blackmailed into siding with the Chinese Government.[239] We would ask of Madrid: To which of these diverse and contradictory versions of Roman Catholicism shall we convert?

On July 16, 2021, Pope Francis issued his *motu proprio* *"Traditionis custodes,"* severely restricting the celebration of the Traditional Latin Mass (TLM) and demanding assent to the modern eucharistic liturgy of Vatican II. Scarcely will be found a more relevant modern application of Ignatius' dictate from the early second century to "have but one Eucharist … as there is one bishop."[240] According to canon lawyer Raymond Cardinal Burke, the clear intent of the *moto proprio* was "to eliminate any celebration" of the Latin Mass, and to universalize the liturgical reforms of Pope Paul VI at Vatican II.[241] Based on the earnest convictions of Roman apologists who cite Ignatius on

---

237 Sungenis, Robert. "The Old Covenant: Revoked or Not Revoked?" *Culture Wars*, 23 Apr. 2020, culturewars.com/news/the-old-covenant-revoked-or-not-revoked?rq=shea+jews.

238 Hahn, Scott. "Scott Hahn's Response." *Unam Sanctam Catholicam*, 1 Oct. 2009, unam-sanctamcatholicam.blogspot.com/2009/10/scott-hahns-response.html.

239 Voris, Michael, director. *Church Militant Evening News*, 28 July 2021, www.churchmilitant.com/video/episode/even-2021-07-28.

240 Ignatius of Antioch, to the Philadelphians, 7.

241 Arroyo, Raymond, director. *The World Over with Raymond Arroyo. YouTube*, Eternal Word Television Network (ETWN), 22 July 2021, www.youtube.com/watch?v=mBfJeRcD4Og.

this point—that there ought to be "one eucharist"—we expected Roman Catholics around the world to fall in line joyfully behind their "one bishop" in unity so they may "have but one eucharist." But that has not happened. Instead, traditionalist and conservative sheep have dug in their trotters and kicked against Francis' goad, debating among themselves whether Francis is a "wicked" bishop issuing valid, binding commands, or a valid bishop issuing "wicked," nonbinding commands. Unable to know with certainty, they have resorted to "Paschal's wager" to determine whether they should obey a wicked pope's valid commands or disobey a valid pope's wicked commands, with eternity hanging in the balance. Hedging their bets, they claim either that the *motu proprio* is not clear, or that such dictates on the liturgy are outside of Francis' jurisdiction, or that we cannot really be sure of what Francis has commanded because he has not issued the command in Latin, the official language of Roman Catholicism.[242] So much for "one eucharist" under "one bishop" in the "True Church"! It is no longer about who is "pope," but rather about what each Roman Catholic *personally believes* based on his *private interpretation* of history, tradition and the valid magisterial teachings of whatever his personal perception of Roman Catholicism happens to be. Again, we ask Madrid: Which of these squabbling factions and sects shall we join if we accept his invitation to return to Rome?

Roman Catholicism, as it turns out, is full of autonomous theologians—both clerical and lay—each examining Tradition, Scripture and the Magisterium for himself to discover his own personally tailored version of Roman Catholicism, then holding fiercely *to that version* of "the True Church." In fact, all he has found is his own private interpretation of it—the very thing Madrid thinks he has avoided, and the very thing of which he would invite Protestants and Orthodox to repent in order to join Romanists in their "unity." We are not persuaded.

---

242 Gordon, Timothy, director. 5 Catholics Debate the Motu and SSPX. YouTube, Rule for Retrogrades, 22 July 2021, www.youtube.com/watch?v=NWgsG3I2tiI.

The Phantom "Unity" of Roman Catholicism

While apologists like Madrid invite Protestants and Orthodox to join Roman Catholicism so that "all may be one," what becomes clear is that the promised "unity" of Roman Catholicism is and always has been imaginary and fleeting. Roman Catholics are not "one" at all because in reality each individual Roman Catholic—including Madrid—believes in a "True Church" of his own imagination, arriving at a different conclusion by relying on his own personal interpretation of church history, patristic writings, the catechisms, church councils, papal statements, the visions of Mary and the Scriptures. Each decides for himself what the real church ought to look like, aligning with whichever one most closely aligns with his preferences, and submitting to the version that comports with his personal convictions and beliefs. This is why layman Patrick Madrid can arrive at one conclusion with utmost sincerity—"Lefebvre was a schismatic worthy of excommunication"[243]—and a Roman Catholic archbishop can arrive at another with equal confidence—"I consider Archbishop Lefebvre an exemplary confessor of the faith."[244] One man's "unending succession of bishops" is another man's "international gay crime syndicate,"[245] and one man's "teaching magisterium" is another man's "crowd of mitred monsters."[246] Examples of such divisions *within Roman Catholicism* are manifold, and indeed have existed throughout history. Cyril of Jerusalem (350 AD) acknowledged as much when he wrote, "If you hear that bishops advance against bishops, and clergy against clergy, and laity against laity even unto blood, be not troubled; for it has been written before."[247] In truth, within "Roman Catholicism" there exist, and for centuries have existed, so many warring and contrary factions that the only true "unity" they have ever really enjoyed is in their vacuous claim of unity!

---

243 Madrid, *More Catholic than the Pope.*

244 Archbishop Carlo Maria Viganò, response to *Catholic Family News (September 1, 2020).* *Translated by Giuseppe Pellegrino (https://www.marcotosatti.com/2020/09/02/vigano-mons-lefebvre-an-exemplary-confessor-of-the-faith/).*

245 Voris, G. Michael, director. *Striking Back. The Vortex*, Church Militant, 12 July 2021, www.churchmilitant.com/video/episode/vortex-striking-back.

246 Voris, G. Michael, director. *Silence and Obedience. The Vortex*, Church Militant, 13 July 2021, www.churchmilitant.com/video/episode/vortex-silence-and-obedience.

247 Cyril of Jerusalem, Catechetical Lecture 15 7.

Madrid laments that there "are literally thousands of Protestant denominations today, each of which ardently claims that it has the truth, taken straight from the Bible," utterly blind to the fact that there are literally thousands of private divisions and public factions within the Roman Catholic religion today. If this is Rome's realization of "unity," on what basis does Madrid criticize Protestants who claim that they, too, are one, under their Heavenly Shepherd, Jesus Christ?

The truth is that Madrid has attempted to wield a definition of "unity" so carefully crafted that it can contain within it every particular schism, squabble, faction, "civil war" and petty doctrinal dispute on one side of the Tiber river, but while excluding such divisions on the other bank. And that is the fatal flaw of his claim that *his* "True Church" is the one that ought to be the custodian of the "unity" for which Christ prayed. "Unity" to Madrid is not an organic or even a synthetic doctrinal conformity, but rather a situational attribute based on which side of the river one's preferred *disunity* happens to exist. Madrid has thus once again stumbled into his besetting sin of assuming what it was his duty to prove, essentially declaring "unity" on the basis that Roman Catholics are not Protestant or Orthodox, and then asking them to join him in that "unity." That is a very convenient definition of "unity."

Very well. If each side in this debate is allowed to define "unity" for himself, then Protestants have "unity," too. The only difference between Protestant "unity" and Roman "unity" is where our Shepherd resides. Ours is in heaven. Madrid's is in Rome. Whatever divisions may exist among Protestants, at least we have no faction arguing whether Jesus is a wicked Shepherd or just a Good Shepherd issuing wicked commands, or claiming that Jesus and His "mitred monsters" have organized an "international gay crime syndicate." We will stay with our *Heavenly* Shepherd, thank you very much.

Madrid's Presumptuous Interpretation of Scripture

At this point, Madrid attempts to provide objective evidence that Roman Catholicism is the "True Church." He writes,

> [I]n spite of one's sincerity and heartfelt desire to serve the Lord, what are the objective evidences we can examine that can help us discover which of all the Christian groups out there, including the Catholic Church, contains the "fullness" of Christianity that Christ wants us all to have? ... how can we know ... which is the one, true Church established by Jesus Christ?

To set the stage, Madrid appeals to three Scripture verses to establish the attributes of the "True Church," so that it might be more easily discerned. First, Matthew 5:14 says "You are the light of the world. A city set on a hill cannot be hidden." He informs us that "this means that the Lord didn't go to all the trouble of establishing His Church only to hide it from view, making it difficult or impossible to locate or enter." Jesus must have "imbued His Church with certain clear, recognizable characteristics." Second, Matthew 5:15 says "Nor do people light a lamp and put it under a basket, but on a stand, and it gives light to all in the house." To Madrid, this means Jesus wants "His Church to radiate the light of His truth in all places and at all times." Third, Matthew 28:20 says "Lo, I am with you alway, even unto the end of the world." Madrid informs us that "this means that from that moment forward, there never would be a time when his Church didn't exist."[248]

Those, of course, are Madrid's private interpretations of those verses. As we have noted in the chapter on *The Word of God*, Roman Catholicism has interpreted only very few Bible verses, leaving individual laymen like Madrid to interpret the rest on their own. Lacking any teaching authority, and lacking an infallible interpretation of the verses, Madrid expects his readers to accept his flawed opinions. We object to such nonsense.

---

248 Madrid, pp. 67-73

The Sermon on the Mount, from which Matthew 5:14-15 are cited, is directed toward individual Christians. Read in context, Mathew 5:13-16 calls Christians "salt" and "light," and by these analogies, Jesus exhorts Christians by their good works to be visibly holy in an otherwise dark and lost world so that the Father may be glorified in them: "Let your light so shine before men, that they may see your good works, and glorify your Father which is in heaven" (Matthew 5:16). It is not a discourse on the *visibility of the church* but on the *visibility of our good works*. In an age when the Vatican is embroiled in doctrinal, financial, homosexual, pederastic, real estate, administrative and Hollywood scandals, we suggest Madrid ought to ask himself whether those are the visible "good works" that Jesus had in mind. If not, then why ought we to interpret these verses to reveal to us the religion of Rome?

Likewise, in Matthew 28:20 Jesus promised to be with us to the end of the world, but this, too, was given in the context of Jesus' teachings on how His people should behave: "Go ye therefore, and teach all nations … to observe all things whatsoever I have commanded you" (Matthew 28:19-20). We are certain that Jesus would not have erected an idol of the Inca fertility goddess Pachamama in the temple in Jerusalem, and we may safely conclude that Pope Francis erecting that idol in a church in Rome is not "whatsoever I have commanded you." All three verses indicate that Jesus' people will be known by their good works, something the Roman Catholic church can hardly claim to have satisfied, and something Madrid completely overlooked in his interpretation.

Clearly, Madrid has read these three verses through Rome-colored glasses, through which he invites the reader to discover that Roman Catholicism is the "True Church" Jesus founded. However, when read in the context of the fruits Christians ought to display, we see these verses as evidence that Roman Catholicism is certainly not the church of Jesus Christ. Of course we believe Jesus will always be with us, "even unto the end of the world." We just do not believe the filthy Roman sludge pump of perpetual vice is the way He has kept that promise.

Madrid's "Simple Test"

Having misconstrued Matthew 5:14-15 and 28:20 to refer to the church rather than to good works of individual Christians, Madrid then takes us on a fanciful trip through history, thinking to have found the "True Church" at each stop, assuming that Rome is the only organization that meets his criteria:

> Here's a simple test you can conduct to verify this and test the Catholic Church's claim. Today you will find the Catholic Church around the world teaching its particularly Catholic teachings.[249]

Madrid then attempts an exercise of retroactive continuity to prove that the Roman religion of today is exactly the same church Jesus founded two thousand years ago. On his fanciful journey, Madrid makes the outlandish claim that at every stop can be found the very same Roman Catholic religion:

> Dial back five hundred years. You'll find the same Catholic Church … Now go back another five hundred years. … there you will see the Catholic Church… Go back another five hundred years. Now you're in the Middle Ages. … you find unfurled gloriously … the capital 'C' Catholic Church.[250]

Such claims are of course debatable. We do not deny that the Roman Catholic religion has spread its errors throughout the world. Nor do we deny that Roman Catholicism may be traced to the medieval era. We deny, however, that it originated with the apostles or that it remains unchanged in all the intervening years, as a simple illustration will prove.

Today, we find a post-Vatican II Roman Catholicism that administers the Lord's Supper under the species of bread alone and adapts itself to every religion and secular philosophy in the world, considering Protestants to be "separated brethren" but not so separated

---

249 Madrid, p. 71.
250 Madrid, pp. 71-72.

that they are eternally lost. Five hundred years ago Protestants
were being burned alive for not kneeling before the consecrated
bread of the Eucharist. Five hundred years before that, the Nicæan
prohibition of kneeling during the Eucharistic liturgy was still
in effect,[251] and communion was celebrated under both species
of bread and wine after the recitation of the *Agnus Dei*, which
itself had only been added to the liturgy in seventh century by
Pope Sergius.[252] Five hundred years before that, the liturgy did not
include the Agnus Dei, and Pope Gelasius of Rome was maintaining that "the substance and nature of bread and wine do not cease
to be" after the consecration of bread and wine in the Supper.[253]
A hundred years before that, the Eucharist offering was limited
to bread, wine, "new grain, or ears of wheat, or bunches of grapes
in their season,"[254] and a hundred years still earlier, the Eucharist
offering took place prior to the consecration and included "the
fruits of the first harvest,"[255] figs, pomegranates, olives, pears,
apples, blackberries, peaches, cherries, almonds, plums, cheese, oil,
milk, honey and water,[256] either for distribution to the poor, for use
as catechetical devices for novices, or as a communal love-feast,
or agape meal, for the Christian community. If we find a different
liturgy at every stop—and indeed we do—on what basis does
Madrid suppose that the church is exactly the same today as it was
back then?

    In a few pages we will explore the sordid history of how the
Eucharist offering of the subapostolic church originated as a tithe
of the first fruits of the harvest, offered *prior to the consecration*
of bread and wine for the Supper, but was later restricted to the
offering of bread and wine *after the consecration*, misleading the
late fourth century proto-medieval writers into thinking the
Eucharist had always been an offering—either symbolically or
literally—of the body and blood of Christ. To our point here, even
on the matter of "the source and summit," the very apex of the

---

251 Council of Nicæa, Canon 20
252 *Catholic Encyclopedia*, Agnus Dei (Liturgy).
253 *De duabus naturis in Christo, adversus Eutychen et Nestorium, 496 AD.*
254 Apostolic Constitutions, 8 XLVII.3.
255 Hippolytus, Anaphora, 20.
256 Hippolytus, Anaphora, 5, 6, 21, 30, 32 (see also Cyprian of Carthage, *Epistle 69* 2.

Roman Catholic religion—the Eucharist offering itself[257] —Madrid's silly claim that at every stage in history we will "find the same Catholic Church" is patently false. In the late fifth century even Pope Gelasius understood that the bread and wine were not substantially changed by the consecration, but by the ninth century ministers were expected to confess that the bread and wine were literally Christ's body and blood, and by the twelfth, kneeling to worship the consecrated bread was added to the liturgy, and public Eucharistic processions and adoration flourished throughout Europe. The inquisitions shortly followed as people were put to death for not bowing down to the Eucharist—a Eucharist that had originated in the early centuries as nothing but a simple thank offering before the Supper! No, we do not "find the same Catholic Church" in every age. To the contrary, we find a different, and increasingly diabolical, "Catholic Church" at every stop.

Madrid's laughable assertion is made even more so as he confronts an inevitable historical reality: He simply cannot trace his religion back to the apostles. As he continues dialing back the clock to the earliest centuries, he begins to waver in his resolve because he cannot find his church there:

> Now, cast your gaze back across the remaining few centuries, the fourth, third, second. Now you are near the end of the first century … the close of the Apostolic age. And here we see the Catholic Church, teaching and proclaiming the faith in seed form, developing a new theological vocabulary on the fly.... The Church is still in its infancy. It doesn't yet have many of the external features and characteristics it will eventually acquire;[258]

Faith "in seed form," a church "still in its infancy" lacking characteristics that it will "eventually acquire" is Madrid's tacit confession that he is unable to uncover his religion in antiquity, but is also unwilling to acknowledge that it did not exist in those early centuries. To justify

---

257 CCC, 1324.
258 Madrid, p. 73 (Emphasis added).

the gross discontinuity between early Christianity and his late fourth century Roman novelty, Madrid resorts to John Henry Newman's "development of doctrine" hypothesis to excuse the historian who cannot find Roman Catholicism in the apostolic and subapostolic era. Like Newman, Madrid simply assumes that "the clear light of the fourth and fifth centuries may be fairly taken to interpret to us the dim, though definite, outlines traced in the preceding."[259] So he assumes that all data from the early centuries, no matter how contrary, can be safely interpreted as early evidence of Roman Catholicism:

> [T]he Church ... grows and develops. And just as you don't today resemble very closely how you looked when you were a one-year-old baby, even so, you are the very same person. ... The same is true of the Catholic Church.[260]

Here Madrid echoes Newman's realization that the early church does not look like the malformed and novel Roman religion. Cardinal Newman, a nineteenth century Anglican convert to Roman Catholicism, formally acknowledged the dissonance between modern Roman Catholicism and the ancient church in his *Essay on the Development of Doctrine*. The catalyst for his work was that nineteenth century Roman Catholicism could not look into the mirror of the first three centuries and see herself looking back. Something was vastly different, and such a vast difference required an explanation. Thus was born Newman's "Development of Doctrine" hypothesis to explain, in his own words, the "want of accord between the early and the late aspects of Christianity."[261] The objective of his essay was to show that the differences between the early church and Roman Catholicism could all be accounted for by the gradual "development of doctrine." He assumed without proof that his nineteenth century Roman Catholic medieval novelties must have been the result of an unbroken, continuous process of doctrinal development since the apostolic era. The fatal flaw of Madrid's (and Newman's) approach is to assume that

---

259 Newman, *On the Development of Christian Doctrine*, Chapter 4, Section 3.
260 Madrid, p. 74.
261 *John Henry Cardinal Newman, Essay on the Development of Doctrine, Introduction, paragraph 20.*

his religion is the "grown-up" version of the infant church, and to search for ancient evidence of his religion "in seed form." To attempt that impossible feat, he reads later novelties such as Roman primacy, the "Real Presence of Christ" in the Eucharist and Purgatory into the ancient writings, hoping to show that Rome's novelties originated earlier than they really did. We will therefore address each in turn.

Roman Primacy

Clement's Letter to the Corinthians

Madrid appeals to the epistle of Clement of Rome to the Corinthians as first century evidence of Roman primacy. "Look at the year A.D. 80," Madrid writes. "You'll see the bishop of Rome, Pope St. Clement I, issuing a letter of encouragement and admonition to another important diocese. … we see one of the very first popes exercising authority in another established church."[262] Madrid bases his conclusion on three statements in Clement's letter:

- "Accept our counsel and you will have nothing to regret." (chapter 58)
- "If anyone disobey the things which have been said by Him [the Lord] through us, let them know that they will involve themselves in transgression and in no small danger." (chapter 59)
- "You will afford us joy and gladness if being obedient to the things which we have been written through the Holy Spirit, you will root out the wicked passion of jealousy." (chapter 63)

In their immediate context, none of these can carry the weight of Madrid's exegesis, and in the broader context of the early church, Madrid's claims are shown to be either willfully obtuse or grossly disingenuous. The first exhortation to "accept our counsel" follows immediately upon Clement's admonition that the seditious parties "submit yourselves to the presbyters, and receive correction so as to repent." That "correction" was based on Proverbs 1:23-33, which Clement had quoted in full, and in which Wisdom implores the simple to "turn at my reproof" in order that he may "dwell in safety." Thus,

---

262 Madrid, p. 74-75.

Clement introduces his admonition by saying, "Let us, therefore, flee from the warning threats pronounced by Wisdom [Proverbs 1:20] on the disobedient...."[263] Clement's counsel was that the seditious ought to obey the warnings of Wisdom in Proverbs, and turn at her reproof, to which the Corinthians were advised to submit. Of course they were. It is sound advice from the Scriptures.

The second citation simply continues on the first. Whereas Clement initially exhorted the seditious with the positive benefits of repentance (Proverbs 1:23,33), he next admonishes them with the negative penalties of their sin, for "the complacency of fools destroys them" (Proverbs 1:24-32). When Clement writes that these recommendations ought to be followed lest the factious parties find themselves "in transgression and in no small danger," he is simply referring to the lengthy citation from Proverbs that he had just quoted. Clement had not invoked his own authority but the Scriptural authority of "Wisdom" in Proverbs.

The third citation is a simple encouragement to the seditious to press onward to repentance. Madrid's rendering, that the seditious ought to be "obedient to the things which we have written through the Holy Spirit" (supported by Lightfoot (1869)[264] and Kleist (1949)[265]), attaches "through the Holy Spirit" to "the things which we have written," ostensibly indicating that Clement believed his letter was inspired by the Holy Spirit, an implication we find quite dubious. Clement elsewhere describes the Scriptures as "the truths of the Holy Spirit."[266] Lightfoot's and Kleist's renderings therefore imply Clement thought his letter was "Scripture," conveying "the truths" of the Holy Spirit to the Corinthians. However, other renderings (supported by Hoole (1885)[267] and Keith (1895)[268]) instead

---

263 Clement, *To the Corinthians*, 58.
264 Clement, and J. B. Lightfoot. *St. Clement of Rome, the Two Epistles to the Corinthians: A Revised Text with Introduction and Notes*. Macmillan and Co., 1869.
265 Kleist, James A. *The Epistles of St. Clement of Rome and St. Ignatius of Antioch*. Newman Press, 1949.
266 Chapter 45. τας αληθεις "the true sayings" (Migne, P.G., Vol. 1 col. 300).
267 Hoole, Charles H., et al. *The Apostolic Fathers: The Epistles of S. Clement, S. Ignatius, S. Barnabas, S. Polycarp, Together with the Martyrdom of S. Ignatius and S. Polycarp*. Rivingtons, 1885.
268 Clement, *To the Corinthians*. Translated by John Keith, trans. *The Ante-Nicene Fathers: Translations of the Writings of the Fathers Down to AD 325*, edited by Alexander Roberts and James Donaldson, 10 volumes, 1885–1887, volume 9.

attach "through the Holy Spirit" to the desired repentance of the seditious, encouraging them to "root out the lawless wrath of your jealousy" *by the power of the Holy Spirit*. This rendering is much more in keeping with the tenor of Clement's letter in which he repeatedly invokes the Holy Spirit's movement in the believer toward an attitude of repentance.[269] Thus, in the immediate context of Clement's letter, his exhortations mean nothing more than what he plainly affirms throughout: that Proverbs 1:23-33 indicates that Wisdom "will pour out My spirit unto you," and thus the seditious ought to follow the leading of the Spirit to repent, lest they face very serious consequences. This point is drawn out by Clement not based on Roman primacy but rather from the Scriptures.

But even more than that, the broader context of the early church militates so strongly against Madrid's conclusion that we have to wonder whether he is as familiar with the early church as he claims. The church at Philippi wrote to Polycarp, bishop of Smyrna, to ask his advice, and Polycarp wrote back to the Philippians "because you have invited me to do so."[270] At another time, a schism had erupted in Rome, whereupon Cyprian of Carthage wrote to the warring presbyters there, demanding that they "acquiesce in these my letters,"[271] which both parties were only too happy to do.[272] Shall we conclude from these that Polycarp of Smyrna was the "pope" of the Philippians and that Cyprian of Carthage was the "pope" of the Romans? Of course not!

We understand, as Madrid surely must also know, that the early church communicated by means of such letters. Yes, it is true, Corinth wrote to Rome, and Clement wrote back to the church at Corinth, and asked the Corinthians to let him know how they were progressing.[273] Ignatius, the bishop of Antioch, wrote letters to Ephesus, Tralles, Magnesia, Rome, Philadelphia and Smyrna, and asked them to write letters back to him[274] and asked

---

269 See paragraphs 7, 8, 13, 16, 56 and 57.
270 Polycarp, *to Philippi*, 3.
271 Cyprian, to the Roman schismatics, *Epistle 43*.
272 Letter to Cyprian, *Epistle 45* Cornelius to Cyprian; *Epistle 49* Maximus and the Other Confessors to Cyprian.
273 Clement, to the Corinthians, 65.
274 Ignatius, *to the Smyrnæans*, 11.

Polycarp to "write to the adjacent Churches" and notify them of his instructions.[275] The church at Philippi wrote to Polycarp to ask his advice,[276] and to request that their letter be duplicated and forwarded to Antioch, and that Ignatius' letters be copied and sent to Philippi. Ignatius wrote to Polycarp requesting that the letter from Philippi be forwarded to him. Polycarp agreed to all of these requests.[277] And when Polycarp died, the church at Smyrna wrote to Philomelium, greeting "all the parishes of the holy Catholic Church in every place,"[278] and requesting that their letter be copied and sent to other churches that were even more remote.[279]

Take any one of these letters in isolation, as Madrid does with Clement's, subject it to a clinical analysis intent on a preferred interpretation, and one can "prove" the primacy of any episcopal seat in the early church. But such a fraudulent analysis requires that we ignore the plain ecclesiological expressions in those very letters. When read in context, the emergent ecclesiology of the early church does not derive episcopal authority from a chief shepherd presiding in Rome. Rather it demonstrates a mutual, fraternal collegiality among them, none presuming to be in charge of the others, Christ alone being the Chief Shepherd of them all.

Ignatius' Letter to the Romans

Madrid appeals to Ignatius of Antioch[280] to suggest that he recognized the primacy of Rome early in the second century. Madrid offers the citation without commentary, but two statements by Ignatius are apparently intended by Madrid to prove to us that the church at Antioch deferred to the church of Rome:

- "to the church which holds the presidency, in the location of the country of the Romans, ... and, because you hold the presidency in love, named after Christ and named after the Father ..." (To the Romans, Greeting)

---

275 Ignatius, *to Polycarp*, 8.
276 Polycarp, *to Philippi*, 3.
277 Polycarp, *to Philippi*, 13.
278 Eusebius, *Church History*, IV.15.
279 *The martyrdom of Polycarp*, 20.
280 Madrid, pp. 75-76.

- "You have envied no one, but others you have taught. I desire only that what you have enjoined in your instructions may remain in force." (To the Romans, 3)

Again, in the immediate context of Ignatius' letters, neither of these citations can carry the weight of Madrid's inferences. And in the broader context of the early church writings, the inferences we are expected to draw from Madrid's citations (as he provides no commentary) are simply laughable.

The first citation in which Ignatius says the Roman church "holds the presidency … in love" can hardly mean that Ignatius believed Rome had the primacy over all other churches. Ignatius called the presbyters of Tralles "the sanhedrin of God, and assembly of the apostles,"[281] and wrote that the bishop of Magnesia "presides in the place of God," and the Magnesian presbyters "in the place of the assembly of the apostles."[282] Did these, too, hold universal episcopal primacy? In the second citation, Ignatius says the Roman church had taught others and desires that such teaching remain in force. But in another letter, Ignatius claimed that he, too, had taught others in order to ensure that all "hold the same opinion."[283] Was Ignatius the universal primate on this account? In another letter he told the Ephesians that others ought to be "instructed by your works."[284] Was Ephesus the therefore the chief city of Christendom? Of the Smyrnæans, Ignatius said that they had been "perfected in an immoveable faith,"[285] and that their bishop was "an immoveable rock,"[286] a Petrine appellation bestowed on no other church in Ignatius' epistles. Was Smyrna therefore the seat of the universal episcopate? Of course not, as anyone familiar with Ignatius' letters would know.

Fundamentally, what is missing in Madrid's assessment is that Ignatius described all congregations in such flowery, magnanimous and superlative language that we cannot possibly read any more into them than the author's earnest affection for them. Take Madrid's

---

281 *Ignatius of Antioch, to the Trallians 3.*
282 *Ignatius of Antioch, to the Magnesians 6.*
283 Ignatius of Antioch, to the Smyrnæans 4.
284 Ignatius of Antioch, to the Ephesians 10.
285 Ignatius of Antioch, to the Smyrnæans 1.
286 Ignatius of Antioch, to Polycarp 1.

approach to Ignatius' epistle to the Romans, and apply it to his letter to the Trallians, and we must conclude that the universal episcopate of the early church "in seed form" resided in the presbyters of Tralles. What higher authority can exist, after all, than the "sanhedrin of God, and assembly of the apostles"? Or apply Madrid's standard to Ignatius' letter to the Magnesians, and we must conclude that the universal episcopacy of the early church "in seed form" belonged to the bishop of Magnesians. What higher authority can exist, after all, than the bishop who "presides in the place of God"? In fact, since the Corinthians sought counsel from Clement (c. 80 AD), and the Philippians sought counsel from Polycarp (153 AD), and Nazianzen (380 AD) believed that Athanasius was "entrusted with the chief rule over the people ... the charge of the whole world" and was chosen by the Spirit to "breathe on His behalf,"[287] and Chrysostom (390 AD) thought Ignatius was Peter's successor in Antioch because in God's eyes, Antioch was "equivalent to the whole world,"[288] and—in history's unkindest cut—the church at Rome sought counsel from Cyprian (c. 256 AD), we can conclude nothing else than this: the whole early church was a veritable "Pope-a-palooza," with every bishop in every city exercising global, universal episcopal authority "in seed form" over every other bishop in the world. Madrid has driven us to this madness with his foolish and grossly selective inferences from Ignatius. To put it another way, if everyone was pope back then, then nobody was, and in truth Madrid is absolutely unable to find proof of his desired "Roman primacy" in Ignatius.

Irenæus' Against Heresies

Madrid's third citation in support of early Roman primacy is from Irenæus' voluminous work, *Against Heresies*.[289] Before addressing the citation itself, it is best to understand the context in which it was written. Irenæus and Florinus had studied together under Polycarp in Smyrna, who himself had been schooled by the apostle John in Asia Minor.[290] Irenæus was called to the western reaches of the empire in

---

287 Gregory Nazianzen, Oration 21 7.
288 Chrysostom, Homily on Ignatius 4.
289 Madrid, p. 75-77.
290 Eusebius, *Church History*, V 15, 20.

Lyons in the middle of the second century, by which time the Gnostic error had made its way into Europe and had taken root in Rome, where Florinus now lived. Gnosticism's most vocal proponent there, Valentinus, had been a candidate for bishop of Rome, but when he was not selected, he "broke with the church" and advanced his errors separately.[291] To Irenæus' dismay, his dear friend Florinus had succumbed to Valentinus' charms. *Against Heresies* therefore, while indeed a valuable compendium and refutation of the errors of the Gnostics, was also Irenæus' endearingly personal appeal to his friend to reconsider the errors into which he had fallen and return to the apostolic orthodoxy of his youth.[292] Irenæus' focus was therefore twofold: first, to challenge those of the school of Valentinus in Rome to consider the apostolic origins of that church and repent of their schism, and second, for Florinus to consider the apostolic teaching he had received in his youth from Polycarp in Asia and return to the orthodox faith.

The reason this brief historical context of *Against Heresies* is so important is that Madrid relies on only one part of it, focusing geographically on Rome (where Florinus had stumbled) and on the apostles Peter and Paul (who had preached there), but omitting Irenæus' equal emphasis on Asia (where Florinus had learned the truth) and the apostle John (who had led the church there). Focusing only on Irenæus' statements on Rome, and studiously avoiding his emphasis on the church in Asia, Madrid would lead his readers to believe Irenæus had written a general treatise on heresy and had prescribed a particular Roman antidote to it. But that is not true. Irenæus had written a particular treatise on the errors into which his friend in Rome had fallen and had prescribed a general apostolic antidote. Quite notably, that antidote could be found both in Rome where the Valentinians had ensnared Florinus, and in Asia where Polycarp had discipled him.

With that in mind we now turn to Madrid's misuse of Irenæus. There are three statements in his citation from which he would have us conclude that Irenæus held to the primacy and authority of the city of Rome in the early church:

---

291 Tertullian, Against the Valentinians 4.
292 Irenæuus, *Against Heresies* I preface.

- "Matthew also issued among the Hebrews a written Gospel in their own language, while Peter and Paul were evangelizing in Rome and laying the foundation of the Church ..." (*Against Heresies*, 3.1.1)
- "But since it would be too long to enumerate in such a volume as this the succession of all the churches, we shall confound all those who, in whatever manner, whether through self-satisfaction of vainglory, or through blindness and wicked opinion, assemble other than where it is proper, by pointing out here the succession of bishops of the greatest and most ancient church known to all, founded and organized at Rome by the two most glorious apostles, Peter and Paul ... ." (*Against Heresies*, 3.3.2)
- "With that church [i.e., with Rome], because of its superior origin, all the churches must agree, that is, all the faithful in the whole world, and it is in her that the faithful everywhere have maintained the apostolic tradition." (*Against Heresies*, 3.3.2)

By these three citations, Madrid attempts to fabricate in Irenæus a conviction that the foundation of the church exists in Rome, that the Gospel comes down to us from the succession of bishops in Rome and that all churches in the world must agree with the church of Rome. But Irenæus expressed no such conviction. Madrid's carefully extracted citations reflect neither the substance of Irenæus' convictions, nor even his particular concern for his friend, Florinus.

Laying the Foundation of the Church

In the first two books of *Against Heresies*, Irenæus focused on the errors of the Gnostics, but here in Book 3, he changes his focus to equipping Florinus. Jesus "gave to His apostles the power of the Gospel," and thus Irenæus attempts to elicit "from the Scriptures" the tools Florinus will need to combat the error.[293] In the next sentence Irenæus says the Gospel preached by the apostles and handed down to us in the Scriptures is "the ground and pillar of our faith," which is to

---

293 Irenæus, *Against Heresies*, 3 preface.

say that the Gospel is foundation of the church.[294] Irenæus' statement that Peter and Paul were "evangelizing in Rome and laying the foundation of the Church" is just one piece of a much broader point he was making—namely that the apostles everywhere had laid the foundation of the church by preaching the Gospel. Isolating and removing that statement from its broader context, Madrid then cloaks Irenæus' narrower point upon which he expounds in the very next sentences: that the same foundation laid down by Matthew to the Hebrews and by Peter and Paul in Rome had also been laid down by Mark and Luke in their Gospels, and had been laid by John in Asia Minor:

> After their departure, Mark, the disciple and interpreter of Peter, did also hand down to us in writing what had been preached by Peter. Luke also, the companion of Paul, recorded in a book the Gospel preached by him. Afterwards, John, the disciple of the Lord, who also had leaned upon His breast, did himself publish a Gospel during his residence at Ephesus in Asia.[295]

The importance of those two geographic references—Rome and Asia Minor—can only be understood in the context of Irenæus' concern for Florinus, who had been discipled in Asia Minor by Polycarp and afterward was led astray in Rome by Valentinus. To discover Roman primacy in Irenæus, Madrid must not only obscure that broader point—that *all of the apostles* had laid "the ground and pillar of our faith" by the preaching of the Gospel—but also the very narrow and particular geographic attention he pays to the spiritual well-being of his dear friend from his youth. Rome (where Florinus stumbled) and Asia (where Florinus first believed) were equally custodians of the same apostolic faith, to which both Florinus and the Valentinians could easily refer to discover the truth. There is nothing in Irenæus to suggest he thought Rome was the sole custodian. Indeed, Irenæus' summary remark on this exact point—in fact his very next sentence— is that "these [Matthew, Mark, Luke, John, Peter and Paul] have all

---

294 Irenæus, *Against Heresies* 3.1.1.
295 Ibid.

declared to us" *the same truth*, whether in Italy or in Asia.[296] Lacking
evidence for Roman primacy in Irenæus, Madrid has attempted rather
to fabricate the evidence and obscure the facts in the hope that his
reader will arrive in ignorance at his same invalid conclusion.

"The Succession of Bishops"

Madrid repeats the error his second citation, highlighting "the
succession of bishops" after Peter and Paul *in Rome* (where the
Valentinians had seduced Florinus), but ignoring Irenæus' appeal
to "those men who have succeeded Polycarp down to the present
time" *in Asia* (where Florinus had been so ably schooled). The Valentinian schism *in Rome* had separated from the church *in Rome*
and began to meet separately *in Rome*, and thus Irenæus attempts
to "confound all those who … assemble other than where it is
proper" (referring to the Valentinians *in Rome*). Instead of reciting
the succession of all the bishops in every city, Irenæus focuses on
the city where the offense had occurred. He concludes, "In this
order, and by this succession, the ecclesiastical tradition from
the apostles, and the preaching of the truth, have come down to
us."[297] This is where Madrid would prefer we stop reading, and that
Irenæus stop writing, so he can move on to his next point.

But Irenæus does not stop. Rather, he follows upon the succession of bishops *in Rome* (for the benefit of the Valentinian
detractors there) with a discussion on the succession of bishops
from John *in Asia* (with whom Florinus was personally familiar),
focusing on the city from which Florinus had come:

> But Polycarp also was not only instructed by apostles, and
> conversed with many who had seen Christ, but was also,
> by apostles in Asia, appointed bishop of the Church in
> Smyrna, whom I also saw in my early youth …. To these
> things all the Asiatic Churches testify, *as do also those*
> *men who have succeeded Polycarp down to the present time*
> — a man who was of much greater weight, and a more

---

296 Ibid.
297 Irenæus, *Against Heresies* 3.3.3.

steadfast witness of truth, than Valentinus, and Marcion, and the rest of the heretics.[298]

That Irenæus understood the Asian foundation (upon which Florinus' faith was built) was equal to and as authoritative as the Latin foundation (from which Florinus had fallen) is evidenced first by his remarkable reference to Polycarp's teachings "which alone are true," and second by his recollection that Polycarp had come to Rome, not to learn the truth but to teach it, having received "this one and sole truth from the apostles" in Asia!

> Polycarp … always taught the things which he had learned from the apostles, and which the Church has handed down, and which alone are true. … coming to Rome in the time of Anicetus … proclaiming that he had received this one and sole truth from the apostles — that, namely, which is handed down by the Church.[299]

The equivalence of the Latin and Asian foundations is also seen graphically in Irenæus' assertion that "the apostolic tradition of the Church" may be found in "a most powerful letter to the Corinthians" from Clement of Rome,[300] but may also be found in "a very powerful Epistle of Polycarp [in Asia] written to the Philippians."[301] As far as Irenæus was concerned, the truth was easily accessible in the two locations of interest to the spiritual condition of his dear friend: Italy and Asia.

From that perspective Irenæus concludes not only the church at Smyrna under Polycarp, but also "the Church in Ephesus, founded by Paul, and having John remaining among them …is a true witness of the tradition of the apostles."[302] Thus, both Rome (where the Valentinians departed) and Asia (from which Florinus had come) were so sufficiently rooted in apostolic truth that either would suffice to correct

---

298 Irenæus, *Against Heresies* 3.3.4
299 Ibid.
300 Irenæus, *Against Heresies* 3.3.3
301 Irenæus, *Against Heresies* 3.3.4
302 Ibid.

the Valentinian errors. By missing the overarching concern Irenæus expresses at the outset for his friend from Smyrna, Madrid both obscures the geographic significance of Irenæus' emphasis on the apostolic roots in both locales, presuming to have found in Irenæus an early witness to Roman primacy. Such a conclusion is completely overturned by Irenæus' explanation that Polycarp had brought with him to Rome the "sole truth from the apostles" from Asia and that those teachings "alone are true"!

"All the Churches Must Agree"

In the third citation from Against Heresies, Madrid thinks he has found evidence that the church at Rome was the standard of orthodoxy because Irenæus appears to suggest that "all the churches must agree" with Rome. There are several problems with such a conclusion, not the least of which are these: First, nobody actually believed or practiced what Madrid thinks Irenæus means; second, Irenæus himself disagreed with Rome and affirmed other great men who had; and third, the Latin upon which Madrid's conclusion is based is known to be a barbaric translation of Irneæus' original Greek.

As we have already noted, so many ancient men disagreed with Rome that we could well-nigh prove that disparaging, mocking, rejecting, ridiculing and overturning the nonsense emanating from Roman church was a universal pastime of the early church, including the congregations of Rome! When Polycarp went to Rome (c. 160 AD), he refused Anicetus' request that he abandon the Eucharistic practices he had learned from "John ... and the other apostles."[303] Polycrates of Ephesus (c. 190 AD) not only refused to bow to the dictates of bishop Victor of Rome, but attested to the "great multitude" of eastern bishops who joined him in his rejection of Roman arrogance.[304] Tertullian (c. 220) mocked bishop Callistus of Rome as "pontifex maximus" for presuming to issue an edict as if he possessed imperial powers.[305] Hippolytus of Rome (c. 225 AD) recalls that he "frequently" opposed the bishops of

303 Eusebius, *Church History* Book V, chapter 24, 14-24.
304 Eusebius, *Church History*, Book V, chapter 24, paragraph 7-8.
305 Tertullian, On Modesty 1.

Rome, "refuted them, and ... forced them reluctantly to acknowledge the truth."[306] Firmilian of Cæsarea (256 AD), far from *agreeing* with Rome, complained instead that Rome had "disagreed with so many bishops throughout the whole world, breaking peace with each one of them" so as to "cut himself off from the unity of love ... with the madness of contumacious discord!"[307] Dionysius of Alexandria (256 AD) rebuked Bishop Stephen for claiming falsely that his novelties originated with the apostles.[308] Under Bishop Cornelius such a severe schism broke out in Rome that the warring parties had to write to Cyprian of Carthage for guidance, and both parties wrote back thanking him for his intervention.[309] Afterward Cyprian demanded that his letters be read aloud to the Roman congregation so that error and schism "may be all purged out of the ears and of the hearts of the brethren, chastising Cornelius for being so easily disturbed by the heretics.[310] Cyprian (256 AD) later pointed out "Pope" Stephen's "error in endeavouring to maintain the cause of heretics against Christians,"[311] and when asked to weigh in on the ordination of bishops in Spain, responded that Stephen's opinion carried no weight and could be ignored.[312] We need hardly go on. Obviously, nobody in the early church seems to have believed *or even heard* that agreeing with the bishop of Rome was a condition of orthodoxy!

To these examples we add Irenæus' own disagreement with Rome, and his personal approval of others who disagreed as well. Irenæus joined with many other bishops in "sharply rebuking" Victor for his attempt to standardize the date of Easter by fiat,[313] and "fittingly admonishes Victor that he should not cut off whole churches of God which observed the tradition of an ancient custom."[314] In that letter, Irenæus reminded Victor that "when the

---

306 Hippolytus, Refutation of All Heresies, Book IX, chapter II.
307 Firmilian, to Cyprian, Epistle 74 6.
308 Dionysius, to Stephen of Rome.
309 Cyprian, to the Roman schismatics, epistle 43; Letter to Cyprian, Epistle 45 Cornelius to Cyprian; Epistle 49 Maximus and the Other Confessors to Cyprian; Epistle 54.
310 Cyprian, Epistle 54, to Cornelius against the Heretics, 2, 20.
311 Cyprian, to Pompey, Epistle 73 1.
312 Cyprian, To the Clergy and People Abiding in Spain, Epistle 67.
313 Eusebius, *Church History*, Book V, chapter 24, 10-11.
314 Eusebius, *Church History*, Book V, chapter 24, 11.

blessed Polycarp was at Rome in the time of Anicetus, and they disagreed a little about certain other things," the bishop of Rome was unable to "persuade Polycarp" to change what he had received from John "and the other apostles with whom he had associated."[315] At that point, "Pope" Anicetus simply "conceded the administration of the eucharist in the church to Polycarp, manifestly as a mark of respect."[316] Clearly, neither Irenæus, *nor even the Bishop of Rome*, believed that "all churches must agree" with Rome!

Finally, there remains yet one more challenge to Madrid's interpretation. Irenæus' original Greek works survive only in fragments and the complete manuscript of his valuable treatise, *Against Heresies*, survives only in a "barbarous" Latin translation. Dr. Alexander Roberts, who translated *Against Heresies* into English, observed,

> Irenæus, even in the original Greek, is often a very obscure writer. ... And the Latin version adds to these difficulties of the original, by being itself of the most barbarous character. In fact, it is often necessary to make a conjectural re-translation of it into Greek, in order to obtain some inkling of what [Irenæus] wrote ....[317]

While Irenæus' original Greek exists for other citations, in this case Madrid has been forced to rely on the "barbarous" Latin translation *that is known to be unreliable.* That barbarous Latin is obviously overturned by more reliable sources from manifold witnesses indicating that Irenæus (with others) not only disagreed with *the church at Rome but also approved of others who did.*

Additionally, we have the testimony of a Roman Catholic patristic scholar who sees, both from the immediate context of Irenæus and from the broader testimony of the early church,

---

315 Eusebius, *Church History*, Book V, chapter 24, 16.
316 Eusebius, *Church History*, Book V, chapter 24, 17.
317 *The Ante-Nicene Fathers: Translations of the Writings of the Fathers Down to A.D. 325*, vol. I, Edited by Alexander Roberts and James Donaldson, 1885, Introductory Note to Irenæus *Against Heresies*, (Repr., New York: Charles Scribner's Sons, 1903), 312.

that the meaning is quite nearly the opposite of what Madrid has imagined. The relevant Latin passage in *Against Heresies* is:

> *Ad hanc enim ecclesiam propter potiorem principalitatem*
> *necesse est omnem convenire ecclesiam.*[318]

"Convenire" is rendered "agree" in Madrid's translation, but it rather has the sense of coming together, as in "to convene" or "to gather." For three hundred years after the apostolic age, the surrounding churches had to meet with Rome to help her and correct her, admonishing and restraining her intractable propensity to inflict damage upon herself and others. Rome was at the crossroads of an empire. Unchecked, her errors would quickly metastasize and spread, and she thus required the constant attention of the surrounding churches. To that end, one Roman Catholic translator has the apostolicity of the church in Rome *being preserved by faithful churches on every side*, rather than the apostolicity of the churches on every side *being preserved by Rome*. This yields a much more natural and believable translation, which, as it turns out is more consistent with history:

> For to this Church, on account of more potent principality,
> it is necessary that every Church, that is, those who are on
> every side faithful, **resort**, in which (Church) ever, by those
> who are on every side, has been preserved that tradition
> which is from the Apostles.[319]

Clearly, it was not those in Rome who preserved the apostolic tradition of "those who are on every side," but rather "those who are on every side faithful" who preserved the apostolic tradition of the oft wavering, frequently schismatic and occasionally heretical church in Rome. Not only is this translation consistent with the abundant testimony of the early church, but it is also consistent with the particular examples of the same phenomenon recorded by Irenæus

---

318 Migne, P.G. Vol VII, 849.
319 Berington & Kirk, *The Faith of Catholics*, vol. I, 2nd ed. (New York, 1885), 248 (emphasis added).

himself. Chrysostom informs us that Ignatius of Antioch was sent to Rome because "they who dwelt in Rome … required more help."[320] Hippolytus resisted the heresies of bishops Zephyrinus and Callistus,[321] and Polycrates with "a great multitude" of Asian bishops rebuked Victor of Rome for his overreach.[322] During the Montanist controversy, "the brethren in Gaul set forth their own prudent and most orthodox judgment,"[323] and with "the faithful in Asia … rejected the heresy,"[324] while hapless Eleutherius in Rome was actively supporting it, only rescinding that support under pressure from without.[325] As these examples illustrate, the perception—and indeed *the reality*—of the early church was not that Rome guarded the orthodoxy of the churches of the world, but quite the opposite: The churches of the world often had to correct and restrain the Roman church to keep it within the bounds of orthodoxy, and that with only limited success because the bishop of Rome was so frequently given to kicking against the goad!

Irenæus' written record is similarly objective regarding the need to for Rome to be held within the bounds of orthodoxy from without. In *Against Heresies*, Irenæus describes Polycarp coming to Rome in the days of Anicetus to assist in putting down the heresies flourishing there.[326] Eusebius described Irenæus joining with other bishops to rebuke Victor for his gross impudence,[327] and Phillip Schaff observes that Irenæus himself "was sent to Rome with letters of remonstrance against the rising pestilence of heresy," only to find "the Montanist heresy patronized by Eleutherus the Bishop of Rome."[328] After visiting Rome, Irenæus attests to his own exhaustive efforts to correct the Gnostic error to which his friend succumbed in that very city,[329] a task for which the bishop of Rome was clearly unequipped.

---

320 Chrysostom, Homily on Ignatius of Antioch 4.
321 Hippolytus, Refutation of All Heresies, Book IX, chapter II.
322 Eusebius, *Church History*, Book V 24.8.
323 Eusebius, *Church History*, Book V, chapter 3, paragraph 4.
324 Eusebius, *Church History*, Book V, chapter 16, paragraph 10.
325 Tertullian, Against Praxeas 1.
326 Irenæus, *Against Heresies*, Book III chapter 3, paragraph 4.
327 Eusebius, *Church History*, Book V 24.10-11.
328 *The Ante-Nicene Fathers*, vol. I, 309.
329 Irenæus, *Against Heresies* preface to Book I.

It is against that historical backdrop that the "barbarous" extant Latin must be measured when it says "all the faithful in the whole world" must agree with Rome. Neither Irenæus himself nor "all the faithful in the whole world" had agreed with Rome to that point, except upon those rare ancient occasions when Rome and her bishops managed to strike an apostolic chord, or could be persuaded, if briefly, to hold to the truth of the apostles. When soberly weighed in the fullness of his personal concern for Florinus and the subject matter being addressed, it is clear that Roman primacy can nowhere be found in Irenæus. Madrid's attempts to find it are based not only on his apparent ignorance of Irenæus's objectives in *Against Heresies,* but also upon the ignorance of the "barbarous" translator who tried unsuccessfully to render it in Latin. In the end, Irenæus' true meaning and true purpose in writing *Against Heresies*, were to remind his beloved friend Florinus that the apostolic truths of the faith could be found *either* in the ministry of Peter and Paul and the apostolic successors in Rome where Florinus ended up, *or* in the ministry of Paul, John and the apostolic successors in Asia where Florinus began. In either case a man must "agree to these truths," whether originating in Asia or Rome, to be a member of Christ's church.[330]

The "Real Presence of Christ" in the Eucharist

Madrid next attempts to show that the early church universally embraced the modern Roman Catholic belief in the "Real Presence" of Christ in the Eucharist.[331] On the night before He died, Jesus celebrated His Last Supper and instituted what we now call the Lord's Supper. Since that night, Christians have celebrated it as a memorial meal in which the bread and wine are blessed and we consume by faith the body and blood of Christ under the symbols of bread and wine. In Roman Catholicism, however, it is not just a memorial meal, but a participation in the very sacrifice of Calvary. The priest, acting in the person of Christ, consecrates the bread and wine, changing them into the actual body, blood, soul and divinity

---

330 Irenæus, *Against Heresies* 3.1.2.
331 Madrid, pp. 77-78.

of Christ, and then offers them to the Father as a sacrifice for sins.
The teaching that the bread and wine truly become Jesus Christ—
body, blood, soul and divinity—is called the doctrine of "the Real
Presence." The Roman Catholic celebration of the Lord's Supper
as a sacrifice of consecrated bread and wine originated late in the
fourth century, but the Roman Catholic apologist is ever eager to
discover earlier proofs of his novelties, thinking to find "the Real
Presence of Christ" in every ancient reference to the Supper. Madrid
is no exception. He offers three ancient citations in support of his
medieval novelty: two from Ignatius of Antioch (107 AD) and one
from Justin Martyr (150 AD). "Consider these three representative
quotes from the first and second centuries regarding the early
Christian belief in the Real Presence of Christ in the Eucharist."[332]
None of them support the doctrine.

Ignatius of Antioch

To the Romans

As evidence of early belief in "the Real Presence of Christ" in the
Supper, Madrid offers Ignatius' epistle to the Romans in which he
wrote, "I desire the bread of God, which is the flesh of Jesus Christ
… and for drink I desire his blood, which is love incorruptible."[333]
Madrid's use of this citation as early evidence for a belief in the
"Real Presence of Christ" is easily dismissed. As we have noted
in this chapter, Ignatius of Antioch tended to use flowery, metaphorical language, illustrating his messages with analogies and
similes even when they served no obvious purpose except to adorn
his letters with figures of speech. While in transit to Rome, he
says he is "bound to ten leopards" and then quickly adds, "I mean
a band of soldiers" (*To the Romans* 5). He warns against "herbage
of a different kind," and then quickly adds, "I mean heresy" (*To
the Trallians* 6). Closer to our point, in his letters he employed
the figures of flesh, blood, bread, wheat and leaven for various
meanings that were very obviously not to be understood literally:

332 Madrid, p. 77.
333 Ignatius of Antioch, to the Romans, 7.

- "Wherefore, clothing yourselves with meekness, be ye renewed in faith, that is the flesh of the Lord, and in love, that is the blood of Christ." (*To the Trallians*, 8).
- "I am the wheat of God, and let me be ground by the teeth of the wild beasts, that I may be found the pure bread of Christ." (To the Romans, 4)
- "Lay aside, therefore, the evil, the old, the sour leaven, and be changed into the new leaven, which is Jesus Christ." (To the Magnesians, 10)

We will not begrudge Ignatius his predilection for metaphors and analogies and for whom there was no figure that could not be stretched to suit his purpose. But Madrid must surely recognize that the figurative language of such a man cannot possibly serve as proof of belief in the literal presence of Christ in the Supper. If faith "is the flesh of the Lord"; and the bread of God "is the flesh of Jesus Christ"; and love "is the blood of Christ"; and Ignatius himself is "the wheat of God" ground into "the pure bread of Christ"; and the Magnesians are "changed into the new leaven, which is Jesus Christ", in what meaningful way can Ignatius confirm that *wine* literally becomes the blood of Christ at the consecration? Would Madrid also conclude from this that the bread is transubstantiated into "faith," Jesus' blood into "love," Ignatius into "bread," the Magnesians into Jesus, the Roman guards into leopards and herbs into heresy? There are much better arguments to be made for early evidence of the "Real Presence" in the early writers, as we shall see next, but Ignatius' obvious nonliteral, figurative reference in his letter to the Romans is not one of them.

To the Smyrnæans

Madrid's first citation revealed his ignorance of Ignatius' writing style, but his second citation rather reveals his ignorance of the ancient liturgy. This is a common mistake made by many Roman apologists and Madrid is not exceptional in committing it. Madrid cites Ignatius' letter to the Smyrnæans as follows:

> Take note of those who hold heterodox opinions on the
> grace of Jesus Christ which has come to us, and see how
> contrary their opinions are to the mind of God. ... they
> abstain from the Eucharist and from prayer because
> they do not confess that the Eucharist is the flesh of our
> Savior Jesus Christ, flesh which suffered for our sins and
> which that Father, in his goodness raised up again. (*To the
> Smyrnœans*, 6-7)[334]

Madrid omitted a single sentence that overturns his interpretation, but the omission was neither malicious nor mendacious. He
simply did not realize what it meant. We shall return to it shortly.
To the gullible and the ignorant (and we include some Reformers
and Protestants among them), the citation appears to show that
Ignatius believed the bread of the Lord's Supper had been literally
changed into "the flesh of our Savior Jesus Christ." In reality, both
mentions of the "Eucharist" here refer to bread that was not yet
consecrated, and thus Ignatius offers no support at all for the "Real
Presence," but rather provides evidence of how far Rome's novel
liturgy has diverged from that of the early church. A little comparative history will shed some much needed light on the passage, and
upon the three mistakes Madrid makes as he interprets it.

The Novel Roman Liturgy

In Roman Catholicism, the bread for the Supper is brought forward
to the altar, consecrated by the priest and ostensibly changed into
the body and blood of Christ by the recitation of Christ's words:
"This is My body."[335] The Eucharistic "body and blood of Christ" is
then offered to the Father as a sacrifice for sins, and then administered to the participants as a meal. When the bread is presented to
the recipient, the priest pronounces, "This is the body of Christ," to
which the communicant responds, "Amen," affirming belief that
the bread has been literally changed into the body of Christ and
offered as a sacrifice for sins. After the sacrificial meal is completed,

---

334 Madrid, p. 78.
335 CCC, 1412.

the assembled communicants are dismissed, which is why the Supper is also called "the Sacrifice of *the Mass*," or literally from its Latin origin, "the sacrifice of *the dismissal*," because it occurs at the end of the liturgy when the communicants are dismissed.[336]

Thus, when Ignatius says the heretics abstain *from the Eucharist* because they do not "confess" that the Eucharist *is the flesh of Christ*, Madrid takes it to mean that the heretics did not participate *in the Supper* because they refused to say "Amen" to the words "This is the body of Christ." The suggestion is preposterous, and is born of Madrid's chronic ignorance of the ancient liturgy. In reality, Ignatius' words mean very nearly the opposite of what Madrid suggests, for the ancient "confession" to which Ignatius refers was spoken over unconsecrated bread!

The Original Eucharist

Through the prophet Malachi, the Lord condemned the unacceptable burnt offerings of the Jews, foretelling a day when "in every place incense shall be offered unto my name, and a pure offering...among the heathen" (Malachi 1:10-11). The apostles left instructions that sacrifices must and would continue under the New Covenant, but these new sacrifices would take the forms of "praise...the fruit of our lips giving thanks" (Hebrews 13:15), doing good works and sharing with others (Hebrews 13:16), "spiritual sacrifices" (1 Peter 2:5), providing for those in need (Philippians 4:18), and "your bodies a living sacrifice" (Romans 12:1). Such sacrifices are "holy" and "acceptable" (Romans 12:1, 1 Peter 2:5) and well-pleasing to the Lord (Philippians 4:18, Hebrews 13:16). A new temple of living stones had been constructed so that these new sacrifices would continue (1 Peter 2:5).

The early church understood these apostolic instructions as a fulfillment of Malachi's prophecy, and included thank offerings—in Greek, εὐχαριστία *(eucharistia)*—in the liturgy. The Sunday gathering was the venue for those offerings, as tithes of the harvest were collected and distributed to "orphans and widows and...all

---

336 *Catholic Encyclopedia*, "The Sacrifice of the Mass."

who are in need."[337] According to Irenæus, "the very oblations" of
the church consisted of the tithes of the Lord's people: Christians
"set aside all their possessions for the Lord's purposes," just as the
widow had in the Gospels (Mark 12:42, Luke 21:2),[338] "offering the
first-fruits" to care for the needy,[339] hungry, thirsty, naked, and
poor.[340] Tertullian believed the sacrifices prophesied by Malachi
were fulfilled in "the ascription of glory, and blessing, and praise,
and hymns"[341] and "simple prayer from a pure conscience."[342]
Athanasius understood the sacrifice of Malachi 1:11 to be fulfilled
in thanksgiving, "a joyful noise," "praise and prayer"[343] when we
"take up our sacrifices, observing distribution to the poor."[344] For
this reason, the early Eucharist offering occasionally included
a banquet of unconsecrated food in order for the poor and the
hungry to be satisfied.[345] That Eucharist sacrifice of the early
church is the predecessor of our modern offertory.

The purpose of "the Eucharist of the oblation" was to "share it
with strangers" for which reason the Eucharist was to be brought
"to the bishop for the entertainment of all strangers."[346] Ignatius of
Antioch insisted that "a proper Eucharist" is administered either
by the bishop or his delegate, as it "is not lawful without the bishop
either to baptize or to celebrate a love-feast."[347] Unsurprisingly,
the Eucharist included not only bread and wine, but other needful
things such as oil, cheese, olives,[348] oxen, sheep, "a batch of dough,"
"a jar of wine or of oil,"[349] figs, pomegranates, pears, apples, black-

---

337 Justin Martyr, *First Apology*, 67.
338 Irenæus, *Against Heresies*, 4 18.2.
339 Irenæus, *Against Heresies*, 4 18.4.
340 Irenæus, *Against Heresies*, 4 17.6.
341 Tertullian, *Against Marcion*, 3 22.
342 Tertullian, *Against Marcion*, 4 1.
343 Athanasius, *Festal Letter*, 11.
344 Athanasius, *Festal Letter*, 45.
345 The Didache portrays this as a feast in which God is thanked for providing it to His people
(*Didache* 9-10). Ignatius of Antioch refers to the Eucharist as a love-feast (*to the Smyrnæans* 8);
Tertullian confirms that the poor and hungry are fed at the love-feast, "with the good things of
the feast we benefit the needy," (*Apology*, 39) and "the Eucharist [is] to be eaten at meal-times"
(*De Corona* 3), consistent with Matthew 26:26, "as they were eating, Jesus took bread..."
346 *Didascalia* 9 (*The Didascalia Apostolorum in English*, Gibson, Margaret Dunlop, M.R.A.S,
LL.D. trans (London: Cambridge University Press, 1903, p. 53).
347 Ignatius of Antioch, *To the Smyrnæans* 8.
348 Hippolytus, *Anaphora*, 4, 5, 6 (Easton, 35-37).
349 *Didache* 13.

berries, peaches, cherries, almonds, plums, milk and honey and even water.[350] On the day of their baptism, catechumens in the early church became eligible to contribute to the offering for the poor, and were thus instructed to bring their own Eucharist with them for the oblation on the day of their baptism.[351] According to the *Didascalia* (230 AD), the gift we offer to God is "our prayer and our Eucharist,"[352] a simple summary of the ancient offering of tithes with gratitude to the One Who had provided them. That state of affairs continued well into the fourth century, until the Eucharist began to be limited to an offering of bread and wine, and wheat and grapes "in their season."[353]

What these early writers were describing is a liturgical offering of the first-fruits with gratitude — "the Eucharist and prayer," in Ignatius' words — and that offering occurred in the liturgy *before anything was consecrated for the Lord's Supper*. Thus, while the Eucharistic oblation of the early church included bread and wine, as well as oil, cheese, olives, almonds, honey, etc… *it could not have included the body and blood of Christ*—symbolic or literal—because the offering was completed *prior to* the consecration. To put a fine point on it, in Ignatius' day, "the Eucharist" offering was not consecrated bread and wine,[354] and therefore Ignatius provides no support for the "Real Presence" of Christ in the Eucharist, a phrase that would have been puzzling to the early church.

The Original "Sacrifice of the Mass"
Because Jesus had given thanks to His Father immediately before instituting the Supper of which only believers can partake, only believers were allowed to participate in the thank offering that preceded it. The unbeliever, the catechumen, the backslider or anyone at odds with his brother was therefore excused or excluded from the liturgy prior to the tithe offering. As Justin Martyr noted, only he "who has been convinced and has assented to our teaching"

350 Hippolytus, Anaphora, 5, 6, 21, 30, 32 (see also Cyprian of Carthage, *Epistle 69* 2).
351 Hippolytus, *Anaphora* 20 (Easton, 45).
352 *Didascalia*, 11 (*The Didascalia*, p. 63).
353 Apostolic Constitutions, 8 XLVII.3.
354 See for example the *Didache* 9-10 in which the Eucharist is a love-feast of bread and wine without a consecration, in which only the baptized may participate.

is invited to "offer hearty prayers" with the brethren "for all things wherewith we are supplied"[355] — that is, to offer "Eucharist and prayer." Jesus said gifts ought not be offered in discord (Matthew 5:23-24), and Paul warned against coming together in strife and divisions (1 Corinthians 11:17-18). The early church took these admonitions seriously, and therefore prohibited anyone from participating in the tithe offering unless he was a professing believer and was not harboring resentment or a spirit of discord against a brother.[356] Such a dismissal was necessary because without Christ, or with unconfessed sin, one could not offer thanks in good faith, with a pure conscience. The tithe oblation thus came to be called by the abbreviated *missa*, and later, the *oblationem missa* in Latin, which is literally "the sacrifice of dismissal," or, in its modern English transliteration, the Sacrifice of the Mass—the tithe offering *immediately following the dismissal* of the unbeliever, the catechumen, the divisive or the backslidden. It was called the Sacrifice of the Mass not because *believers* were dismissed *after the Supper,* but rather because *unbelievers* were dismissed *before the tithe.* Thus, still speaking of unconsecrated food at the Eucharistic love-feast, *the Didache* says, "But let no one eat or drink of your Thanksgiving (Eucharist), but they who have been baptized."[357]

The origin of the term "Sacrifice of the Mass" is significant to our discussion because it explains in part why the heretics would "abstain from" the Eucharist and prayer in the first place. They did not believe Jesus had a body, or that He had suffered, or that His body was raised from the dead, and therefore did not believe the Gospel, and would have been dismissed prior to the tithe offering of first-fruits and prayer, which is precisely what Ignatius meant by "they abstain from the Eucharist and from prayer." As Justin Martyr noted, those who had not "assented to our teaching" were not allowed to participate in the Eucharist. That is, they were not

---

355 Justin Martyr, *First Apology,* 65, 67.
356 Didache [c. 100 A.D.], 14; Justin Martyr [c. 150 A.D.])., First Apology 13, 65, 66; Irenæus, Against Heresies IV.18.4 [189 A.D.]; Hippolytus, Anaphora 20 [215 A.D.]; Nicæa, Canon 11 [325 A.D.]; Athanasius, Apology Against the Arians, I.28 [341 A.D.]; Ambrose, Epistle 20 4-5 [385 A.D.]).
357 *Didache* 9.

allowed to participate in *the tithe offering*, and thus were dismissed before it was offered.

The Apostolic "Amen"

Based on Paul's instructions in 1 Corinthians 14:16, an "Amen" was spoken after the thanksgiving, and therefore the people said "Amen" at the completion of the Eucharist, signifying *the completion of the oblation*. The evidence for the apostolic "Amen" immediately after the ancient tithe offering but before the consecration is plentiful: Justin Martyr (c. 150 AD) wrote that "all the people present express their assent by saying Amen" immediately after the officiant "offers prayers and thanksgivings (εὐχαριστίας, eucharistias)," the "Amen" being spoken, quite notably, before the consecration is uttered.[358] Irenæus of Lyons (189 AD) described the "Amen, which we pronounce in concert,"[359] and had the Eucharist offering occurring prior to the consecration,[360] implying that the "Amen" to conclude the oblation would have been spoken prior to the consecration for the Supper, a liturgy he confirmed later in *Against Heresies*, and again in *Fragment* 37.[361] Tertullian of Carthage (208 AD) considered the Eucharist to be "the sacrificial prayers" that were offered.[362] He wrote of the "Amen" a person speaks with regard to the *"sanctum protuleris,"*[363] or literally, "the holy offering,"[364] and placed the consecration after the distribution of the bread for the Supper, implying an "Amen," and therefore the completion of the Eucharistic sacrifice, before the bread and wine

---

358 First Apology 65, 67, Migne, P.G. vol 6 col 429.
359 *Against Heresies*, 1 14.1. Nowhere in the ancient liturgies is "Amen" spoken at or after the consecration. Because Irenæus has bread becoming the Eucharist when it is tithed (*Against Heresies*, 4 18.5), and then has the Eucharist becoming the body of Christ when it is consecrated (*Against Heresies*, 5 2.3), the "Amen" pronounced "in concert" would have occurred after the offerings, but before the consecration.
360 Irenæus, *Against Heresies*, 1 13.2.
361 The Greek of *Against Heresies* 5 2.3 indicates that the consecration is spoken over food that has already been Eucharisted, and *Fragment* 37 states plainly that "the oblation of the Eucharist" occurs *before* the bread and wine are consecrated for the supper.
362 Tertullian, *On Prayer* 19.
363 Migne, P.L. vol I, col 657.
364 Tertullian, *The Shows* 25. (Because Tertullian has the Eucharistic sacrifice separate from and prior to the Supper (*On Prayer* 19), and has an "Amen" spoken over the holy offering (*the Shows* 25), but has the consecration spoken only after the distribution of the bread into the hands of the recipient (*Against Marcion* 4 40), what he calls "the sacrificial prayers," or "the Eucharist" or "the participation of the sacrifice" (*On Prayer* 19), and what he describes as the "Amen" spoken over it, can neither refer to an offering of consecrated bread and wine, nor to an affirmation of a liturgical sacrifice of Christ's body and blood).

were consecrated. Hippolytus of Rome (215 AD), disciple of Irenæus, referred to the liturgical "Amen" that "we simultaneously utter,"[365] and carefully placed the Eucharist offering prior to the Consecration,[366] which implies an "Amen" between the sacrificial offering and the consecration for the Supper. Cornelius of Rome (251 AD) wrote of an "Amen" spoken by the communicant "as he takes the bread" after the minister "has made the offerings," but before the blessing is pronounced over it.[367] Dionysius of Alexandria (255 AD) described a man "who had heard the giving of thanks (ευχαριστιας) and joined in repeating the Amen" before the Supper took place.[368] In his 11th *Festal Letter*, Athanasius of Alexandria described the liturgical thanksgiving oblations of prayers and praise, by which "a pure sacrifice is offered to God" for the care of the poor, at which point the people "in common send up a song of praise and say, Amen."[369] For three hundred years, that apostolic "Amen" occurred immediately after the Eucharistic tithe offering, *but before the consecration of bread and wine for the Supper*. That ancient liturgy utterly rules out any possibility of a liturgical offering of Christ's body and blood in the early church, for the offering was complete before the bread and wine were consecrated.

The original placement of the apostolic "Amen" between the thanksgiving sacrifice (Offertory) and the consecration (for the Supper) is liturgically significant. It had the dual effect of completing the oblation prior to the consecration while also ensuring that consecrated bread and wine of the Supper were not included in the oblation. But at the end of the fourth century, the liturgy evolved into something the early church would not have recognized. With the content of the tithe offering being reduced to bread and wine, and the consecration moved *liturgically prior to the offering*, the ancient Eucharistic tithe offering morphed into a liturgical sacrifice of the body and blood of Christ. At the same time, the liturgical "Amen" was moved after the consecration, no longer serving as an affirmation of gratitude, becoming instead an affirmation that the consecrated bread and wine

---

365 Hippolytus, *Refutation of all Heresies*, Book VI, 34, 37 (Hippolytus follows Irenæus on this, and we read him accordingly).
366 Hippolytus, *Refutation of All Heresies*, 6, 34.
367 Eusebius, *Church History*, Book VI, chapter 43, 18-19.
368 Eusebius, *Church History*, Book VII, chapter 9, 4, (Migne, P.L. vol V, col 98).
369 Festal Letter 11 11.

was truly Christ's body and blood.[370] Madrid's first mistake was to read Ignatius' first century liturgy through the lens of a late fourth century novelty, of which Ignatius knew nothing.

The Original Consecration

According to Cyprian of Carthage (255 AD), on the day of a new convert's baptism, some of the oil from the Eucharist was used to anoint the newly baptized.[371] According to Hippolytus of Rome, on the day of a convert's baptism, some of the bread, wine, milk, honey and water that had been offered in the Eucharist was given to the newly baptized to taste, as the bishop instructed him about the church and the history of the people of God and the symbolic meaning of each item.[372] All of this was done prior to the consecration for the Supper. Just as some of the oil from the Eucharist was used to anoint the convert, and milk and honey from the Eucharist were used to instruct him, some of the bread and wine from the Eucharist were then consecrated for the Supper. As Irenæus observed, bread becomes the Eucharist when it is set aside for the tithe,[373] and then "the Eucharist becomes the body of Christ" when it is consecrated for the Supper.[374]

---

370 Cyril of Jerusalem [350 AD], *Catechetical Lectures* 23 21; *Apostolic Constitutions* [c. 375 AD] VIII 13; Ambrose of Milan [c. 387], *On the Mysteries* 54; Augustine [c. 405 AD] *Contra Faustum*, XII.10.

371 Cyprian of Carthage, *Epistle 69*, 2.

372 Hippolytus, *Anaphora* 21; Tertullian, *De Corona* 3.

373 Irenæus, *Against Heresies* 4 18.5. For the correct rendering, see *A Library of the Fathers of the Holy Catholic Church, Anterior to the Division of the East and West*, Volume 42, *Five Books of S. Irenaeus Bishop of Lyons Against Heresies*, Rev. John Keble, M.A., translator, James Parker & Col., 1872, 361. In his Greek original, Irenæus had used the term "ecclusin," or "summoned," referring to bread when it is "summoned" (as in Malachi 3:10) by the Lord for the tithe. Irenæus therefore says, "For as the bread, which is produced from the earth, when it receives the summons (ἔκκλησιν, ecclusin) of God, is no longer common bread, but the Eucharist, consisting of two realities, earthly and heavenly...." To Irenæus, the bread thus takes on a heavenly reality when it is set aside for the Lord's purposes as a tithe, and is offered as such: a tithe offering. Because the barbaric Latin manuscripts took root long before the Greek original entered circulation in 1743, the accepted rendering of Irenæus for centuries was that the bread took on earthly and heavenly realities when it received the "*invocationem Dei*," suggesting transubstantiation. Upon discovery, the Greek should have corrected the barbaric Latin, but the reverse occurred: the barbaric Latin was used to correct the original Greek! While Migne acknowledged Irenæus' original ἔκκλησιν, he added a footnote to make the Greek comport with the Latin, saying "ἐπίκλυσιν" (invocation) is the preferred reading (Migne (1857), *PG*, 7: 1028n)!

374 Irenæus, *Against Heresies* 5 2.3.

That consecration was performed by reciting Jesus' words of institution over them—"this is my body, which is broken" (1 Corinthians 11:24) and "this is my blood … which is shed" (Matthew 26:28)—as attested by Justin,[375] Irenæus,[376] Clement,[377] and Tertullian.[378] According to Irenæus, Jesus took the cup and "confessed" it "to be His blood," having done the same with the bread.[379] To put it another way, the consecration was performed by *confessing* not-yet-consecrated bread to be the body of Christ and *confessing* not-yet-consecrated cup to be His blood.[380] To *confess* that the bread was the body of Christ was not an acknowledgement that it had just been consecrated, *but rather was the consecration itself*. To *confess* that the cup was the blood of Christ was not an acknowledgement that it had just been consecrated, *but rather was the consecration itself*. Madrid's second mistake was to misunderstand the "confession" to be an acknowledgment of the consecration. In truth, when Ignatius says the heretics "do not confess that the Eucharist is the flesh of our Savior Jesus Christ," he was simply saying that they do not consecrate the Eucharist, for they were unwilling to pronounce Jesus' words, "this My body, which is broken."

Madrid's Anachronism

We mentioned earlier that Madrid omitted a portion of Ignatius' words, not realizing its significance. Having walked through the ancient liturgy of the church, we now return to Madrid's omission. Madrid did not realize that by "the Eucharist and … prayer," Ignatius had been referring to the love feast and tithe offering for the widow and orphan and the stranger. Nor did he realize that the heretics would have been dismissed before the Eucharist was offered and the love feast celebrated, which is why Ignatius said the heretics "abstain from the Eucharist and from prayer." In his

---

375 *First Apology* 66.
376 *Against Heresies* 4 17.5, 5 2.3.
377 *Paedagogus* 2.2.
378 *Against Marcion* 4 40.
379 Irenæus, *Against Heresies*, 4 17.5.
380 See for example, Irenæus' description of the original consecration: "the cup likewise … He confessed to be His blood" (Against Heresies, 4 17.5).

ignorance, Madrid omitted a single sentence that contextualizes Ignatius' liturgy, unaware of its monumental significance. Here is the full citation of Ignatius, now with Madrid's omission included (in brackets):

> Take note of those who hold heterodox opinions on the grace of Jesus Christ which has come to us, and see how contrary their opinions are to the mind of God. [They have no regard for love; no care for the widow, or the orphan, or the oppressed; of the bond, or of the free; of the hungry, or of the thirsty.] They abstain from the Eucharist and from prayer because they do not confess that the Eucharist is the flesh of our Savior Jesus Christ, flesh which suffered for our sins and which that Father, in his goodness raised up again. (*To the Smyrnæans*, 6-7)

Now reading him in his full context, it is clear that Ignatius' reference to the Eucharist and prayer is a reference to *a love feast and tithe offering* prior to the consecration, whereby the early church provided for the needs of the widow, the orphan, the oppressed, the hungry and the thirsty. The reason the heretics abstained from *the Eucharist and the Eucharistic prayers* is because unbelievers were not allowed to participate in the tithe and prayer and were therefore dismissed before the offering. That is why the tithe offering was called the sacrifice of the dismissal, or in its latinized form, "the sacrifice of the mass." In his ignorance of that ancient liturgy, Madrid's third mistake was to omit the context Ignatius provided, and then backload his medieval superstitions onto Ignatius, obscuring what Ignatius was actually saying.

Ignatius' Apostolic Liturgy

With this information we may reconstruct the apostolic liturgy of Ignatius of Antioch and uncover Madrid's misrepresentation. Under the ancient liturgy, the people gather for the reading and preaching of the Scriptures; the unbelievers, heretics and backslidden are dismissed when it is time for the love-feast and the offering of prayers of thanks and food for the help of the widow, the orphan, and the stranger. After the offertory and agape meal, some of the bread from the Eucharist is distributed to those present and then consecrated by confessing it to be His body—"This is my body, broken." When Ignatius writes that heretics "abstain from the Eucharist and from prayer," he refers to the Gnostic heretics who were dismissed before the Eucharist (the tithe offering and agape meal and prayers) because unbelievers were not allowed to participate in them. When Ignatius writes, "They do not confess that the Eucharist is the flesh of our Savior Jesus Christ ... which suffered," he is simply acknowledging that the heretics do not consecrate their offerings by saying, "This is My body, broken" because they do not believe Jesus had a body, suffered, died and rose from the dead. Ignatius' words were consistent with the subapostolic liturgy and had nothing to do with the "Real Presence" of Christ in the Supper. When understood this way, it is clear that Ignatius' words— "they do not confess that the Eucharist is the flesh of our Savior Jesus Christ"—do not suggest that heretics denied the *consecrated* bread to be the body of Christ but rather that they refused to "confess" the consecratory words, "This is My body" over the unconsecrated bread.[381] As Ignatius well knew, the Gnostic heretics of his day were not allowed to participate in the Christian Eucharist, and would never have "confessed" Jesus' words in their own liturgies.

So far removed is the liturgy of Ignatius from Madrid's novelty of sacrificing the "Real Presence" of Christ that we can only conclude that Ignatius and Madrid are talking about two different liturgies from two different religions. The former is consistent with what Protestants do today, in which the only liturgical offering is that of the tithe with prayers of gratitude, and the latter is a medieval novelty utterly foreign to the Scriptures and the early church.

---

381 Tertullian, by way of illustration, said the consecration, rather than affirming the reality of transubstantiation, instead "affirms the reality of His body" (*Against Marcion* 4 40).

Justin Martyr

Justin did not believe in Transubstantiation

Madrid next appeals to Justin Martyr (c. 150 AD) as proof of an early belief in the "Real Presence," because Justin is alleged to say that the Eucharistic prayer turns the bread and wine into the Eucharist, which in Justin's words, is "the flesh and the flood of that incarnated Jesus."[382] Madrid errs again, which is apparent when Justin's words are examined. In paragraphs 65 to 67 of his *First Apology*, Justin writes that the minister "offers prayers and thanksgivings" over the food just as Jesus did the night before He died, after which the people "express their assent by saying Amen" in accordance with 1 Corinthians 14:16, and then the deacons distribute that food "over which the thanksgiving was pronounced."[383] When Justin says, "this food is called among us the Eucharist,"[384] he still has not mentioned the consecration. And when he does mention the consecration, he says it is spoken over "eucharisted food"[385] that had already been distributed to the communicants, indicating that the food was already the Eucharist offering before it was consecrated. It did not become the Eucharist by being consecrated, and it was not offered after the consecration.

It is important to understand this first to show that the early church knew nothing of the "Real Presence of Christ" in the Eucharist offering, but also to show the great lengths to which the Roman apologist will go to obscure that fact. When we examine Madrid's citation of Justin, we find that it has been carefully crafted in an attempt to move the consecration prior to the offering in order to give the appearance that Rome's novel medieval liturgy is older than it really is. Madrid cites Justin's *First Apology* as follows:

> For not as common bread nor common drink do we receive these; but since Jesus Christ our Savior was made incarnate by the word of God and had both flesh and blood for our salvation, so too, as we have been taught, the food which

---

382 *Justin Martyr, First Apology, 66.*
383 Justin Martyr, *First Apology, 65.*
384 Justin Martyr, *First Apology, 66.*
385 Justin Martyr, *First Apology*, 66, εὐχαριστηθείσαν τροφήν *(Migne, P.G. VI, 428).*

has been made into the Eucharist by the Eucharistic prayer set down by him, and by the change of which our blood and flesh is nurtured, is both the flesh and the flood of that incarnated Jesus.[386]

Before we can understand what Justin did write, we must first acknowledge what he did not write, and we may begin by saying that the word "Eucharist" only occurs once in the original Greek. Madrid's errant translation comes to us from William A. Jurgens' *The Faith of the Early Fathers*,[387] in which an additional "Eucharist" is inserted to fabricate support from Justin. That subtle wordcraft serves two purposes: first, to create the impression that Justin has the bread turned into the Eucharist by the consecration, when in fact Justin states explicitly that it was already the Eucharist before it was consecrated; second, to suggest that the consecration occurred prior to the offering such that the bread is consecrated by the "prayers and thanksgivings" rather than by the recitation of Christ's words of institution after the offering. Jurgens' clever redaction creates the appearance that the liturgical offering of the ancient church was the flesh and blood of Christ, and is provided by Madrid as evidence of an ancient belief in the "Real Presence." However, Justin did not write what Jurgens claimed.

We note as well that Madrid has attempted to press Justin into service to affirm Transubstantiation by his reference to a change that occurs in the bread and wine. However, it is one thing to say the bread and wine are changed by the consecration into the body and blood of Christ, but quite another to say the bread and wine are the body and blood of Christ and "our blood and flesh is nurtured" through a change that takes place in them. The former would imply Transubstantiation, but is not what Justin wrote; the latter is what he wrote, but speaks rather of a change that occurs by digestion, not by consecration. In this case, Justin has used the Greek word "μεταβολήν" (metabolen), from which we derive our modern English word for "metabolism." Justin uses the same term

---

386 Madrid, p. 78 (Emphasis added)
387 Jurgens, William A. *The Faith of the Early Fathers*, Vol I: the Pre-Nicene and Nicene Eras (Collegeville, MN: The Liturgical Press (1970)) §128.

other times in his *First Apology* to indicate a change (μεταβάλλειν) of mind,[388] a change (μετάβολιυν) of seasons,[389] a change (μετέβαλον) of face,[390] and quite notably the change (μεταβολήν) by which the elements will one day be dissolved (i.e., "resolved into fire").[391] All involve a total change by which one thing completely and visibly changes into another. None of these can refer to the Roman Catholic Eucharist, which is alleged to change substantially but not visibly into something else, when it is consecrated. What Justin is describing is not a substantial invisible change that occurs *at the consecration* but rather a total change that occurs when the digestive system *metabolizes* what has been eaten for the Supper.

Thus, Justin has simply asserted that the food of the offering is called "Eucharist" and when consecrated the bread and wine are Jesus' body and blood, and that bread and wine, through the digestive process, nourish our flesh and blood when we partake of it.[392] On this we agree with Justin, for he is consistent with Paul, "For we being many are one bread, and one body: for we are all partakers of that one bread" (1 Corinthians 10:17). "For we are members of his body" (Ephesians 5:31).

Having corrected Jergens' redactions and Madrid's appeal to them, we can more clearly understand the parallel Justin fashioned — "in like manner ... so likewise" — to describe both the form and the benefit of the Eucharistic liturgy. His description thus conveys a much simpler meaning, cleansed of Madrid's medieval novelties:

> In the same way Jesus was made incarnate by the Word of God, taking on flesh and blood for our salvation, so likewise we have been taught that the eucharisted food that is consecrated by the prayer of His word is the flesh and blood of

---

388 Justin Martyr, *First Apology* 12 (Migne P.G. VI 345)
389 Justin Martyr, *First Apology* 13 (Migne P.G. VI 346)
390 Justin Martyr, *First Apology* 16 (Migne P.G. VI 352)
391 Justin Martyr, *First Apology* 20 (Migne P.G. VI 357)
392 Note that Irenæus makes a similar observation: "He has acknowledged the cup (which is a part of the creation) as His own blood, from which He bedews our blood; and the bread (also a part of the creation) He has established as His own body, from which He gives increase to our bodies" (*Against Heresies*, 5.2.1). The *substantial* change that occurs in the consecrated Eucharist is a result of digestion, not of consecration.

Jesus, and by the metabolic process of digestion, our flesh and blood are nourished by His.

This more reasonable rendering[393] preserves Justin's Biblical teaching that the bread is "My body" and the wine is "My blood"— which Protestants, too, believe — but strips out the transubstantiation that Jergens attempted to import into it. Such a rendering removes any suggestion either that the bread and wine are substantially changed by the consecration, or that they are liturgically offered as a sacrifice of Jesus' body and blood. This, as we shall now demonstrate, is consistent with Justin's other observations on the Supper.

Justin did not believe in a liturgical offering of Jesus' body and blood

That Justin did not believe in a liturgical offering of Jesus' body and blood is also proven by his description of what the church actually offers. In his *Dialogue with Trypho*, when describing the sacrifice of the church, Justin absolutely ruled out an offering of the body and blood of Christ by saying that the only thing the church offers is prayers and thanks:

> Now, that prayers and giving of thanks, when offered by worthy men, are the only perfect and well-pleasing sacrifices to God, I also admit.[394]

That is not something Justin would have written if he believed the perfect and well-pleasing sacrifice of the church is Jesus' body and blood.

What is more, when discussing the prophecy of Malachi 1:11 ("and in every place incense shall be offered unto my name, and a pure offering"), Justin acknowledges that the bread and wine Jesus

---

393 See, for example, John Kaye's translation: "so are we taught that this food, ... blessed by prayer and thanksgiving, is turned into the nourishment and substance of our flesh and blood, and is in some sense the flesh and blood of the incarnate Jesus." (Kaye, John The First Apology of Justin Martyr (London: Griffith, Farran, Okeden & Welsh (1889)) 90
394 Justin Martyr, *Dialogue with Trypho* 117 (emphasis added).

gave us to eat with thanksgiving were given "in remembrance of His being made flesh" and "in remembrance of His own blood":

> Now it is evident, that in this prophecy [allusion is made] to the bread which our Christ gave us to eat, in remembrance of His being made flesh for the sake of His believers, for whom also He suffered; and to the cup which He gave us to drink, in remembrance of His own blood, with giving of thanks.[395]

This we do not deny. But if Justin believed in transubstantiation, he would have said the Malachi 1:11 prophecy refers to the flesh Jesus gave us to eat and the cup of His own blood He gave us to drink. But saying the bread was to remind us "of His being made flesh," and the cup to remind us "of His own blood" is a different matter entirely. It is in no way consistent with a belief that bread and cup were "His own" flesh and blood to be offered in the liturgy. Either Jesus gave us "His own" literal blood to drink (as Madrid believes), or He gave us something else "in remembrance of His own blood," as Justin wrote. The two positions are mutually exclusive.

Justin confirms this for us elsewhere when he say says the Malachi prophecy anticipated "all the sacrifices which we offer ... i.e., in the Eucharist of the bread and the cup, and which are presented by Christians in all places throughout the world."[396] Here he identifies the bread and wine as the offering of the church, but as we noted above, at the time of the offering in Justin's liturgy, the bread and wine are not yet consecrated, and as such cannot possibly be construed to be an offering of the "Real Presence" of Christ. Only when the people say "Amen," after the Eucharist offering is complete, are the bread and wine consecrated "by the prayer of His word," at which time, Justin says, the bread and wine are solely to stimulate our senses and bring to mind Jesus' body and blood:

---

395 Justin Martyr, *Dialogue with Trypho*, 70.
396 Justin Martyr, Dialogue with Trypho, 117.

...in the remembrance effected by their solid and liquid food, whereby the suffering of the Son of God which He endured is brought to mind.[397]

If the bread and wine are presented to the Lord as a Eucharistic tithe offering as "the only perfect and well-pleasing sacrifice" before the consecration, and if the people then say "Amen" at the conclusion of that offering, and if the Eucharist is then distributed, and only then is consecrated so that the solid and liquid food might stimulate our senses to remind us of Christ's sacrifice, we are at loss to understand how Justin's liturgy is very different from that of Protestants today. For the same reason, we do not understand how Justin's liturgy can possibly be construed to support Madrid's medieval novelty without his translator's misleading editorial redactions. It is clear that Justin did not believe that the "Real Presence" of Christ was offered in the Eucharist, and it is clear that he did not believe the bread and wine were converted into the "Real Presence" of Christ at the consecration.

The "Real Presence" of Christ in the Cheese

The ancient Eucharist offering of olives, cheese, oil, milk, honey, bread, wine, water, plums and blackberries is, quite obviously, *not* the Lord's Supper. The ancient church would be as baffled at the medieval Romanist's claim of the "Real Presence" of Christ in the Eucharist as the medieval Romanist is that the ancient Eucharist included an offering of oil, cheese and olives. The early church would wonder what on earth Jesus' "Real Presence" was doing in the cheese, while the modern Romanist would wonder why cheese was even being offered. Such is the galactic dissonance between what the early church practiced and what Roman Catholicism claims, and such is the gap between ancient church history and Madrid's wishful reconstruction of it. The ancient Eucharist is easily understood if one sets aside the Roman novelties, and grasps what the Eucharist actually meant to the early church: a thank offering, a tithe of the first-fruits of the harvest set aside as a love

---

397 Ibid.

feast and an offering for the poor, in which only the initiated were allowed to participate.

So far removed from the apostles is Madrid's "Real Presence" that it did not even occur to anyone to kneel before the consecrated bread until late in the eleventh century. Kneeling on Sunday was prohibited by the twentieth canon of Nicæa (325 AD), a prohibition that was maintained all the way through first canon of the Fourth Council of Constantinople (870 AD). Even the *Catholic Encyclopedia* acknowledges that elevation of the consecrated bread for adoration during the Supper "is not known to have existed earlier than the close of the twelfth century,"[398] and "kneeling during the Consecration was introduced ... in the same period."[399] How could Madrid's ostensibly apostolic religion fail for over a thousand years to realize that it was supposed to be kneeling before Christ's "Real Presence" on Sunday mornings? We can only conclude that there are two different liturgies from two different religions— one authentic liturgy originating from the apostles in which the church gratefully offers the tithe of the harvest to the Lord and then consecrates some of it for a meal but does not worship it, and an abominable mutation in which ignorant men attempt to change the food into Jesus' body and blood, sacrifice it and worship it. In any case, Madrid's "three representative quotes" on the "Real Presence" in the ancient church fail to prove that the early church believed what Madrid claims.

Purgatory

Madrid next attempts to prove that the early church believed in Purgatory.[400] According to the *Catechism of the Catholic Church,*

> All who die in God's grace and friendship, but still imperfect-
> ly purified, are indeed assured of their eternal salvation; but
> after death they undergo purification, so as to achieve the

---

398　*Catholic Encyclopedia*, The Elevation.
399　*Catholic Encyclopedia*, Genuflexion.
400　Madrid, pp. 78-80.

holiness necessary to enter the joy of heaven. The Church
gives the name Purgatory to this final purification…[401]

Although the doctrine of Purgatory was most fully formu-
lated "at the Councils of Florence [1431-1449 AD] and Trent
[1545-1563 AD],"[402] Madrid provides three citations from the early
church—Tertullian of Carthage, Cyprian of Carthage and Cyril of
Jerusalem—without elaboration or commentary. Madrid assumes,
we suppose, that these citations from the early church stand on
their own and therefore require no elucidation. Because Madrid
does not, we shall provide a brief compendium of ancient support
for Purgatory and then show that the early church could not have
received Purgatory as an apostolic tradition.

2 Maccabees 12:36-45

"Old Testament" support for the doctrine of Purgatory is ostensibly found in the Roman Catholic apocryphal book of 2 Maccabees.
During the Maccabean revolt against the Greeks, Judas Maccabeus
came across some of his fellow countrymen who had fallen in
battle. When their bodies were recovered they were found to
possess pagan amulets under their garments, from which those
present observed that their grave sin must have been "the reason
these men had fallen" (2 Maccabees 12:40). Judas then took up
a collection "for a sin-offering" (2 Maccabees 12:43). The author
of 2 Maccabees concludes in view of the resurrection that it was
laudable to "pray for the dead" and to make "atonement" for "their
sin" (2 Maccabees 12:44-45). From what little can be gathered from
the story, it is clear that those who had sinned had clearly "sinned
unto death," and that the author believed it was a good thing to
pray for the dead. However, the Apostle John corrects that error,
saying, "There is a sin unto death: I do not say that he shall pray
for it" (1 John 5:16). Thus, we can say the author of 2 Maccabees
inserted his errant opinion into the text and the apostle John's
authoritative opinion on the matter is to be received instead. If

---

401 CCC, 1030, 1031.
402 CCC, 1031.

2 Maccabees is presumed to provide evidence the existence of purgatory, that presumption is clearly erroneous.

The Acts of Paul and Thecla (160 AD)

Recorded in the *Acts of Paul and Thecla* is the story of a woman whose daughter appeared to her in a dream requesting prayers, "that I may be transferred to the place of the righteous."[403] A woman's dream about her recently departed daughter a century after the apostolic era hardly suffices as evidence of an apostolic tradition, but is instead a violation of God's commandment against necromancy (Deuteronomy 18:11).

Epitaph of Abercius (190 AD)

Apparently Abercius, "a citizen of a prominent city," arranged for his burial plot while he was still alive, and erected a monument as a marker, inscribing upon it a humble request: "May everyone who is in accord with this and who understands it pray for Abercius." This is taken by Roman Catholics to suggest that belief in prayer for the dead, and therefore Purgatory, originated early in the life of the church. There are several problems with such a conclusion. First, we do not derive the tenets of our faith from epitaphs inscribed on real estate markers. Second, the inscription includes highly metaphorical language about a man's life and journeys and cannot serve as unambiguous evidence of *any* apostolic teaching. Finally, Abercius clearly erected the monument "while living" so that *later* he would have a marked place for his burial: "that in due season I might have here a resting-place for my body." Thus, by his own testimony, he clearly understood that the marker would be seen and read *while he was still alive*. Therefore, his request to "pray for Abercius" cannot be interpreted to mean that he wanted people to pray for him *in death*. The entire epitaph is 22 lines long, only the last three of which can be taken unambiguously as postmortem instructions to those who may consider violating his tomb:

---

403 *Acts of Paul and Thecla.*

17. These words, I, Abercius, standing by, ordered to be inscribed.

18. In truth, I was in the course of my seventy-second year.

19. Let him who understands and believes this pray for Abercius.

20. *But no man shall place another tomb upon mine.*

21. *If one do so, he shall pay to the treasury of the Romans two thousand pieces of gold,*

22. *And to my beloved fatherland Hieropolis, one thousand pieces of gold.*[404]

Clearly, Abercius wanted to reserve a burial plot and, *while still living,* wanted people to know of his journeys. A subjective reading with a view toward justifying controversial doctrines looks upon this as evidence for a belief in prayer for the dead. An objective reading, however, sees *a living man* reserving a burial plot, *while living,* and asking people in the meantime to pray for him, *while living,* when they see the marker, which they certainly would before he died. There is no proof for Purgatory here.

Clement of Alexandria (c. 200 AD)

Clement is believed to have taught a form of purgation in Book 6 of his *Stromata.* It is sufficient to point out here, however, that the alleged evidence from Clement is actually his opinion on degrees of glory after entering heaven, rather than levels of purgation beforehand. What is more, Clement acknowledges that he is engaging in theological speculation, guessing at what heaven might be like. He even confesses his guesswork as he introduces the topic, stating his "opinion" that the degrees of glory in heaven might be like the order of church offices.

Since, according to my opinion, the grades here in the Church, of bishops, presbyters, deacons, are imitations of the angelic glory, ... these taken up in the clouds [1

---

404 Epitaph of Abercius (Quasten *Patrology*, v. 1, p. 172).

> Thessalonians 4:17] … will first minister [as deacons], then
> be classed in the presbyterate, by promotion in glory. [405]

Upon that assumption, Clement expounds in the next chapter
that "there are various abodes, according to the worth of those
who have believed," and through knowledge, "the perfect inheritance belongs to those who attain to 'a perfect man,' according
to the image of the Lord."[406] All of this knowledge is ostensibly to
be gained *in heaven*, for Clement's entire narrative is about what
happens after entering heaven as those in glory continue being
promoted through the ranks. This is not Purgatory "in seed form,"
as Madrid might have supposed, but an entirely foreign construct
that Clement himself acknowledges to be "my opinion." Such
speculative guesswork can hardly supply evidence of an apostolic
tradition.

The Martyrdom of Perpetua and Felicity (202 AD)

In this account a woman received a dream of her seven-year-old
brother who had "died miserably with disease," and was apparently
still suffering terribly in the afterlife. Inspired by the vision, she
believed her prayer "would bring help to his suffering," and later
she received another dream by which she "understood that he was
translated from the place of punishment," and therefore that her
prayer had been answered.[407] A silly dream of a bereaved sister
hardly rises to the level of apostolic revelation and is another mani-
festation of the sin of necromancy.

Origen of Alexandria

We need not spend much time with Origen, as his meanderings are
inspired by those who are to be caught up "to meet the Lord in the
air" (1 Thessalonians 4:17), and his opinion is similar to that of his
fellow Alexandrian, Clement. Origen speculates about "some place
of instruction, and, so to speak, [a] class-room or school of souls,
in which they are to be instructed," and where they "will in order

---

405 Clement, *Stromata* 6.13.
406 Clement, *Stromata* 6.14.
407 *The Martyrdom of Perpetua and Felicity* 2:3–4.

pass through all gradations." Notably Origen believed these various "gradations" were the "many mansions" to which Jesus referred in John 14:2, each gradation being based on the aggregation of "knowledge," he says, "if indeed the result should follow according to our expectations."[408] Such is the guesswork in which Origen engaged as well, and those gradations are based on knowledge acquired *in heaven*. Since Origen and Clement have the same opinion, and both were of the Alexandrian school, we see this as an Alexandrian phenomenon, and not an apostolic teaching to which two ancient writers separately attest. They themselves acknowledge that what they have written is just what they think might be the case, but do not know with certainty.

Madrid's Citations on Purgatory

Having walked through some of the more ancient sources, we now turn to the authors Madrid provides without commentary, on the apparent assumption that they speak for themselves.

Tertullian of Carthage

In his treatise *On the Soul* (210 AD), Tertullian interprets Matthew 5:25-26 to refer to a kind of spiritual prison "out of which there will be no dismissal until the smallest even of your delinquencies be paid off in the period before the resurrection."[409] This passage from Tertullian is not cited by Madrid, but Madrid's reliance upon it will become apparent in a moment. For now, it is important to understand first that Purgatory, according to the *Catechism*, "is entirely different from the punishment of the damned,"[410] while the Sermon on the Mount is very much about the punishment of the damned. In Matthew chapters 5 to 7, Jesus contrasts sons of heaven and sons of hell, and ultimately the difference between the narrow way that "leadeth unto life" and the broad way that "leadeth to destruction" (Matthew 7:13-14). He repeatedly warns his audience of the dangers of judgment and hell fire (Matthew 5:22, 29, 30). The punishment of the damned is in view. Would Tertullian have

---

408 Origen, *De Principiis* Book II, Chapter 11 On Counter Promises, paragraph 6.
409 Tertullian, *On the Soul* 35.
410 CCC, 1031.

us believe that in the midst of His sermon on the narrow path to heaven and the broad path to hell, Jesus paused momentarily to mention the discomfort of Purgatory that makes the path to heaven equally broad? Are we to believe He taught being angry "without a cause" and calling someone "fool" places one "in danger of hell fire" (v. 22), and looking on a woman lustfully places one in danger of hell (29, 30), and that swearing by heaven, by earth or by one's own head "cometh of evil" (37) but failing to agree with one's adversary only puts one at risk of the indefinite and temporary flames of Purgatory? Was that Jesus' nuanced message in Matthew 5:25-26? We jest, of course. It is a silly argument, but one that Madrid apparently finds appealing.

To support his belief, Madrid quotes from *On Monogamy* (212 AD), in which Tertullian alleges that unless a woman prays for the soul of her dead husband, "and requests refreshment for him meanwhile, and fellowship (with him) in the first resurrection," then she is guilty of divorce.[411] That is a ridiculous teaching that contradicts Paul's statements that "if the husband be dead, she is loosed from the law of her husband … but if her husband be dead, she is free from that law." (Romans 7:2-3).

Neither of these citations from Tertullian can possibly substantiate an apostolic tradition, but it is also noteworthy that they both came during Tertullian's Montanist period. Tertullian's writings after 206 AD began to reflect his Montanist heresy, so these writings from 210 and 212 AD are clearly suspect, but in addition, they also twist, disregard and contradict the Scriptures.

Cyprian of Carthage (253 AD)

Madrid's next citation is from Cyprian of Carthage, a man, by his biographer's confession, who advanced too soon to the bishopric in violation of Paul's proscription (1 Timothy 3:6).[412] Cyprian's speculation on its face appears to be derived from Tertullian's treatise On the Soul, mimicking Tertullian's interpretation of Matthew 5:25-26 to justify his view. In this citation, Cyprian contrasts the faithful

---

411 Tertullian, *On Monagamy* 10.
412 Pontius the Deacon, *Life and Passion of St. Cyprian* 3.

martyrs who have already attained to glory and the recently repentant lapsed who, for a moment unfaithful, will nevertheless join the martyrs in glory one day. In his contrast, Cyprian assumes a kind of Purgatorial suspension for the repentant lapsed between their death and Judgment Day:

> It is one thing to stand for pardon, another thing to attain to glory; it is one thing, when cast into prison, not to go out thence until one has paid the uttermost farthing; another thing at once to receive the wages of faith and courage. It is one thing, tortured by long suffering for sins, to be cleansed and long purged by fire; another to have purged all sins by suffering. It is one thing, in fine, to be in suspense till the sentence of God at the Day of judgment; another to be at once crowned by the Lord. (*Letters* 51)

At first glance, Cyprian appears to have discovered in Matthew the same evidence for Purgatory that Tertullian did. But upon closer inspection, it is clear that Cyprian had only found Tertullian's Montanist error. As the *Catholic Encyclopedia* concedes, Cyprian likely only had access to the Scriptures and to the writings of Tertullian:

> We have always to remember that his experience as a Christian was of short duration, that he became a bishop soon after he was converted, and that he had no Christian writings besides Holy Scripture to study besides those of Tertullian.[413]

Lacking theological training, violating the Pauline proscription against novices advancing to the bishopric, and relying on the writings of a Montanist heretic, we are not surprised Cyprian arrived at the same error Tertullian did. Not only do we lump Cyprian and Tertullian together as a single unreliable source here, we also observe that the arguments these Carthaginians make for Purgatory are a far, far cry from the high standard of apostolicity.

---

413 *Catholic Encyclopedia*, "Cyprian of Carthage."

Cyril of Jerusalem (350 AD)

Madrid cites Cyril's 23rd *Catechetical Lecture* in which an argument is made for offering sacrifices for the dead. Cyril notes that during the liturgy, "we make mention of those who have already fallen asleep," because "it will be of very great benefit to the souls of those for whom the petition is carried up, while this holy and most solemn sacrifice is laid out."[414] We offer two notable observations: First, in the early centuries, it was not uncommon to offer sacrifices to commemorate the dead, but they were commemorative sacrifices to celebrate lives well-lived, not propitiatory sacrifices to benefit the departed. By way of illustration, the disciples of Polycarp "celebrate[d] the anniversary of his martyrdom," which celebrations were regularly performed "both in memory of those who have already finished their course," but also to inspire and prepare "those yet to walk in their steps."[415] The *Catholic Encyclopedia* acknowledges that "commemoration services of the martyrs" were held "on the anniversaries of their death."[416] In those early years of the church, the day of the martyr's death was affectionately referred to as his *birthday*, and thus "the *anniversary* of his martyrdom" is more accurately translated "the *birthday* of his martyrdom." The purpose was not to commemorate his death but rather to commemorate his translation to glory, or his "birth" into eternity.[417] Cyprian, too, acknowledges the practice, reporting that "[w]e always offer sacrifices ... as often as we celebrate the passions and days of the martyrs in the annual commemoration."[418] It was not uncommon to celebrate the lives of the martyrs by offering sacrifices during the liturgy, but those sacrifices were of the same order as the Eucharistic offerings—commemorative and celebratory rather than propitiatory—not unlike the modern practice of donating poinsettias in memory of a loved one.

By the end of the fourth century, however, the consecration for the Supper was moved before the Eucharistic tithe offering,

---

414 *Catechetical Lectures 23:5-9.*
415 *Martyrdom of Polycarp 18.*
416 *Catholic Encyclopedia*, "Martyr."
417 So it is rendered in the original Greek, "μαρτυρίου αὐτοῦ ἡμέραν γενέθλιον," and then rendered into Latin, accordingly, "*natalem martyrii ejus diem*" (*P.G.*, vol. 5, cols. 1043, 1044).
418 Cyprian of Carthage, Epistle 33, paragraph 3.

and thus the Eucharist sacrifice became a propitiatory offering of the body and blood of Christ. Cyril's lecture is from that period, and he, too, began to understand the Eucharist offering to be "that sacrifice of propitiation."[419] It was in that period of transition that the departed, instead of being merely named and commemorated in the offerings, were also alleged to benefit from them, and thus the common teaching emerged that the Eucharistic propitiatory sacrifice was offered for the dead. It was a novelty that did not originate with the apostles, which leads us to our second point.

Even in Cyril's day there was widespread resistance to the practice of offering sacrifices for the benefit of the dead. In the very same *Catechetical Lecture*, Cyril observes, "I know that many say, what is a soul profited, which departs from this world either with sins, or without sins, if it be commemorated in the prayer?"[420] Jerome, too, found himself having to defend against similar criticism, hitting the peak of his vitriolic stride when attempting to defend against Vigilantius' critique of the novel practice of offering prayers and sacrifices for the dead.[421] Sacrificing for the benefit of the dead was a novelty and was immediately met with resistance.

On that note, let us now take inventory of the ancient evidence for Purgatory we have provided here: an apocryphal account (2 Maccabees 12) that contradicts the Scriptures and contradicts even Roman Catholicism's own definition of Purgatory, a woman's conversation with her dead daughter in a dream (*Acts of Paul and Thecla*), some guy's burial plot marker for his later use (*Epitaph of Abercius*), Clement's and Origen's speculation on the degrees of glory *in heaven*, a girl's dreams and conversation with her dead brother (*The Martyrdom of Perpetua and Felicity*), heretical Montanist writings from Tertullian and writings from Cyprian that are obviously derived from them, and Cyril's and Jerome's frustration at the firm and widespread resistance they encountered when trying to foist prayers and sacrifices for the dead upon the church. Not exactly a ringing apostolic endorsement of the doctrine.

---

419 Cyril of Jerusalem, *Catechetical Lecture* 23.8.
420 Cyril of Jerusalem, *Catechetical Lecture* 23.10.
421 Jerome, *Against Vigilantius*, 7-8.

Madrid Fails His *"Simple Test"*

As we reviewed the three topics upon which Madrid's "Simple Test" was based—Roman Primacy, the "Real Presence" of Christ in the Eucharist and Purgatory—we found that his hypothesis did not hold water. He invited us "to verify … the Catholic Church's claim" to antiquity, offering a sampling of quotes, and thumped his chest triumphantly, concluding,

> these kinds of powerful authoritative statements of early Christian belief in doctrines such as the authority of the Bishop of Rome and the Real Presence of Christ in the Eucharist could be multiplied practically endlessly with regard to the other Catholic teachings mentioned above.[422]

That such halting attempts to find Roman Catholicism where it did not exist could be multiplied endlessly we certainly agree, but that they are "authoritative" or "powerful" proof of its Apostolic origins, we emphatically deny. What we find instead is a desperate apologist attempting to paper over the soft white underbelly of Rome, hoping we will not notice that he cannot close that three-hundred-year gap between his novel anti-Christian religion and the faith once delivered by the apostles. Instead of finding ancient evidence for the authority of Rome, we found instead an ancient distrust of her bishop and disparagement of the Roman church because it frequently thought above its station and was constantly in need of supervision from without. Instead of finding ancient evidence of the "Real Presence" of Christ in the Eucharist we found instead that the ancient Eucharistic "Sacrifice of the Mass" was a tithe offering after the dismissal of the unbeliever but before the consecration for the Lord's Supper, and therefore the sacrifice of the "Real Presence" had not even entered the mind of the early church. In fact what we found was that even after the consecration of the bread and wine for the Supper, the early church still held that the bread and wine served as sensible reminders of His body and blood, but were not literally so. Rather than finding ancient apostolic

---

422 Madrid, p. 80.

evidence for Purgatory we found rather that Rome's unbiblical doctrine is founded not upon the apostles but upon necromancy, speculation, heresy and the dreams of silly women, and repeatedly met with resistance from a scripturally literate populace. Indeed, Madrid has dramatically failed his own "simple test."

A Biblical Snapshot

To conclude his lengthy chapter on the True Church, Madrid plants his flag on Matthew 28:18-20 to make his closing arguments. Jesus instructed the apostles, and based on that instruction Madrid notes that the church Jesus founded must have the authority to go forth in Christ's name, to make disciples, administer the sacraments, teach in Christ's name, and have the attribute of perpetuity:

> And Jesus came and spake unto them, saying, All power is given unto me in heaven and in earth. Go ye therefore, and teach all nations, baptizing them in the name of the Father, and of the Son, and of the Holy Ghost: Teaching them to observe all things whatsoever I have commanded you: and, lo, I am with you alway, even unto the end of the world. Amen.

In Madrid's eyes, the only logical interpretation of the passage is that the Roman Catholic religion is the church Jesus founded. We shall interact with him briefly on each point to conclude the chapter.

The Authority to Go Forth in Christ's Name

Madrid suffers here from his intractable assumption that the Roman Catholic religion originated with the apostles, and then expects his reader to embrace the conclusions he invalidly draws from that false assumption. He writes, "Christ sent this Church (represented here by the eleven remaining apostles, the first bishops) into the world on a mission."[423] Those "first bishops," in Madrid's mind, constitute the "Roman Catholic Church," an

---

423 Madrid, p. 81.

assumption we absolutely deny and which Madrid in this chapter
has utterly failed to prove. What Madrid is attempting here is to
make the Eleven into Roman Catholic bishops, and thereby to
elicit from his reader the invalid inference that Jesus conferred His
teaching authority on Roman Catholicism, and then finally that
it is our bounden duty to hear and believe the religion of Rome,
lest we be guilty of rejecting Jesus. It is consistent with Madrid's
chapter on Catholicism in which he essentially substitutes the
Roman religion in the place of Christ. In a remarkable error, Madrid
says Jesus conferred his authority upon the Eleven by saying to
them in Luke 10:16, "He who hears you hears Me, and he who
rejects you rejects Me." But Jesus did not say that to the *Eleven*. He
said that to the *Seventy,* who marveled at the authority with which
they, too, had been endowed. Jesus "in that hour" turned to His
Father to praise Him for conferring such knowledge, wisdom and
authority on men *who were not apostles* (John 17:21). If Madrid does
not even understand that the Seventy, too, were endowed with
authority to go forth in Jesus' name, and not only the Eleven, why
are we to believe him when he says the Eleven represent Roman
Catholicism, a religion that we must accept lest we reject Jesus?

Protestants deny neither that the apostles were apostles (they
were) nor that Jesus sent them forth authoritatively (He did). But
Roman Catholicism is an apostate religion that originated *as a
departure from apostolic truth*, and we are under no moral obligation to follow her into her damnable errors and apostasy. Madrid,
for his part, remains unable to prove that his religion originated
any earlier than late in the fourth century, but has very success-
fully demonstrated repeatedly that the only evidence he can bring
forward for her apostolic origins is his own assumption that she
is of apostolic origin. We require proof for such claims, and he has
been manifestly unable to produce it.

A Mandate to Make Disciples of All Nations
On this point, Madrid again brings his invalid assumptions to
the text. We all agree with Jesus' command to make disciples of
all nations. From this, Madrid concludes that Jesus "doesn't want

anyone to settle for anything less than the one, true Church He had established."[424] We agree. However, neither the Scriptures nor the historical record identify Roman Catholicism as that "one, true Church."

Sacramentality

Based on Mark 16:15-16, Acts 2:37-39, 8:36 and 22:14-16, which are about baptism, Madrid concludes that the "Church's mission would have a distinct sacramental dimension."[425] We observe that these verses cannot possibly substantiate Rome's system of sacraments by which grace is ostensibly distributed. In the Scriptures we find evidence of two ordinances—baptism and the Lord's Supper—which we have addressed elsewhere in this book. We do not deny that baptism accompanies the preaching of the gospel, or that Jesus commanded His disciples to commemorate His death in the Supper. What we deny is the sacraments as the instrument of justification and means of salvation.

The Authority to Teach in Christ's Name

Madrid invokes Matthew 16:18-19 and Matthew 18:18, which we have already addressed elsewhere. As above, Madrid here again invokes Luke 10:16, "He who listens to you listens to me."[426] As we noted above, Madrid thinks Jesus said this to the Eleven, and concludes that we are to listen to Roman bishops. The Scripture does not mean what Madrid supposes, since Jesus said this not to the Eleven but to the Seventy, and we can say with confidence that the early church did not believe it the way Madrid does. We have already shown in this chapter how frequently the early church rejected, corrected and even ridiculed bishops of Rome without thinking they had rejected Christ.

Perpetuity

Madrid concludes this section by saying that Rome's "unique ability to demonstrate continual existence from the time of Christ

---

424 Madrid, p. 82.
425 Madric, p. 83.
426 Madrid, p. 84.

to the present day" proves that Roman Catholicism is the church Jesus founded.[427] As we have demonstrated repeatedly, however, Roman Catholicism is manifestly unable to prove that it originated any earlier than the late fourth century. Since Jesus' promise, "lo, I am with you always" was made *to the church He actually founded*, not to the medieval monstrosity that emerged centuries later, we do not accept Madrid's premise that Jesus promised that He would be with Roman Catholicism to the end of the age. Nay, the fact that Rome has stumbled into apostasy, error and heresy indicates rather that Jesus is most certainly not with Roman Catholicism, and that Roman Catholicism is not His church.

Madrid perpetually interprets the evidence through the lens of his original assumption—that Roman Catholicism is the True Church—and then supposes that the evidence has proven his assumption true. He writes, "All this evidence when taken together shows that Jesus Christ established a particular Church, not some loose confederation of like-minded believers."[428] And yet from the Scriptures and the historical record, a "loose confederation of like-minded believers" is precisely what we find. We know very well that Paul and Barnabas could not agree in their ministry to recent converts and "the contention was so sharp between them, that they departed asunder" but continued "strengthening the churches" separately (Acts 15:38-41). We also know that the church in Smyrna had a bishop ordained by the apostle John, and Rome had a bishop ordained by Peter,[429] but the church at Corinth, established by Paul, had a plurality of elders, or presbyters, elected by a simple majority of the congregation.[430] We also know that Polycarp of Smyrna and Anicetus of Rome in the mid-second century celebrated the Lord's Supper so differently that neither could persuade the other to change his ways.[431] Indeed, our forebears were loosely confederated with each other, but were like-minded — one church, founded and shepherded by Christ.

---

427 Madrid, pp. 84-85.
428 Madrid, p. 85.
429 Tertullian, *Prescription Against Heretics*, chapter 32 (215 A.D.).
430 Clement, *To the Corinthians*, paragraph 54 (90 AD).
431 Eusebius, *Church History*, Book V, chapter 24, paragraph 16.

Madrid's fundamental error is to think that it would be impossible to have one, true church unless it was centrally administered by a man in Rome. Assuming that all the evidence must lead him to that conclusion, Madrid unsurprisingly arrives at that very conclusion from the evidence. But when viewed objectively, the evidence rather works against him. There was no "Catholic" church in the way Madrid imagines it, for the churches in fact disagreed on tradition (the Lord's Supper and Easter), ministry (Paul and Barnabas), ecclesiology (presbyterian or episcopal government) and yes, even on what constituted the Scriptures, for a definitive canon of the Old and New Testaments was still centuries away when the term "Catholic Church" was first used. Christians know well enough that Christ's church is administered by the Chief Shepherd in heaven (1 Peter 2:25), and it is "Catholic" only in the sense that *all Christians belong to it.* Christians of various denominations today may disagree with one another and may establish different local customs, but that does not mean they are any less "Catholic" than the early church which experienced similar differences even while apostles were still among them.

To conclude this section, and to rebut Madrid, we cite Irenæus' rebuke of "Pope Victor" in which Irenæus reminds him that the Lord had indeed established a "loose confederation of like-minded believers," not a global, Roman-administered, papally administered carnal episcopate. When Victor attempted to establish monolithic, centrally managed, universal conformity among the congregations regarding the date and day to celebrate the Resurrection, Irenæus had to remind him that since the days of the apostles *the church had been loosely confederated and heavenly shepherded,* and it was not Victor's place to change that:

> For the controversy is not only concerning the day, but also concerning the very manner of the fast. For some think that they should fast one day, others two, yet others more; some, moreover, count their day as consisting of forty hours day and night. And this variety in its observance has not originated in our time; but long before in that of

our ancestors. It is likely that they did not hold to strict accuracy, and thus formed a custom for their posterity according to their own simplicity and peculiar mode. Yet all of these lived none the less in peace, and we also live in peace with one another; and the disagreement in regard to the fast confirms the agreement in the faith. ... And yet though not observing it, they were none the less at peace with those who came to them from the parishes in which it was observed; although this observance was more opposed to those who did not observe it. ... And they parted from each other in peace, both those who observed, and those who did not, maintaining the peace of the whole church.[432]

---

432 Eusebius, *Church History*, V.24.12-17.

Salvation?

When asked the question, "If you died tonight, would you go to heaven?" Madrid answers, "If I die in a state of grace when I die, I will go to heaven, guaranteed."[433]

But what does it mean to die in a state of grace? Madrid understands that living in a state of grace "means obeying Christ's commands, avoiding sin, and clinging to Christ's grace for our salvation."[434] The idea of being in a "state of grace" is synonymous with being saved in the Roman Catholic scheme of things. To be in a "state of grace" is to be saved. To fall from a "state of grace" is to lose salvation. Madrid does not elaborate on the extent of each criterion to keep one in a "state of grace," stating only that one must die in this so-called "state of grace" to reach heaven. The opposite of dying in a state of grace is to die in a state of mortal sin, in which case such a person would go to hell.

Before analyzing the proof texts for such a foundation of salvation we must reiterate that the Roman Catholic religion is fond of inventing terms to describe Her doctrine. She then searches the Bible for validation of Her terms. We have seen this in the

---

433 Madrid, p. 85.
434 Ibid., p. 91.

concepts of Roman Catholic Purgatory, Indulgences, Treasury of Merit, Assumption of Mary, and Papal infallibility, to name a few. In this section we notice that the Bible does not contain the terms "state of grace" or "mortal sin." These are Roman Catholic ideas, not biblical doctrine.

So what is Rome's conception when it comes to the formulation of her understanding of salvation? Rome believes that salvation is by God's grace, given freely through man's faith (faith is a gift of God but is useless unless employed by man) whereby we are transformed from a state of sin to a "state of grace." Once dead in sin, a man is now alive in Christ through grace. However, "one who is alive in Christ can throw away that gift and kill his soul through mortal sin."[435]

Rome is clear that once anyone uses God-given faith to receive the gift of grace he is then in a "state of grace." But then he is responsible to keep himself in this "state of grace" and hope to die in it to be saved. If he does not keep himself in this "state of grace" and throws it away, he will lose his salvation. Listen to Madrid citing a portion of Romans 11:

> This means that those who receive the gift of salvation by grace through faith (the Roman Christians to whom St. Paul was writing being a good example of this), are "in the state of grace." *But, of course, they can choose to forfeit that gift of grace and lose their salvation.*[436]

There is much confusion in reading Madrid's defense of Roman Catholic salvation. In fact, it is more a defense of losing one's salvation than an explanation of how one is saved.[437] But one theme remains consistent throughout Madrid's defense. He is convinced that one must keep oneself in a "state of grace" to gain heaven. This is done through the Roman Catholic sacraments. But how does one get to

---

435 Ibid., p. 86.
436 Ibid., p. 87. Emphasis mine.
437 As we shall see the words "saved" and "salvation" are radically different concepts between the Roman Catholic religion and Christianity. In Rome baptism is necessary for salvation as well as faithful attendance to the other Roman Catholic sacraments. In Rome salvation is dependent upon sacraments. In Christianity salvation is dependent upon faith alone in the finished work of Christ alone, quite apart from sacraments.

Madrid's "state of grace"? According to Madrid, "The Lord doesn't desire that we remain passive and inert in this process of our justification, sanctification, and eventual salvation."[438]

> Our faith in Christ is a gift, but yet it is we who must exercise that faith in order for it to be efficacious.[439]

After saying that our faith (if used) brings us to a "state of grace," Madrid says:

> We are the ones who have been enabled by His grace to have faith in Him—it is something we do. And it is, in a very real sense, a "work."

How does one comprehend that grace and faith are gifts of God and yet totally dependent upon man's faithful use to be effective? In Rome grace and faith are gifts from God but only some will use them to gain "a state of grace." Faith does nothing unless activated by man. Grace is impotent unless actuated by man. Faith is something we do, and it is in a very real sense a "work." Truly, in Rome salvation is of man! If man fails to perform, he is doomed to Hell. It seems that salvation in Rome is principally accomplished by man. Faith is made effectual by man and is a work of man. But this is not all. There is much left to do in Rome to gain this "state of grace." This is borne out as we look at what Madrid leaves out of what it takes to gain salvation in Roman Catholicism.

Madrid leaves out quite a bit of information regarding Roman Catholic salvation. For instance, the role of baptism in Roman Catholic salvation is critical but left out entirely by Madrid in his chapter on salvation. Listen to the New Catholic Catechism (NCC):

> The Lord himself affirms that Baptism is necessary for salvation.[440]

---

438 Madrid, p. 94.
439 Ibid.
440 New Catholic Catechism, paragraph 1257.

> By Baptism all sins are forgiven, original sin, and all personal sins, as well as all punishment for sin.[441]

> Baptism not only purifies from all sins, but also makes the neophyte [newcomer] "a new creation," an adopted son of God, who has become a "partaker of the divine nature," a member of Christ and co-heir with him, and a temple of the Holy Spirit.[442]

Madrid leaves out the necessity of Roman Catholic sacraments. One would think that something so necessary for salvation would be mentioned in a chapter on salvation. However, Madrid has a different agenda. He is most interested, as we shall see, in promoting the Roman Catholic dogma that one can throw away his "state of grace" (salvation) and retrieve it only through Rome's sacraments.

However, we think it necessary to include a couple of NCC statements to the discussion on how one gets into a "state of grace" in the first instance. Let us listen to the *Catholic Catechism* once again.

> The Church affirms that for believers *the sacraments of the New Covenant are necessary for salvation.* "Sacramental grace" is the grace of the Holy Spirit, given by Christ and proper to each sacrament.[443]

> The sacraments are efficacious signs of grace, instituted by Christ and entrusted to the Church, *by which divine life is dispensed to us.*[444]

Although left out by Madrid, these components of Rome's salvation fill in the blanks of what it means to "die in a state of grace." Perhaps it is difficult even for a defender of Rome to reconcile how

---

441 Ibid., paragraph 1263.
442 Ibid., paragraph 1265.
443 Ibid., paragraph 1129.
444 Ibid., paragraph 1131. Italics mine.

someone who through baptism is "a new creation," an "adopted son of God," a "partaker of the divine nature," "member of Christ," "co-heir with Him," and "a temple of the Holy Spirit" could possibly throw it all away by failing to continue in the sacraments of Rome.

It's all up to you!

Rome asserts salvation (state of grace) is a "free gift" while at the same time making salvation conditioned upon faithfulness to the Roman Catholic system of grace dispensing and the best efforts of man. Ultimately, salvation is not really a "free" gift in Rome. Salvation is free to the one who navigates the Roman Catholic sacramental scheme. The system is free for the choosing but salvation (state of grace) is dependent upon a method, technique, and structured arrangement of obligations. God's grace introduces you to the procedure. You can take it or leave it at any point. It is all up to you. Jesus Christ made salvation possible. But that is it. Jesus saves those who save themselves by availing themselves of the free system arranged by the grace of God.

The Use of the Bible

Ironically, Madrid appeals to a passage in the Bible normally used to refute Rome's scheme of salvation:

> But God, being rich in mercy, because of His great love with which He loved us, even when we were dead in our transgressions, made us alive together with Christ (by grace you have been saved), and raised us up with Him, and seated us with Him in the heavenly places, in Christ Jesus, in order that in the ages to come He might show the surpassing riches of His grace in kindness toward us in Christ Jesus. For by grace you have been saved through faith; and that not of yourselves, it is the gift of God; not as a result of works, that no one should boast. For we are His workmanship, created in Christ Jesus for good works, which

God prepared beforehand, that we should walk in them. (Ephesians 2:4-10)[445]

This passage appears to teach the opposite of what Rome teaches on salvation. But in the hands of a Roman Catholic interpreter, it becomes his ally.

Madrid starts out on the wrong foot in his analysis of this passage. He says, "We see how this transformation from sin to grace is likened to being raised from the dead."[446] However, the verse does not teach that we are transformed from sin to grace. It says that *by grace* we have been *saved*. We are not transferred into a state of grace that we must maintain within a system. We are rather "*saved*" from spiritually dead to spiritually alive in Christ. The apostle reiterates that we have been "*saved*" by grace through faith and not of ourselves. The apostle drives home the point that to be "*saved*" is to be raised up with Christ and seated in the heavenly places (positionally) with Christ. We are "*saved*" through faith and faith itself is a gift made certain by the regeneration of the Holy Spirit. In short, to be born of the Holy Spirit is to be given faith that works. It is no dormant faith awaiting activation by man. This passage does not teach that one is transformed into a state of grace that can be killed by sin or kept alive through a routine of sacraments and God-aided good works.

The apostle Paul writes in Ephesians 2:4, "But God, being rich in mercy, because of His great love with which He loved us, even when *we were dead* in our transgressions, *made us alive together with Christ* (by grace you have been saved)... ." Madrid interprets this to mean that "He (God) *extends* that grace to me, but I am always free to accept it or reject it; free to remain in it or to throw it away and turn my back on it."[447] But this passage does not teach this. It teaches the opposite. God does not simply extend grace. God makes that which is dead alive. God *saves* poor 'dead in sin' sinners. They are His workmanship, created in Christ Jesus. It is not because of works lest any man should boast. If, as Madrid contends, one can

---

445 Unless otherwise noted, Mr. Zins cites the *New American Standard Bible* throughout.
446 Madrid, p. 86.
447 Madrid, p. 86.

take it or leave it, then it is all up to me and my boasting would not be eliminated. Madrid puts into capsule form the gospel of Rome:

> If I accept His grace, embrace it, and live according to it, I will be saved.[448]

Madrid continues to interpret this passage by asserting that faith, if *used properly*, will eventually bring about salvation (state of grace) through the Catholic system. Faith if *used properly* will enable us to be obedient to the commands of Christ, which are good works. Remarkably, Madrid cites Ephesians 2:10 to prove his point that faith *if used properly* will obey the commands of Christ to do good works. Does Ephesians 2:10 teach us that if we use our faith appropriately, we will be able to obey Christ's commands, which are to do good works?

Ephesians 2:10 teaches no such thing. Here is the passage:

> For we are His workmanship, created in Christ Jesus for good works, which God prepared beforehand, that we should walk in them. (Ephesians 2:10)

The apostle Paul is clear that all those saved by grace, through faith, not of their own doing, and not because of works are God's workmanship. The text literally states, "We are His work." We are created in Christ Jesus. We are created for good works. These good works have been previously prepared by God so that His new creation in Christ should walk in them. The good works of the Christian are a result and goal of God's creating Christians in Christ. They are the effect of salvation, not the cause. It is safe to say that all of God's elect will walk in good works prepared before the foundation of the world. These works are part of God's plan of salvation through sanctification.

> But we should always give thanks to God for you, brethren beloved by the Lord, because God has chosen you from the

---

448 Ibid., p. 87.

beginning for salvation through sanctification by the Spirit
and faith in the truth. (2 Thessalonians 2:13)

For Rome, every aspect of salvation is dependent upon man to
accept the grace of God and use it properly. Because of this there is
absolutely no certainty that anyone will take on board the gift of
grace or faith at all. And if one begins by accepting the grace of God
there is no guarantee that he will continue in either grace or faith.
Hence there is no certitude that good works will be accomplished,
which leads to Rome's conclusion that assurance of salvation is a
myth and those who believe that they are undoubtedly *saved* are
guilty of the sin of presumption.

Not by Works Righteousness

Considering our investigation into how Rome defines the terms
"gift", "grace", "faith", and "salvation" we would find disingenuous
the claim that "The Catholic Church does not now teach, nor has it
ever taught, a doctrine of salvation based upon works righteousness."[449] The Council of Trent defies the boast of Madrid. Here is
what Trent, the foremost doctrinal council of the Roman Catholic
religion, has to say about works righteousness:

> If anyone says that the *good works* of the one justified are in
> such manner the gifts of God that they are not also *the good
> merits of him* justified; or that the one justified *by the good
> works that he performs* by the grace of God and the merit
> of Jesus Christ, whose living member he is, *does not truly
> merit an increase of grace, eternal life*, and in case he dies
> in grace, the attainment of eternal life itself and also an
> increase of glory, let him be anathema.[450]

As we can plainly read from this citation, Madrid's confidence
that Roman Catholicism does not teach a doctrine of salvation
based upon works righteousness is at odds with his own religion.

---

449 Madrid, p. 93.
450 Council of Trent Session 16, Canon 32. Italics mine.

Madrid's exact words are not used by the Council of Trent, but the concept of a merit-based, good works righteousness which achieves eternal life is undeniably clear. In Rome good works are good merits that justify and truly merit eternal life.

How does Madrid avoid apparent contradictions in terms of understanding the basis of salvation and justification? As quoted above, Madrid claims that Roman Catholicism does not teach a doctrine of salvation based on "works righteousness." Yet earlier in his chapter on salvation Madrid has this to say:

> Anyone who tells you that the central message of the Gospel is "justification by faith alone" doesn't understand the central message of the Gospel.[451]

So if justification and salvation are not based on "works righteousness" and not based on "faith alone," then what are they based upon? The answer is that salvation and justification are based on good works done in faith (produced by God if man allows God to aid him) through the Roman Catholic grace dispensing scheme of things. In short, Rome teaches that God, through the death of Jesus Christ, has left mankind a labyrinth or maze of religious obligations which, if done appropriately, will land the Roman Catholic in nothing less than Purgatory, where he will ultimately pay his last punishments for sin.

In contrast, when Christians say they are saved by grace through faith apart from works they mean it. God's grace saves His church, and this salvation is real and eternal. In Rome grace merely makes salvation possible. For Christians faith is a gift that receives authentic salvation that is eternal. For Rome faith makes salvation possible. For the Christian, trust in Christ by God's grace through faith alone guarantees salvation. Not so with Rome. Madrid explains:

> Clearly our faith is the instrument by which we receive and maintain the grace of salvation but notice what this

---

451 Madrid, p. 89.

entails: Our faith in Christ is a gift, but it is we who must exercise that faith for it to be efficacious. Or, to say it differently, God does not have faith in himself for us. We are the ones who have been enabled by His grace to have faith in Him—it is something we do. And it is, in a very real sense, a "work."[452]

It seems clear-cut that one cannot have it both ways. One cannot deny salvation by "works of righteousness" and then claim that grace produces faith, which is then termed a righteous work. What better example is there of salvation by a "work of righteousness" than to claim that faith is that righteous work? Madrid freely admits that God makes us cooperators in the process of justification, sanctification, and eventual salvation.[453] At the end of the day our faith is a work, our works wrought by God (if we allow Him to work in us) count toward justification, and the way in which we keep ourselves in a "state of grace" is through the Roman Catholic system.

For Christians salvation is the gift of eternal life gained by faith alone in the finished work of Christ alone. Christians add nothing to their salvation. Christians are not lifetime cooperators, hoping to cooperate enough to gain heaven. Heaven is an eternal possession given to all those in Christ by faith alone, apart from works. Salvation is all of God's grace. No kind of work, including so-called God-initiated work, is required by God to be saved eternally. All works of Christians are *the result* of having been saved and are in no way *the cause* or basis of salvation.

> These things I have written to you who believe in the name of the Son of God, in order that you may know that you have eternal life. (1 John 5:13)

---

452 Ibid., p. 94.
453 Ibid.

> And as Moses lifted up the serpent in the wilderness, even
> so must the Son of Man be lifted up; that whoever believes
> may in Him have eternal life. (John 3:14-15)

The Roman Catholic religion nullifies the grace of God by making
faith a righteous work and compelling her adherents to be cooperators through a man-made system of self salvation. When confront-
ed with the anti-Christian doctrine of salvation by meritorious
works Roman Catholics are taught to claim innocence, insisting
that their works are produced by God and therefore not really their
works. And yet behind the scenes they are taught that their works
count as cooperators to gain salvation. The word of God forcefully
resists such claims:

> In the same way then, there has also come to be at the
> present time a remnant according to God's gracious choice.
> But if it is by grace, *it is no longer on the basis of works,*
> otherwise grace is no longer grace. (Romans 11:5-6)

In the above passage the apostle writes the antidote to adding one's
own works (God-initiated or not) to the grace of God. There is no
caveat that says, "Your works count and do no harm to grace if they
are God-produced." The Bible is sure. If it is by grace, it is no longer
based on works, otherwise grace is no longer grace.

> He saved us, *not on the basis of deeds which we have done in*
> *righteousness*, but according to His mercy, by the washing
> of regeneration and renewing by the Holy Spirit, whom He
> poured out upon us richly through Jesus Christ our Savior,
> that being justified by His grace we might be made heirs
> according to the hope of eternal life. (Titus 3:5-7)

Here the apostle Paul gives us the antidote to so-called "deeds of
righteousness we have done" (God-initiated or not). Notice we are
justified by His grace without works being included. It is according
to His mercy, not by works that He has done in us. It is by the

washing of regeneration (born again) by the Holy Spirit, poured out richly through Jesus Christ our Savior. The result of God saving us by faith apart from any kind of works is to be made heirs of eternal life.

> Therefore do not be ashamed of the testimony of our Lord, or of me His prisoner; but join with me in suffering for the gospel according to the power of God, who has saved us, and called us with a holy calling, *not according to our works*, but according to His own purpose and grace which was granted us in Christ Jesus from all eternity. (2 Timothy 1:8-9)

Again, in the above passage the apostle gives the antidote to any question as to whether the gospel is a message of cooperation by man and contribution by man's works (God-initiated or not). Notice Paul writes, "Who has saved us." Paul considered himself to be a saved man. He was called to a holy calling. This call was not according to his own works but according to God's purpose and grace. This grace was granted in Christ Jesus from all eternity. It is not in any way dependent upon man's cooperative good works.

Can Christians Lose Their Salvation?

There is only one correct answer to the question of eternal security in the Roman Catholic religion. Madrid is certain and straightforward.

> The fact is, the Bible is clear that Christians can lose their salvation.[454]

This is perfectly consistent with Rome. Madrid has made it clear that man is a co-contributor with God when it comes to gaining a "state of grace." Man must keep himself in a "state of grace" (salvation) or forfeit eternal life. At any point in the process of salvation, man can keep it or walk away from it. God has done

---

454 Madrid, p. 101.

His share by leaving a method and structure for mankind to follow. Now it is up to man to do it.

The answer to the question "Can a Christian Lose His Salvation?" begins with two radically different blueprints to salvation that can never ever be harmonized. The gulf between them is eternal.

We must go all the way back to the sin of Adam to understand Rome's sacramental salvation. Rome admits that Adam's sin brought displeasure from God but not only for Adam and Eve. Rome rightly assesses that Adam's sin infects all of Adam's posterity through propagation. All that Adam lost in his sin was lost for all mankind, as Adam's sin of disobedience defiled him and by transfusion entered the entire human race. Rome asserts that Adam's sin, transfused to humanity, is sin that kills the soul.

> If any one asserts, that the prevarication of Adam injured himself alone, and not his posterity; and that the holiness and justice, received of God, which he lost, he lost for himself alone, and not for us also; or that he, being defiled by the sin of disobedience, has only transfused death, and pains of the body, into the whole human race, but not sin also, which is the death of the soul; let him be anathema.[455]

It will be the extent of the damage incurred by Adam's sin and the remedy of that infusion[456] that will begin to separate into two radically opposed blueprints for salvation. Rome affirms Adam's sin affected the will of his posterity. The will has been damaged and weakened and now bent in a downward trajectory but by no means extinguished.

> If any one saith, that, since Adam's sin, the free will of man is lost and extinguished; or, that it is a thing with only a name, yea a name without a reality, a figment,

---

455 Council of Trent 5th Session, paragraph 2.
456 Christians are more familiar with the terms "imputed guilt" of Adam's sin to his posterity and the corresponding "inherited corruption" of human nature due to Adam.

in fine, introduced into the Church by Satan; let him be anathema.[457]

If any one saith, that by faith alone the impious is justified; in such wise as to mean, that nothing else is required to co-operate in order to the obtaining the grace of Justification, and that it is not in any way necessary, that he be prepared and disposed by the movement of his own will; let him be anathema.[458]

It is clear in Rome that the will of man has full ability to opt for or against salvation. Mankind has the free will to decide.[459] If an adult decides to take Rome's offer of co-contribution salvation, then the first step is to get rid of Adam's pollution. So, by self-preparation of will, one commences with Roman Catholic baptism. Rome believes that baptism (rightly administered by a Roman Catholic priest) washes away original sin of both infants and adults. The beginning of the Roman Catholic Road to salvation is the declaration that the tarnished (yet free will) must co-operate in salvation (attaining a state of grace). This is the first necessary step. Infants who cannot exercise faith have the faith of their parents or the Roman Catholic religion in general to stand in at their baptism. All Roman Catholic parents are required to have their babies baptized.

For, by reason of this rule of faith, from a tradition of the apostles, even infants, who could not as yet commit any sin of themselves, are for this cause truly baptized for the remission of sins, that in them that may be cleansed away by regeneration, which they have contracted by generation. For, unless a man be born again of water and the Holy Ghost, he cannot enter into the kingdom of God.[460]

---

457 Council of Trent 6th Session, Canon 5.
458 Ibid., Canon 9.
459 By free will Rome does not mean that a man can believe without help. The predisposing work of the Holy Spirit must precede and help for one to believe, hope, love or be repentant as he ought. Man can take or leave this help.
460 Council of Trent 5th Session, paragraph 4.

> If anyone denies, that, by the grace of our Lord Jesus Christ,
> which is conferred in baptism, the guilt of original sin
> is remitted; or even asserts that the whole of that which
> has the true and proper nature of sin is not taken away;
> but says that it is only erased, or not imputed; let him
> be anathema. For, in those who are born again, there is
> nothing that God hates.[461]

Salvation in Rome is established on the belief that Adam's sin
is remitted in baptism for both infants and adults (properly administered by Roman Catholic officials). It is also founded on
the belief that man has the full capacity to cooperate in his own
salvation. With this in mind, Roman Catholic religious obligations
are designed to take adherents from the cradle to the grave and
beyond to keep them in a "state of grace." Given these parameters
it is logical to assume that one can lose his "salvation" (state of
grace) at any point along the way. What you put yourself into you
can take yourself out of. In short, God is said to have outlined the
program (Roman Catholic religion), and man follows it to heaven or
renounces it to hell.[462]

We have argued in our chapter on baptism that Rome has it
wrong from the start. While we agree that Adam's sin affected his
posterity, we disagree with Rome on the extent. We do not find
the Roman Catholic blueprint for salvation in the Bible. Thus, a
different blueprint will lead to a totally different understanding
of salvation. The Bible does not teach that the transfused sin of
Adam is cancelled in baptism. Furthermore, we have argued in our
chapter on baptism that the Bible nowhere teaches infant baptism,
much less the remission of sin for infants through baptism. Rome
is mistaken in her calling baptism the "laver of regeneration." The
entire scheme of Roman Catholic salvation rests upon her belief

---

461 Ibid., paragraph 5.
462 Certainly, since Vatican II Rome has softened her appraisal of other religions and their capability to lead their followers to heaven. Rome goes so far as to find good things in a variety of
religions. Protestants who wholeheartedly disagree with Rome's dogma are called "separated
brethren." Vatican II takes away any necessity to become a Roman Catholic to find salvation.
Considering this, Rome loses much of her vitality but strives to sit at the head of the table and
call herself the queen of Christianity. We are arguing that she does not belong at any table of
Christianity as her doctrines are averse to true Christianity.

that water administered by her priests takes away sin. Rome errs right from the beginning by assigning forgiveness of sins and regeneration to her baptism. Without this sacrament Rome's blueprint for salvation vanishes. We agree with Rome that Adam's sin rendered man unable to believe on his own. Thus, Rome insists that the will must be helped by the Holy Spirit to believe. Where Rome goes astray is in her insistence that man's innate ability to resist or accept the grace of God (which helps him to a state of grace) is unaffected by the fall of Adam. Rome admits that no man on his own can believe, but also declares that every man on his own can resist and deny God's efforts to help. This denial of the Holy Spirit's help is said to be the exercise of man's free will, which trumps the help offered.

However, does the New Testament give us this blueprint for salvation? Positively not in the case of Rome's baptism. How about capability of the will of man to ultimately accept or deny the help of the Holy Spirit? We do not find man's will to be the determining factor in salvation. We find just the opposite. The Bible teaches that man is dead spiritually and must be made alive by God. There is no cooperative will of man that makes man spiritually alive. Rather, the Bible teaches that the natural man cannot understand or accept the things of the Spirit of God. The natural man must be born from above by the Spirit to believe. The work of Holy Spirit cannot be resisted in God's intention to give spiritual life to the spiritually dead. Let us look at a more biblical blueprint for salvation.

> But as many as received Him, to them He gave the right to become children of God, even to those who believe in His name, who were born not of blood, nor of the will of the flesh, nor of the will of man, but of God. (John 1:11-13)

Those who receive Jesus Christ have been born of God and not of the will of flesh or the will of man.

> But a natural man does not accept the things of the Spirit of God; for they are foolishness to him, and he cannot

understand them, because they are spiritually appraised. (1 Corinthians 2:14-15)

To the natural man the things of the Spirit of God are foolishness. The natural man cannot understand them because they are spiritually appraised. God must first make the spiritually dead alive before they can believe. And all who are made alive will believe.

And you were dead in your trespasses and sins, in which you formerly walked according to the course of this world, according to the prince of the power of the air, of the spirit that is now working in the sons of disobedience. Among them we too all formerly lived in the lusts of our flesh, indulging the desires of the flesh and of the mind, and were by nature children of wrath, even as the rest. But God, being rich in mercy, because of His great love with which He loved us, even when we were dead in our transgressions, made us alive together with Christ (by grace you have been saved), and raised us up with Him, and seated us with Him in the heavenly places, in Christ Jesus. (Ephesians 2:1-7)

The natural man is spiritually dead in trespasses and sins. He is by nature a child of wrath. But God makes those dead in transgressions spiritually alive in Christ. God brings to spiritual life those who are dead. It is not the will of man.

No one can come to Me, unless the Father who sent Me draws him; and I will raise him up on the last day. (John 6:44-45)

And He was saying, "For this reason I have said to you, that no one can come to Me, unless it has been granted him from the Father." (John 6:65)

> All that the Father gives Me shall come to Me, and the
> one who comes to Me I will certainly not cast out. (John
> 6:37-38)

No one can come to Jesus unless the Father draws him. This
indicates the spiritual inability of man to save himself. It is not
man's cooperative will but rather the impetus from the Father that
enables him to come to Jesus. John adds that all that the Father
gives to Jesus shall come. Salvation is dependent solely upon the
Father. If one is given by the Father to Jesus, he will come to Jesus.

> That which is born of the flesh is flesh, and that which is
> born of the Spirit is spirit. "Do not marvel that I said to you,
> 'You must be born again.' The wind blows where it wishes
> and you hear the sound of it, but do not know where it
> comes from and where it is going; so is everyone who is
> born of the Spirit." (John 3:6-8)

One must be born of the Spirit to see the kingdom of God. Man's
will does not determine who the Spirit births spiritually.

> And a certain woman named Lydia, from the city of
> Thyatira, a seller of purple fabrics, a worshiper of God, was
> listening; and the Lord opened her heart to respond to the
> things spoken by Paul. (Acts 16:13-14)

For even a religious person to understand the gospel, the heart
must be opened by God. The will of man cannot open his own heart
to understand spiritual things.

> And not only this, but there was Rebekah also, when
> she had conceived twins by one man, our father Isaac;
> for though the twins were not yet born, and had not
> done anything good or bad, in order that God's purpose
> according to His choice might stand, not because of works,
> but because of Him who calls. (Romans 9:10-11)

> What shall we say then? There is no injustice with God, is
> there? May it never be! For He says to Moses, "I will have
> mercy on whom I have mercy, and I will have compassion
> on whom I have compassion." *So, then it does not depend on
> the man who wills or the man who runs, but on God who has
> mercy.*" (Romans 9:14-16)

In both citations it is the calling of God, not the will of man or
the works of man, that is efficacious in making God's purposes
according to His choice stand. It does not depend upon the man
who wills or the man who runs, but on God! It seems perfectly clear
that salvation is of the Lord and not of man. Man is not a coopera-
tor in regeneration (again born). Rather, it is the Holy Spirit giving
spiritual life that is expressed in faith by those who have been truly
born from above. This is of God and not of man. Luke tells us in
Acts 13:48 that the Gentiles who had been appointed to eternal life
believed. The appointment comes from God first, before faith. John
tells us in 1 John 5:1 that whoever believes that Jesus is the Christ
is born of God. Peter tells us in 1 Peter 1:3 that God has caused us
to be born again. We could list illustration after illustration from
the Bible showing that God is sovereign in salvation and man is
not called to cooperate through a man-made religion system of any
kind.

All this is to say that anyone appointed to eternal life, called by
God, given to the Son by God, born from above by the Holy Spirit,
and made spiritually alive by God (who has caused them to be born
again) cannot lose their salvation. It is secure in heaven and all
in Christ by faith alone will go to heaven. This is the blueprint of
salvation given to us in the Bible. Roman Catholicism has no part in
this.

What About the Warning Passages?

Roman Catholic defenders like Patrick Madrid like to use the
warning passages in the New Testament to prove that someone
who is saved can lose his salvation if he does not do enough works.
A few comments should be considered at this point. First, Rome

errs in taking for granted that those who utterly fail to obey the commands of Christ have been born again of the Holy Spirit. The apostle Paul writes his letters to those whom he hopes to have been born again. However, he is cautious lest he has run in vain. He is aware that not all those who say "Lord, Lord" are truly converted. With this the apostle John agrees.

> Children, it is the last hour; and just as you heard that antichrist is coming, even now many antichrists have arisen; from this we know that it is the last hour. They went out from us, but they were not really of us; for if they had been of us, they would have remained with us; but they went out, in order that it might be shown that they all are not of us. (1 John 2:18-20)

Considering the disturbances created by false teaching, most of Paul's writings address the issue of false brethren and heresies. It is much more plausible from Scripture to assume those who have rejected Christ have not been converted to the gospel. Perhaps this is why Paul writes these overall words of warning to the church at Corinth:

> Test yourselves to see if you are in the faith; examine yourselves! Or do you not recognize this about yourselves, that Jesus Christ is in you — unless indeed you fail the test? But I trust that you will realize that we ourselves do not fail the test. (2 Corinthians 13:5-6)

We notice here that the concern of the apostle is whether his readers were sincerely in the faith. Any departure from the gospel or lack of fruit in the lives of those to whom he is writing might signal that they simply were not authentic believers.

Secondly, it is important to focus on Madrid's selection of biblical passages that he thinks prove conclusively that a Christian can lose his salvation (state of grace) if he fails to do certain things. Madrid quotes Romans 11, where the apostle Paul mentions that those who *continue in the Lord's kindness* will not be cut off. Continuing in the Lord's kindness hardly equates to keeping oneself in a "state of grace" through Roman Catholic sacramentalism. He next mentions Matthew 10, where the Lord says whoever denies Him before men He will deny before His Father in heaven. Again, no mention that sticking with the Roman Catholic religion equals not denying the Lord. In fact, there is not one single word in any warning passage that suggests a failure to be involved in the Roman Catholic sacramental salvation leads to a loss of salvation. Or vice-versa. Attendance in the Roman Catholic religion does not carry with it biblical salvation. Madrid quotes Luke 6:46, where the Lord asks, "Why do you call Me Lord, Lord but do not the things I tell you?" Still no mention that not doing the things that the Lord tells us is the same as departing from Rome's system. Madrid quotes John 15:9, where Jesus says, "If you keep my commandments, you will abide in my love…" He thinks that "abiding in my love" is the same thing as "remaining in a state of grace" which, of course, means receiving grace from Rome. But this link and leap is nowhere taught in scripture. Without laboring the point too much we see that for Madrid "obeying the gospel" is shorthand for keeping oneself in "a state of grace," which means obeying Christ's commands by careful pursuit of the Roman Catholic blueprint for ultimate salvation. But this has no biblical support.

Third, there is absolutely no appeal to any of the Roman Catholic sacraments to remedy those who seem to have fallen away from the faith or have been mesmerized by false teachers. There is no command to confess one's sins to a New Covenant priest or do penance to receive forgiveness. There is no appeal made to have one's sins forgiven by ingesting Jesus Christ in the form of a wafer of bread in the Roman Catholic Mass. As we have shown in our section on Purgatory there is no appeal made in scripture to this after-life punishment for sins either. There is simply no mention that obeying the gospel or the command of Christ has any reference to participating in the Roman Catholic religion. In stark contrast, there is the simple promise from scripture:

> If we confess our sins, He is faithful and righteous to forgive us our sins and to cleanse us from all unrighteousness. (1 John 1:9)

Further Analysis of Roman Catholic Use of the Bible

We must remember the mindset of Patrick Madrid as he approaches warning passages. He is defending the Roman Catholic blueprint of salvation. Hence, he equates salvation with being in "a state of grace" which must be maintained by man to be effectual. Because of this Madrid sees individual salvation as nothing more than an elevated "a state of grace" which comes with the great burden of maintaining this "state of grace." Thus, salvation does not mean eternal life or being eternally secure. It means being elevated to a heightened relationship with God that requires self-preservation. Given this definition of salvation, it is easy to see why Roman Catholic apologists insist salvation can be gained and lost and gained again. Roman Catholic salvation is not eternal life guaranteed by the promises of God in Christ.

What comes from this man-made definition of salvation is a forced biblical interpretation to defend the Roman Catholic religion. For instance, Madrid misrepresents the warning of Paul in Romans 11. The context informs us that Paul is writing about God's dealings with a national Israel and the Gentile nations. Madrid sets forth this passage as pertaining to the personal salvation of individuals. Those who have been saved (in a "state of grace") are in danger of losing their salvation (losing their "state of grace"). However, Christians and Roman Catholics are operating under two different blueprints of salvation. Christians affirm that real salvation is not merely being transferred into a "state of grace," to be gained and lost based upon man's best efforts in Rome's system. Rome essentially redefines salvation and then claims it can be lost. Since Rome puts her devotees (by virtue of baptism) in a "state of grace" (salvation), it is easy to see every warning passage as illustrating a loss of salvation, i.e., forfeiting their "state of grace." For instance, Madrid quotes 2 Timothy 2:11f., "if we deny him, he also will deny us; if we are faithless, he remains faithful…" A Christian sees those who deny Jesus Christ as faithless, i.e., never having been saved. Madrid sees them as losing their salvation, i.e., their "state of grace." Again, Madrid quotes Matthew 10:32f., "…whoever denies me before men, I also will deny before my Father who is in heaven." To Madrid these are saved people (in a state of grace) who lose their standing by denying Jesus. For the Christian those who deny Jesus before men were not saved to begin with. To be succinct, all the passages marshaled to prove a loss of salvation are linked to Rome's false concept of salvation. Not a thought is given in Rome that the culprits in the severe warnings (dogs returning to vomit and pigs to mire) are not saved in the first place.

Rome has no doctrine of the perseverance of the saints and the preservation of God for His elect. She does not because Rome's religion is entered upon by man-made rituals and lost by failure to perform man-made commandments. It is not the salvation of the Bible. Foreign to Rome are the biblical promises given by our Lord and guaranteed by our Lord.

> Jesus answered them, " I told you, and you do not believe; the works that I do in My Father's name, these testify of Me. But you do not believe because you are not of My sheep. *My sheep hear My voice*, and I know them, and *they follow Me*; and *I give eternal life to them, and they will never perish*; and no one will snatch them out of My hand. My Father, who *has given them to Me*, is greater than all; and no one is able to snatch them out of the Father's hand. I and the Father are one. (John 10:25-30)

Jesus does not say, "You are not my sheep *because you do not believe*, or do good works, or follow the sacraments of Rome, or any other kind effort by man." He says the opposite: "*You do not believe because* you are not my sheep." Those who *do not* believe *are not* His sheep. Those who *do not* follow *are not* His sheep. His sheep follow Him. He gives them eternal life. The Father has given sheep to

Jesus. They will never perish. They will always persevere, and God will preserve them. This is sovereign, majestic, efficacious grace, unconditional love, and authentic salvation. God's promise of salvation is for His sheep and His sheep will love Him, for they have been born from above.

The Papacy

———————— (Kauffman) ————————

The Peter Problem

In this chapter, Madrid attempts to provide ancient evidence for Peter as the first pope, and a succession of Roman popes after him. Unable to provide any explicit evidence from the scripture to support Peter's "special authority," Madrid instead attempts to aggregate various references to Peter so that he may load them with meaning that supports his claim: Peter is named more frequently than any other apostle; Peter is always listed first; only Peter's name was changed by Jesus; Peter received the keys of the kingdom—all of which are purported to reveal to us Peter's "striking prominence," "special primacy," and "special role" in the New Testament. Madrid scoffs at the idea that "[t]he Bible nowhere says anything about Peter being the first pope," and offers a condescending retort: "Perhaps you aren't as familiar with the biblical evidence as you think you are."[463]

Madrid's "evidence" is as silly as his claim. Anyone familiar with the Scriptures can easily discern the fallacy into which he repeatedly stumbles. Is Peter named more frequently than any

---

463 Madrid, p. 106.

other apostle? He certainly is. But God does not assign prominence by such means. Sodom is mentioned more frequently in Scripture than Bethlehem, and Artaxerxes than Melchizedek. What would Madrid have us understand from this? That Sodom and Artaxerxes were more important than Bethlehem and Melchizedek? And who would doubt that Abraham is strikingly prominent and holds a "special primacy" and "special role" in covenantal history. Yet Abraham is mentioned only 250 times compared to Jacob's 377. What is more, Abraham, Isaac and Jacob are frequently mentioned together, and Abraham is often but not always mentioned first. Sometimes he is mentioned *last*, as in Leviticus 26:42, "My covenant with Jacob, and also my covenant with Isaac, and also my covenant with Abraham will I remember."

Doubtless, in the cases of Abraham, Bethlehem and Melchizidek, Madrid would have us assign *their* prominence and significance based on what the Scripture *actually says* about their prominence and significance. Their frequency and order tell us nothing in particular. And that is precisely what the question about Peter ought to have elicited from Madrid: "What makes you think Peter had any special authority or primacy among the apostles?" An easy answer would have been to recite what the Bible says about Peter's prominence and primacy, but Madrid knows well enough that he has no Scriptural case. Unable to offer *actual evidence* of what the Scripture *actually says* about Peter, Madrid instead employs the smoke and mirrors of deflection and spin to give the appearance that the Scripture *says something* based on *the order* in which a man's name appears or *the frequency* of its mention. We will hold to the propositions of Scripture rather than to Madrid's fanciful attempts to make the Scripture say something that it does not.

On that note, we invite the attention of the reader to inspect Madrid's claims closely and skeptically. He says that "whenever the apostles are all listed by name as a group, he is always first."[464] That should hold true no matter how many apostles are mentioned with him, but Peter is not always mentioned first:

---

464 Madrid, p. 106.

But go your way, tell his disciples and *Peter* that he goeth before you into Galilee" (Mark 16:7).

James, *Cephas*, and John, … seemed to be pillars (Galatians 2:9).

Philip was of Bethsaida, the city of Andrew and *Peter* (John 1:44).

Why did the angel not send the witnesses to *"Peter and the disciples"*? Why did not *"Cephas, James and John"* seem to be pillars? Why was Bethsaida not the city of *"Peter and Andrew"*? And why would Madrid omit these references? Madrid knows very well that his premise is flawed, and so his citations are conveniently selective to account for it. Frequency and order are not determinative when evaluating a man's "prominence," "primacy" and "role" in salvation history.

Madrid also says "Only Simon, among all the personages of the New Testament, received a name change."[465] The statement is false, as anyone familiar with the Scriptures would know, for James and John were surnamed "*Boanerges*, which is, The sons of thunder" by Jesus (Mark 3:17).

Madrid highlights the fact that Peter was given the keys of the kingdom:

> He was also chosen by Christ to be the one who would receive 'the keys of the kingdom of heaven.' He was told that whatever he personally bound on earth would be bound in heaven and what he loosed on earth would be loosed in heaven.[466]

Madrid acknowledges that "the rest of the apostles received this authority" in Matthew 18:18, but that Christ conferred it "to Simon Peter alone" in Matthew 16:18-19. But the meaning of this authority was indeterminate in the early church. Tertullian did

---

465 Madrid, p. 106.
466 Madrid, p. 106.

not believe binding and loosing meant the pope could remit "the capital sins of believers."[467] Cyprian of Carthage (250 AD) thought Matthew 16:19 meant "the Church is founded upon the bishops,"[468] *plural*, and Firmilian of Cæsarea (256 AD) held that "the foundations of the Church were laid" upon Peter, but not upon the bishop of Rome.[469] We do not believe "keys," "bind" and "loose" in Matthew 16:19 mean what Madrid thinks they do,[470] and the early church certainly did not think so either. In any case, we see no reason to believe that Peter's role was special here.

Madrid continues his attempts to establish Petrine primacy by reading "primacy" into various Scriptural passages that do not mention it. In order to illustrate Madrid's propensity to read into the Scriptures what they are not saying, we simply note that none of these passages say anything of Peter's special prominence and primacy. Madrid had to read special Petrine prominence and primacy into them. He writes,

> It was to Peter that Christ called to come out of the boat and walk on water (Matt. 14:25-33). It was from Simon Peter's fishing boat that Christ preached to the crowds that pressed against him on the shore of the Lake of Galilee (cf. Luke 5:3). St. John deferred to Peter at the tomb, even though he was younger and ran there faster than Peter, waiting for Peter to enter ahead of him (John 20:6). It was to Simon Peter, first among all the apostles, that Christ's resurrection was revealed and first among the apostles to whom Christ appeared after His resurrection (Mark 16:7). … Peter leads the other apostles in choosing a replacement for Judas, who had committed suicide (Acts 1:13-26). He preaches the first post-Pentecost sermon, leading some

---

467 Tertullian, *On Modesty*, 21.
468 Cyprian, *Epistle 26*, 1.
469 Cyprian, *Epistle 74*, 17.
470 For a detailed discussion on "bind" and "loose" as synecdoches for the preaching ministry of the Good Shepherd, Who was sent "to *bind up* the brokenhearted" and *to loose* "them that are bound" (Luke 4:18; Isaiah 61:1), see Kauffman, Timothy F., Of Broken Hearts and Broken Shackles, parts 1 & 2, *The Trinity Review* 2022 (September – December 2022 (370a-b)). Jesus had been commissioned by the Father to "bind up" and to "loose." Peter (Matthew 16:19) and the rest (Matthew 18:18) would be commissioned to do the same after Him.

three thousand people into the Church through baptism.
The first miracle performed after Pentecost was by Peter
(Acts 3:1-10), and it was he who led the apostles and faced
down the Sanhedrin in Acts 4:1-12. ... In Acts 10:9-16, God
delivers revelation to Peter that Gentiles could now enter
the Church...[471]

None of these verses establish what Madrid claims. He has simply
assumed Petrine primacy, and then read into each passage the
Petrine primacy he already believed before he read it. We could as
easily do the opposite, approaching each passage on the assumption that Peter was the *least* of the apostles. Under that rubric (we
proceed facetiously here to illustrate a point), Christ calls Peter out
of the boat because Peter's faith was smallest of them all, providing
Jesus an opportunity to use Peter's unbelief as an object lesson.
Jesus preaches from Peter's boat because in his unbelief, Peter had
caught the fewest fish, and therefore had the most room available
for an extra passenger. Jesus warned all the apostles that Satan
desired to "sift you (plural) as wheat" (Luke 22:31), but because
the "roaring lion" tends to prey upon the stragglers (1 Peter 5:8),
Jesus prays for Peter alone, "that thy (singular) faith fail not"
(Luke 22:32). The meaning of the linen cloths in the empty tomb
did not register with Peter—weak in faith, and dull of mind and
heart—but John "saw and believed" (John 20:8). When He visited
the disciples at the Sea of Galilee after the Resurrection (John
21:1-6), Jesus gave a sign specifically tailored to prompt Peter's
memory (Luke 5:4-8), but it is perceptive *John*, not the dullard
Peter, who understands the significance (John 21:7). Impulsive
and uncaring, Peter immediately abandons his post, leaving the
heavy lifting to the other disciples, who remained in the boat and
returned the sizeable haul two hundred cubits to shore without
him (John 21:8). By the time Peter finally lends a hand, the fish
are already conveniently near land where the other apostles have
hauled them (John 21:11). After the Ascension, Peter was allowed
to lead the selection of Judas' replacement because, still stinging

---

471 Madrid, pp. 107-108.

from his denial of Christ, he was most in need of a confidence boost. Remembering Peter's weaknesses—how difficult it was for him to comprehend the empty tomb, and how quickly he wanted to return to fishing after his early failures—John becomes his mentor and coach, and stays with Peter to guide him through the next steps of his growth: assisting him with his first miracle and standing with him before the Sanhedrin, knowing that Peter, of all the apostles, is mostly likely to buckle under modest pressure or to succumb to irrational exuberance. It is revealed to Peter that Gentiles could enter the church, but it took three repetitions of the vision for Peter, and even then he still "doubted in himself" what the vision meant (Acts 10:16-17); while Paul by way of contrast was made aware of God's plan for the Gentiles without doubting (Acts 9:15). At the council of Jerusalem, Peter's anemic, ineffectual attempt to settle a bitter dispute (Acts 15:7-11) is met with unre-solved silence (Acts 15:12), so Paul and Barnabas must intervene to bolster his argument with evidence of the miracles God had performed through them (Acts 15:12). Only then does James rise to implore "the apostles and elders" to welcome the Gentiles by letter, and the matter is settled by acclamation—not upon Peter's argument, but upon James'. In response the church elects to send to Antioch the "chief men among the brethren" (Acts 15:22) — Judas and Silas — to deliver the conciliar instruction, but opts not to send the wavering, uncertain, impetuous Peter. Other apostles and deacons tower over Peter in significance and influence in the early church. *Only Nathanael* was called an Israelite (John 1:47). Jesus often fed the apostles, but *only Matthew* ever "made him a great feast" (Luke 5:29). Jesus called himself "Physician" (Luke 4:23) but among all the apostles, *only Luke* was ever called by that title (Colossians 4:14). In the early days of the church all twelve apostles are present in Jerusalem (Acts 6:2), and yet it is Stephen, a mere deacon, who had the leaders of the synagogue tangled in knots: they were "disputing with Stephen. And they were not able to resist the wisdom and the spirit by which he spake" (Acts 6:9-10). Two chapters later, Peter was still in Jerusalem (8:1,14) and was supposed to be devoting himself to the ministry of the word (6:4), but he left the important preaching to Stephen. It is Stephen, rather than Peter, who went before the High Priest to make the case for the gospel. When opportunities arise to preach the gospel to the leaders of the synagogue and to the High Priest, it is Stephen, not Peter, who speaks for the church. Why did Peter wither when it was his time to shine? Was Stephen greater than he?

We are, of course, being absurd in order to demonstrate Madrid's absurdity. If his exegetical methods had any merit at all, he would have to conclude that Paul, Nathanael, Matthew and Luke were Peter's superiors. In fact, by some readings, Peter was even lesser than Stephen the deacon. And what is more, Jesus never called any of *them* Satan (Luke 4:8).

Thus ends our facetious illustration of Madrid's folly. To be clear, we do not believe any of these verses mean Peter was the least of the apostles—we simply offer them as a general illustration of how easy it is for Madrid to read the Scriptures according to his own invalid presuppositions, and a particular illustration of how vulnerable Madrid is to the temptation to infer from the Scriptures what he wishes they implied—to make the Scriptures say what he wants them to say, mean what he wishes they meant. The verses do not explicitly or implicitly support "primacy" or "prominence" or a "special role" for Peter, but neither do they militate for Peter being the least of the apostles. They simply relate events that occurred in the ministry of the apostles.

Madrid's propensity for finding in the Scriptures what he has only imagined in his heart may be seen by his interpretation of Peter's vision in Acts 10. From that vision, Madrid makes the argument that "Peter made binding on the whole Church" the new "food laws" he received from the Lord in Joppa:

> In Acts 10:9-16, God delivers revelation to Peter that Gentiles could now enter the Church *without the need to observe Jewish Kosher food laws*, and this teaching Peter made binding on the whole Church at the Council of Jerusalem in Acts 15.[472]

---

472 Madrid, p. 108.

Madrid is grossly mistaken on three counts. Peter's vision in Acts 10 was not about *food laws*, the Jerusalem council did not *rescind* them, and Peter did not *bind* the church to the *recension* of food laws at the Jerusalem council.

On the first count, Peter tells us what the vision actually meant, and it was not about food laws. He was thrice commanded in his vision to "rise, … kill, and eat" (Acts 10:13), and he thrice refused saying, "I have never eaten any thing that is *common or unclean*" (Acts 10:14). He was thrice reprimanded, "What God hath *cleansed*, that call not thou *common*" (Acts 10:15). At first Peter did not know what the vision meant (Acts 10:17), but continued to ponder it (Acts 10:19), and the next day in Cæsarea, it came to him:

> Ye know how that it is an unlawful thing for a man that is a Jew to keep company, or come unto one of another nation; but God hath shewed me that I should not call any man common or unclean. Therefore came I unto you without gainsaying… (Acts 10:28-29)

The meaning of the vision is obvious: Peter should not call any *man* common or unclean. The application of the vision is to preach the gospel to the Gentiles unreservedly. The food in the vision was not literal food but was *a figure for the Gentiles*. This becomes further apparent when Peter relates the vision to the Jews. After he recounts the vision and its meaning, he again concludes that "God gave them [the Gentiles] the like gift as he did unto us, who believed on the Lord Jesus Christ" (Acts 11:17), and the circumcised responded in kind, "Then hath God also to the Gentiles granted repentance unto life" (Acts 11:18). Note well that neither Peter in Cæsarea, nor the Jews in Jerusalem, at any point understood the vision to mean that *food* was no longer "common or unclean." Rather, the Lord had cleansed the hearts of the *Gentiles* the same way he had cleansed the hearts of those gathered at the council (Acts 15:8-9), so *Gentiles* were no longer "common or unclean."

On the second count, the Jerusalem council did not exempt Gentile converts from Kosher food laws. Kosher food laws prohibit eating meat without first draining the blood (Leviticus 17:12,14), which is why it is forbidden in the Law to eat the meat of "strangled" animals that still have the animal's blood in it. And yet, the council, rather than *releasing* Gentiles from that Kosher precept, actually *reaffirmed* it:

> For it seemed good to the Holy Ghost, and to us, … That ye abstain from meats offered to idols, and from blood, and from things strangled… (Acts 15:28-29)

It is clear from the context of the council that the Gentiles were by no means obligated to observe the law of Moses, but out of deference to the weaker brethren, the Gentiles were nevertheless to refrain from actions that could cause their circumcised brethren to stumble. Such consideration by the new Gentile converts in "Antioch and Syria and Cilicia" (Acts 15:23) would not be too burdensome, James concludes, for the Gentiles in those cities were already well familiar with those Jewish practices:

> For Moses of old time hath in every city them that preach him, being read in the synagogues every sabbath day. (Acts 15:21)

The cities addressed in the conciliar letter all had synagogues where Moses was read weekly, and therefore the Gentile proselytes in those cities would already be familiar with Moses. They would receive the apostolic instruction neither as surprising nor as overly burdensome since the objective of the instruction was simply to avoid offending the weaker brethren, the Jews. As is evident from related passages of Scripture—Acts 21:25, Romans 14:1-17; 1 Corinthians 8:1-13; Revelation 2:14,20—it is the Jews who are considered the weaker brethren on this matter, and the conciliar prohibition against certain activities was promulgated with the aim of minimizing their offense. In that light, it is clear that the council did not release the Gentile Christians from the food laws, but rather *instructed them to abide by them* for the sake of their weaker brethren.

We propose here neither that the Kosher food laws are still in force nor that Peter's vision in Acts 10 is unrelated to the actions of the Jerusalem council. We simply highlight the fact that Madrid must grossly misunderstand the passages in question to conclude that Peter's vision *was about Kosher food laws*, and that the Jerusalem council *exempted Gentiles from them*. Clearly, neither is true, and on this count we remand Madrid to his studies that he may perhaps learn the truth.

On the third count, *Peter* did not bind the church at the council of Jerusalem, as a cursory review of Acts 15 reveals. After the controversy arose, it was decided to appeal "unto the apostles and elders about this question" (Acts 15:2). After hearing the arguments, "the apostles and elders" agreed to send ambassadors to the Gentiles with instructions (Acts 15:22) and "the apostles and elders and brethren" wrote letters to the same effect (Acts 15:23). Three times the authority of the apostles and elders is invoked. At no point did it occur to anyone to appeal to Peter. At no point did Peter decide anything. At no point were letters written in Peter's name to the churches. In fact, what was transmitted in writing and by word of mouth was not Peter's judgment, but James', for James is the only one among them actually to propose a solution to the dispute: "Wherefore my sentence is…" (Acts 15:19). The conciliar letter reflected James' judgment, not Peter's, and James' judgment is the one reflected in the letter from "the apostles and elders."

In sum, Madrid was wrong about Peter's vision in Acts 10, wrong about the substance of the council's judgment in Acts 15, and wrong about Peter binding the church through the council. What Madrid has done, rather, is assume the Lord had rescinded a food law through "Pope" Peter, and interpret the Scripture through the lens of that governing assumption. He simply assumed to be true what he already believed about Peter, and read the passages accordingly.

"As a final example," Madrid concludes, "remember that the great St. Paul himself, after his conversion to Christ and time spent in prayer and preparation, *did not begin his own public ministry until he had first gone up to Jerusalem and checked with Peter* (cf. Gal. 1:18). If nothing else, that alone should give you pause and make you reconsider your argument that Peter had no special primacy."[473] Yet the scales that dropped from Paul's eyes are still firmly obscuring Madrid's vision. The Scripture contradicts Madrid, stating plainly that Paul's public ministry began "straightway," before he ever had the opportunity to "check with Peter":

> And immediately there fell from his eyes as it had been scales: and he received sight forthwith, and arose, and was baptized. And when he had received meat, he was strengthened. Then was Saul certain days with the disciples which were at Damascus. *And straightway he preached Christ in the synagogues*, that he is the Son of God. But all that heard him were amazed, and said; Is not this he that destroyed them which called on this name in Jerusalem, and came hither for that intent, that he might bring them bound unto the chief priests? But *Saul increased the more in strength, and confounded the Jews which dwelt at Damascus*, proving that this is very Christ. (Acts 9:18-22)

Paul's public ministry clearly began in the synagogues of Damascus *immediately after his conversion*, and he "did not ... consult with" Peter for another "three years"! (Galatians 1:16-18).

We could go on and on, but the reader will certainly see the point. Madrid's *modus operandi* is to assume Peter's "primacy" or "prominence" and "special role," and then read that assumption into every Biblical passage about Peter, thinking he has proven that the passages teach exactly what he had assumed before even reading them. We could use the same method to establish the "primacy" or "prominence" or "special roles" of Nathanael, Matthew, Luke, Paul and Stephen—not to mention Sodom and Artaxerxes—were we inclined to engage in Madrid's unfaithful analysis. What Madrid has really demonstrated is that the

---

473 Madrid, p. 108 (Emphasis added).

Scriptures are rather an obstacle to Petrine primacy than proof of it.

In his initial response to the question, Madrid adopted a condescending tone, as if the inquirer must not be familiar with the Scriptures: "Perhaps you aren't as familiar with the biblical evidence as you think you are."[474] In fact, we are sufficiently familiar with both the Scriptures and Madrid's fallacious approach that we can easily discern his error. It is Madrid, ironically, who is not as familiar with the biblical evidence as he claims to be.

The Eastern Problem

Madrid continues by speaking directly to a typical objection raised by the Greek Orthodox. We understand that this particular question is between eastern and western catholic rites, and evangelicals do not "have a dog in the fight." But Madrid's response is illustrative of the underlying weakness of his broader apologetic, and thus it is worth the time to interact with him here. In the introduction to his book, Madrid insisted that the apologist must "be ready always to give an answer to every man that asketh you" (1 Peter 3:15),[475] but to the Greek Orthodox, he only makes a half-hearted attempt, constructing an ineffective argument that relies more on illusion than substance. Once again, he simply assumes what he claims to prove. The Greek Orthodox question was about the authority *of the bishop of Rome*. Madrid dodges the question and argues instead for *the authority of Peter*, and—here is the leap—"by extension, his successors, the popes."[476]

To make his argument, Madrid opts out of providing the allegedly "vast and compelling" "mountain" of evidence from the early church, and instead relies on a citation from an eastern father, John Chrysostom. Madrid cites his *54th Homily on Matthew 16:13* to show that Peter was revered in the east. From this, the reader is expected to believe that Chrysostom understood the bishops of Rome to occupy the seat of authority over the whole church. The citation to which Madrid appeals actually says nothing

---

474 Madrid, p. 106.
475 Madrid, p. 21.
476 Madrid, p. 109.

of the bishops of Rome, but instead challenges those who would diminish Christ in relation to His Father to compare what the Father gave to Peter with what the Son gave to Peter:

> For the Father gave to Peter the revelation of the Son;
> but ... to a mortal man [Peter] He [the Son] entrusted the authority over all things in heaven.

Madrid uses this citation[477] to show an eastern Father's reverence *for Peter*, thinking it ought to suffice for the inquiring Greek Orthodox who questioned the authority of *the bishop of Rome*. We cannot imagine how it could. Chrysostom believed Christ promised to build his church upon "this rock," "that is, *on the faith of his [Peter's] confession*,"[478] and further, that Christ's sheep were entrusted to Peter *and his successors*, by which Chrysostom means *all bishops everywhere*. "For what purpose did He shed His blood?" Chrysostom asks, and then answers, "It was that He might win these sheep which He entrusted to Peter and his successors."[479] By "successors" here, Chrysostom means all bishops, as the context plainly reveals, for he considers himself and Basil to be successors of Peter also.[480] The truth is, there is nothing in Chrysostom to support Madrid's point. Even the *Catholic Encyclopedia* acknowledges that Chrysostom offers "*no clear and direct message in favor of the primacy of the Pope*."[481] Just keep that in mind: the *Catholic Encyclopedia* acknowledges plainly that Chrysostom offers nothing definitive in favor of the primacy of the Pope, *yet Madrid invokes Chrysostom to assure the Greek inquirer that Chrysostom is representative of early Greek fathers acknowledging the primacy of the Pope!* It is Madrid's stock-in-trade to assume that which is his duty to prove, believing the mere assumption absolves him of his duty.

That said, there are indeed some eastern fathers who spoke with sufficient clarity *against* the authority of the bishops of Rome that we can establish that the early eastern fathers did not

---

477 Madrid, p. 110.
478 Chrysostom, *54th Homily on Matthew, 3*.
479 Chrysostom, *On the Priesthood*, Book II, 2.
480 Chrysostom, *On the Priesthood*, Book II, 1.
481 *Catholic Encyclopedia*, volume 8:457A.

recognize Roman authority. Take for example, "Pope" Stephen's insistence that a Trinitarian baptism administered by heretics ought to be recognized as valid. Bishop Firmilian of Cæsarea tersely responded that Stephen was teaching the traditions of men, and that a synod in Iconium had already come to the opposite conclusion, so Stephen's opinion could be ignored:

> But that they who are at Rome do not observe those things in all cases which are handed down from the beginning, and vainly pretend the authority of the apostles; ... Whence it appears that this tradition is of men which maintains heretics, and asserts that they have baptism, which belongs to the Church alone. ... very many of us meeting together in Iconium very carefully examined the matter, and we decided that every baptism was altogether to be rejected which is arranged for without the Church.[482]

Dionysius of Alexandria objected strenuously as well, balking at Stephen's claims that an ancient apostolic tradition justified the recognition of heretical baptisms. How could we accept heretical baptism if the Scripture instructs us to admonish and avoid them? He rejected Stephen, and his successor Xystus:

> How can these comply with the customs of the ancients? ... For as we are told after a first and second admonition to avoid them [Titus 3:10], so must we admonish and converse about them, and after brief inculcation and talk in common we must desist.[483]

> And these are all they that have among us the appellation of heretics. If however we in the least let them have their way or side with them [by recognizing their baptisms], then no longer will the precept to love God with our whole heart be observed in its entirety...[484]

---

482 Cyprian of Carthage, *Epistle 74*, from Firmilian, paragraphs 6, 19.
483 Dionysius of Alexandria to Stephen of Rome.
484 Dionysius of Alexandria to Xystus of Rome.

Here we have two eastern bishops—Firmilian and Dionysius—who predated Chrysostom by more than 100 years, and they see fit not only to reject the teachings of two bishops of Rome, but to use their knowledge of Scripture to argue against their presumptuous arrogance.

Clearly Madrid has done with Chrysostom what he did with the Scriptures: He merely read into the text what he already believed before he read it. He certainly has not proven to the Greek Orthodox skeptic that "the bishop of Old Rome, the 'pope,' has authority over other bishops," or that the early eastern writers believed it to be so from the beginning.

The "Universal Bishop" Problem

Next, Madrid addresses Pope Gregory the Great's rejection of the title "Universal Bishop," but he completely misses the point and argues around it, claiming that Gregory only objected to the way the title was being used.[485] The fact is, Gregory the Great considered *the title itself*—"Universal Bishop"—to be the harbinger of antichrist and demanded that John of Constantinople "relinquish that name of pride," because "this title of pride" was clearly the precursor of the appearance of "the enemy of the human race." Gregory's demand was that no one ever take *the title* at all:

> ...we once and again addressed the same most holy John by letter, bidding him relinquish *that name of pride*, and incline the elation of his heart to the humility which our Master and Lord has taught us. ... But since it is the case, as we see, now that the end of this world is near at hand, that the enemy of the human race has already appeared in his harbingers, so as to have as his precursors, through *this title of pride*, the very priests who ought to have opposed him by living well and humbly, I exhort and entreat that not one of you ever accept *this name*, that not one consent

---

485 Madrid, p. 111.

to it, that not one write it, that not one admit it wherever it may have been written, or add his subscription to it.[486]

That is a wholesale rejection of "this title of pride." It is not a rejection of one interpretation of the title. The mere emergence of "that name of pride" was evidence, to Gregory, of "poisoned infection," and heralded the arrival of "the cunning lier-in-wait," doing great injury to the church in the process. That is not a simple rejection of one possible meaning of the title. *It is a rejection of the title*. Later Popes, of course, adopted the title anyway. And thus, the skeptic Madrid cites is justified: "Why don't you follow what Pope Gregory said?"[487] Indeed, if Pope Gregory said *no one should ever admit the title or subscribe to it*, is it not evident that Gregory believed that *no one should ever admit the title or subscribe to it*?

The early church, in any case, certainly would have had no place for it. The original structure for the church had a bishop over the local congregation, with the understanding that Christ was the Bishop of each bishop, just as Peter describes in 1 Peter 5:1-4:

> The elders which are among you I exhort, who am also an elder ...: Feed the flock of God which is among you, taking the oversight thereof .... And when the chief Shepherd shall appear, ye shall receive a crown of glory that fadeth not away.

As we observed in the chapter on Catholicism, the early church reflected this same order, and there was no *intermediate Roman bishop* between the local bishop and Christ, the Chief Shepherd. The very idea of a "Universal Bishop" between Christ and the individual congregations was foreign to the apostolic church, and did not arise until the carnal ambitions of the Roman bishop finally began to hold sway several centuries later. It certainly was no apostolic tradition.

---

486 *Registrum Epistolarum*, Book IX, Epistle 68 (emphasis added).
487 Madrid, p. 111.

Madrid talks around these historical facts. Instead of facing the truth that "Universal Bishop" was a title unknown in the early church and rejected on its face by Gregory, he rather attempts to prove that Gregory exercised universal authority over the other bishops, and thus, that Gregory must have been "Universal Bishop" even though he himself rejected the title:

> In *Epistle 10*, Pope Gregory ... rejected some candidates for bishop who had already been approved by other bishops. ... In *Epistle 17*, we see Pope Gregory intervening in the affairs of the church at Firmium. ... In *Epistle 81*, Pope Gregory restored Bishop Maximus to communion with the Catholic Church.[488]

By these examples, Madrid believes he has shown that Gregory must have been worthy of the very title he forbade, and therefore he must have accepted implicitly a title that he had rejected explicitly. Very well! Let us use Madrid's own standard to prove that Cyprian of Carthage must also have been the "Universal Bishop" over the Bishop of Rome.

The Roman clergy wrote to "Father Cyprian" of Carthage, confessing their many crimes and shortcomings.[489] The Roman congregation later wrote to Carthage for help when "schismatical parties" rebelled against the lawfully elected bishop and set up their own.[490] Cyprian wrote back demanding that the factious parties "acquiesce in these my letters."[491] Both the Bishop of Rome[492] and the schismatics[493] wrote back to Cyprian to thank him for intervening in the Roman congregation to restore unity there. In *Epistle 54*, Cyprian intervened in the affairs of the church at Rome, writing to "Pope" Cornelius to "both warn and ask" that Cyprian's letters be read aloud to the Roman congregation so that "any contagion of envenomed speech and of pestilent

---

488 Madrid, pp. 114-115.
489 Cyprian of Carthage, *Epistle 30*, The Roman Clergy to Cyprian.
490 Cyprian of Carthage, *Epistle 40*, To Cornelius 2.
491 Cyprian of Carthage, *Epistle 43*, To the Roman Confessors.
492 Cyprian of Carthage, *Epistle 45*, Cornelius to Cyprian.
493 Cyprian of Carthage, *Epistle 49*, Maximus and the Other Confessors to Cyprian.

propagation … may be all purged out of the ears and of the hearts of the brethren," and that their ears and hearts "may be cleansed anew from all the filth of heretical disparagement."[494] In *Epistle 67* Cyprian of Carthage overturned "Pope" Stephen's direction to restore lapsed bishops Basilides and Martialis to the episcopate in Spain.[495] Cyprian wrote not only to "approve, but applaud"[496] the Spanish congregation for electing and installing more respectable bishops Sabinus and Felix in their place. Stephen could be ignored, Cyprian wrote, because he had been "deceived" and "taken … by surprise" and "surprised by fraud."[497] Thus did Cyprian assert himself as the bishop of the bishop of Rome.

Applying Madrid's highly selective standard, Cyprian so insinuated himself into the operation, administration and affairs of the Roman congregation, and so deferential was the Roman congregation to Cyprian, that no other conclusion is possible: The bishop of Rome *had as his bishop* the bishop of Carthage: Cyprian! We hope the point is obvious to the reader. Madrid's propensity to read the historical data with a selective bias toward Roman primacy is nothing short of pathological. If Madrid's inferences were valid, Cyprian of Carthage would have been the Pope's Pope!

The Infallibility Problem

Having argued for the primacy of the Bishop of Rome, Madrid now turns the matter of his infallibility. At Vatican Council I in 1870, the Roman Pontiff was declared to be "infallible" when in his role as the shepherd and teacher of all Christians he defines "a doctrine concerning faith or morals to be held by the whole Church."[498] Such a definition has been much debated in the centuries since Vatican, even within Roman Catholicism. Although the authority by which such a papal statement may be propagated is precisely defined (i.e., "in the exercise of his office as shepherd"), there remains nothing but confusion in the minds of Roman Catholics about when the

---

494 Cyprian of Carthage, *Epistle 54*, To Cornelius 20.
495 Cyprian of Carthage, *Epistle 67*, To the Clergy and People Abiding in Spain.
496 Cyprian of Carthage, *Epistle 67*, To the Clergy and People Abiding in Spain 9.
497 Cyprian of Carthage, *Epistle 67*, To the Clergy and People Abiding in Spain 5.
498 *Pastor Æternus*, 18 July 1870.

pope actually exercises that authority (i.e., "when the Roman Pontiff speaks *ex cathedra*," from the chair of Peter). Evidence of the confusion may be seen simply by asking Roman Catholics how many times the Roman Pontiff has ever spoken *ex cathedra*. They do not know. Some say he has only exercised the charism of infallibility once. Others, twice. Others four times, ... or eleven, ... or eighteen.

> John Vidmar: one time[499]
> Scott Hahn: two times[500]
> Tim Staples: at least four times[501]
> Adam Miller: eleven times[502]
> Leslie Rumble: eighteen times[503]

Roman Catholic apologist Robert Sungenis sums up the problem most succinctly. In an argument with other Roman Catholics whether *Ordinatio Sacerdotalis was* declared infallibly by Pope John Paul II, he lamented:

> The reason someone could question the infallible status of *Ordinatio Sacerdotalis* is that the language John Paul II used in the decree gave some doubt as to whether he was making it infallible. This is why I said earlier that when the Church makes something infallible, I wish they would just do it plainly and clearly, as Canon 749.3 requires.[504]

And that brings us back to Madrid's earlier response on papal infallibility: "Your question is based on a common misunderstanding" that papal *infallibility* means papal *impeccability*.[505] But that is to

499 John Vidmar, O.P. , *The Catholic Church Through the Ages: A History*, (2005) 289; Gary Wills, *Why I Am a Catholic* (2002), xiii.
500 Hahn, Scott, "A Biblical Understanding of Mary," tape 3 of 4, side 1.
501 Staples, Tim, "All Generations Shall Call Me Blessed," tape 2 of 6, side 1.
502 Miller, Adam S., *The Final Word*, (Gaithersburg, MD: Tower of David Publications, 1997), p. 28.
503 Rumble et al., *That Catholic Church: A Radio Analysis*, (St. Paul, MN, Radio Replies Press, 1954), p. 81.
504 Sungenis, Robert (August 5, 2008), blog. Retrieved October 26, 2014 from the world wide web at http://catholicintl.com/question-85-july-2008/.
505 Madrid, p. 119.

sidestep the real issue. Everyone, including every Roman Catholic apologist, already understands and freely acknowledges that popes sin and make mistakes. About that, there is no debate. Everyone, including every informed Protestant apologist, already understands and freely acknowledges that only *ex cathedra* statements are in view when we talk about "papal infallibility." The language of *Pastor Æternus* makes that quite clear.

However, there is a yawning gap that separates the presumption of teaching authority and whether that authority has been duly exercised, and nobody seems to know when the Pope has exercised it. Thus, it is left up to each individual Roman Catholic to determine *on his own* whether or not the Pope has spoken *ex cathedra*. Even battle-hardened Roman apologists do not know! The predictable result is that every Roman Catholic—clergy and lay— is thus faced with the unenviable task of examining every papal statement and comparing it against the Scriptures, the councils, and centuries of other magisterial documents and patristic writings to determine whether the pope has correctly spoken congruently with historical Roman Catholic teaching, or perhaps has made a mistake. It is no simple task, and the Magisterium of the church cannot help.

And yet, in addition to that Gordian knot which no pope or apologist can untie, there is another problem Madrid has created for himself on the topic of infallibility. In his defense of the dogma, he reveals his propensity to read papal and Petrine primacy into every passage of Scripture. In answering the question on infallibility, Madrid insists that Jesus cannot possibly keep His promise of "He who hear you hears me" without the infallibility dogma:

> The Lord's promises, such as 'Whatever you bind on earth will be bound in heaven, and whatever your loose on earth will be loosed in heaven' (Matthew 16:18-19), and, 'He who hear you hears me, and he who rejects you rejects me' (Luke 10:16), would be impossible to keep if He hadn't established some way to ensure that Peter and his successors

did not lead the church into error through teaching as true
what was actually erroneous.[506]

But there is a problem with Madrid's claim. Jesus did not say, "He
who hear you hears me, and he who rejects you rejects me" to Peter.
Nor did He say this to any apostle at all. He said it rather to the
Seventy, among whom not one apostle was to be found. Jesus had
gathered the Twelve together "and gave them power and authority
over all devils, and to cure diseases" (Luke 9:1). Afterward He
appointed *another Seventy* to go out preaching (Luke 10:1). *It is
to the Seventy*—not to Peter or even to the Twelve—that the Lord
said, "He who hear you hears me, and he who rejects you rejects
me." Madrid has thrown down the gauntlet, insisting that such a
promise as this "would be impossible to keep if [Jesus] hadn't established" some mechanism of infallibility. Very well! Using Madrid's
own standard, the Seventy and their successors must have been
infallible! But how on earth will Madrid track down the Seventy
and two thousand years of their successors to be sure he has heard
Christ and not rejected Him? They must have possessed infallibility, as Madrid himself insists: Such a promise "would be impossible
to keep" unless Jesus had conferred infallibility upon them. Will he
adjust his convictions accordingly?

Such is the corner into which the Roman apologist paints
himself when he reads Petrine and papal primacy into every
verse. But there is relief for him if he will only seek it. The Seventy
were fallible, like everyone else. Just as there is no reason to infer
extraordinary magisterial infallibility of the Seventy from *their*
commission to preach in Jesus' name, there is likewise no need to
infer the extraordinary magisterial infallibility of Peter from *his*
commission. After all, Peter (Galatians 2:11) and the Seventy (Luke
10:17-20) were prone to mistakes. And if Jesus could commission
the Seventy without extraordinary magisterial infallibility, surely
He could commission Peter without it, too.

---

506 Madrid, 120-121.

Statues, Icons, and the Sin of Idolatry

—————————— (Zins) ——————————

It is a well-known fact that the Roman Catholic community makes elaborate use of statues, images, and carvings of wood and stone. Boettner points out:

> With this official encouragement (omission of the 2nd commandment) it is not surprising that images of Christ, Mary, the saints and angels are very common in Roman Catholic circles. They are found in the churches, schools, hospitals, homes, and other places. Occasionally one even sees a little image of Jesus or Mary or some saint on the dashboard of an automobile (often the image of St. Christopher, the patron saint of travelers).[507]

This being noted, there is great controversy whether these kinds of things are forbidden by the second of the 10 Commandments. Madrid obviously says they are not. We shall attempt to discern

---

507 Lorraine Boettner, *Roman Catholicism* (Presbyterian and Reformed Publishing Company Phillipsburg, New Jersey), 1962, p. 280.

and reply to his logic in a moment. However, we must first turn our attention to the Roman Catholic use of the second commandment. In a bold display of Roman Catholic disregard for the text of the Bible, She has put together a list of the 10 Commandments to be used in Her catechism classes and schools that omits the second commandment altogether. This is done despite the fact the New American Bible (Roman Catholic standard) and the Old Douay Rheims version of the Bible (former Roman Catholic standard) contain the second commandment as a separate commandment. In short, Rome does not dare take it out of Her Bible translations (this would be outrageous even by Rome's ethics), but She compiles a new list for teaching purposes. To arrive at the number 10, to give impression that She is quoting the Bible, Rome simply eliminates the second and breaks the tenth into two separate command-ments to arrive at the number 10. Let us hear the reason for such underhandedness.

Here is the presumption of the Roman Catholic apologist. Even though Rome's own Bibles have the second commandment in detail both in Exodus and Deuteronomy, Madrid finds a way to justify its elimination in Roman Catholic teaching.

> The first Commandment is against idolatry of any kind, including statue worship. So it's senseless to divide it, as Protestants do, into two separate commandments. To worship a graven image as an idol is the exact same sin as "having strange gods" before God himself.[508]

The problem here for Madrid is that Protestants do not divide one into two. They are divided in the Bible! They are divided in the Protestant and Roman Catholic Bibles. What is not divided is the tenth commandment. It is one single commandment in all versions of the Bible. Yet, Rome divides the tenth into two to suit Her own purpose of eliminating commandment number two!

It is not a stretch to conclude that Rome wants no part in having to explain, in Her schools and Catechism Classes, the full

---

508 Madrid, p. 130.

weight of the second commandment. Here is the second commandment taken from the Roman Catholic *New American Bible Revised Edition*.

> You shall not make for yourself an idol or a likeness of anything in the heavens above or on the earth below or in the waters beneath the earth; you shall not bow down before them or serve them. For I, the LORD, your God, am a jealous God, inflicting punishment for their ancestors' wickedness on the children of those who hate me, down to the third and fourth generation.[509]

Even though Madrid thinks it is "senseless" to separate commandment two from commandment one, his own religion keeps the two as separate in their version of the Bible because that is the way the Bible is written. Knowing this, Madrid cannot simply ignore the true second commandment. So how does he get around it? He does so by insisting that the Lord is only concerned with idolatry and not with the "carving of graven images." Madrid then cites examples of graven images commanded by the Lord in the Old Testament. While it is true that the Lord superintended the building of the temple and commanded the making of a bronze serpent and images of the angels, these things to do not mitigate God's own second commandment. The difference is that God ordered these kinds of things for His purposes. These are not concoctions of man designed to be used in worship. Madrid misses the point of the brazen serpent. Even things ordered by God for the good of His people can be misused and abused. Such was the case of the brazen serpent. Though designed to be an intentional test of faith to protect Israel, it had to be destroyed when the bronze serpent began to be worshipped (2 Kings 18:4). So it is with man. Hence the commandment to not make graven images is fully illustrated in Israel's ultimate misuse of the bronze serpent. It is the sinful nature of man to make an image the object of worship. It

---

509 New American Bible Revised Edition (confraternity of Christian Doctrine) online NABRE edition, Exodus 20:4,5.

is no secret in Rome that Her devotees worship a piece of bread in a gold monstrance, thinking it to be Jesus Christ. However, Rome excuses the excess veneration given to statues. Listen to the council of Trent:

> Moreover, that the *images* of Christ, of the Virgin Mother of God, and of the other saints, are to be had and retained particularly in temples, and that due *honour and veneration are to be given them*; not that any divinity, or virtue, is believed to be in them, on account of which they are to be worshipped; or that anything is to be asked of them; or, that trust is to be reposed in images, as was of old done by the Gentiles who placed their hope in idols; but because the honour which is shown them is referred to the prototypes which those images represent; in such wise that by *the images which we kiss, and before which we uncover the head, and prostrate ourselves*, we adore Christ; and we venerate the saints, whose similitude they bear: as, by the decrees of Councils, and especially of the second Synod of Nicaea, has been defined against the opponents of images.[510]

The commandment is clear that Christians are not to bow down before graven images. Rome wiggles out of this by asserting they are in fact worshipping the prototype. Rome is ignorant of the commandment's intent as well as the heart of man. Man will turn the image into something superstitious. Man will kiss the idol. Rome stands ready to control the mind of man and sell him the worthless idol. Madrid expects Roman Catholics to use images without a hint of superstition. However, a quick look at Rome's "no hint of superstition" is crushed by the endless marketing of Rome's delusory claims for one of her popular medals. When asked why one should wear a St. Benedict medal here is the answer from a Roman Catholic website:

---

510 Council of Trent 25th session. Emphasis mine.

The medal is a way to obtain God's blessing and protection
through the intercession of St. Benedict....

One can go to a website that promotes the top 60 medals in the
Roman Catholic religion. Roman Catholics are taught to give *dulia*
[veneration accorded to saints] to images, *hyperdulia* [heightened
degree of dulia] to Mary, and *latria* [highest form of veneration] to
God alone. These categories of worship are designed to protect the
Roman Catholic practice of violating the second commandment
already removed from their teaching communities.

For the sake of simplicity let us compare the second commandment as stated in the Roman Catholic *New American Revised Edition*
with the *New Roman Catholic Catechism*.

> You shall not make for yourself *an idol or a likeness* of
> anything in the heavens above or on the earth below or
> in the waters beneath the earth; you shall not bow down
> before them or serve them. (New American Bible Revised)

> Following the divinely inspired teaching of our holy
> Fathers and the tradition of the Catholic Church (for we
> know that this tradition comes from the Holy Spirit who
> dwells in her) we rightly define with full certainty and cor-
> rectness that, like the figure of the precious and life-giving
> cross, venerable and holy images of our Lord and God and
> Savior, Jesus Christ, our inviolate Lady, the holy Mother of
> God, and the venerated angels, all the saints and the just,
> whether painted or made of mosaic or another suitable
> material, are to be exhibited in the holy churches of God, on
> sacred vessels and vestments, walls and panels, in houses
> and on streets.[511]

It is no wonder why Roman Catholic apologists wish to hide the
second commandment from their pupils and congregations. The
Roman Catholic propensity to usurp the plain meaning of the

---

511 New Catholic Catechism p. 300 #1161.

Bible and overlay Her man-made religious system is apparent and appalling at every turn.

The Blessed Virgin Mary

————— (Kauffman) —————

M adrid begins his chapter on Mary by acknowledging that the Scriptures refer to Jesus' brothers, but maintains and defends the Roman Catholic belief that she remained a "perpetual virgin" throughout her life. He addresses the matter first from the Scriptures, claiming that the Scriptural term "brothers of the Lord" must not have referred to literal brothers, and then makes a passing comment that "Christian Tradition" has "upheld and affirmed" the doctrine of Mary's perpetual virginity "since the earliest years" of the church.[512] While Madrid acknowledges that there is no dispute over Mary's virginity before Jesus' birth (*ante partum*), he limits the discussion to "whether she remained that way after His birth" (*post partum*), inexplicably omitting the third leg of the Roman Catholic doctrine: her virginity *during* Christ's birth (*in partu*). Mary's virginity *in partu* is an extremely important and indispensable element of the "perpetual virginity" doctrine, which alleges that her physical virginity was not compromised even during childbirth: no labor pangs, no tearing of the flesh, no blood, no opening of the womb. All three elements of the doctrine are important to any conversation on the history of the dogma of Mary's alleged

---

512 Madrid, pp. 134-136.

"perpetual virginity." We shall interact with his arguments and explore the significance of his omission.

The Scriptural Argument

Regarding the Scriptural data, Madrid relies on the hypothesis first proposed by Jerome in 383 AD, namely that while the Greek *adelphos* (brethren) can mean literal brothers, it can also mean relatives, neighbors, countrymen or fellow believers:

> The Greek word for 'brother' is *adelphos*. Not unlike the way the word "brother" is used in modern English, *adelphos* also had a variety of meanings in the New Testament. The literal meaning referred to siblings born of the same mother or father (or both). But *adelphos* was also used in a much wider nonliteral sense, referring, for example, to the first followers of Christ, to any fellow human being, to one's fellow countrymen, to friends, extended family, and neighbors, and also to fellow Christians.[513]

We reject at least one of Madrid's claims, namely that "brethren" can be used to refer "to any fellow human being." That is not true. His proof text for this is Matthew 25:40 in which the goats are separated from the sheep. In that verse, the King says, "Inasmuch as ye have done it unto one of *the least of these my brethren*, ye have done it unto me." Madrid has "brethren" here referring "to any fellow human being," but in context "these my brethren" refers specifically to "these sheep" on His right. It is a reference to fellow believers, not a general reference to any human being on earth. That said, Madrid holds that the various meanings of the word "brethren" must be determined by context. We certainly agree.

The allegorical use of "brethren"

Let us first observe that the reason the words "brethren" and "sisters" may be used so *flexibly* is precisely because of what they are known to mean *literally*: children with a common biological

---

513 Madrid, p. 134.

parent. The New Testament use of "brother" and "sister" as a term of endearment between fellow believers is because through Christ all believers have a common Father (John 20:17). Likewise, the reason "brethren" is used to describe citizens of the same country or neighbors from the same town is because the Greek words for country or hometown (πατρίδα, patrida) have "father" as a common root. In these senses, the "brethren" are so called because they, at least allegorically, have a common parent: God the Father, or the country or town of origin. Thus, the *allegorical* sense only makes sense because of the *literal* meaning.

That said, it is true that Jesus uses the term "brethren" to refer to His countrymen (e.g., Matthew 5:47) and to disciples (e.g., John 20:17), but it is also true that the Gospel writers possessed the means to differentiate between those uses. John distinguishes between "brethren" and "disciples" in John 2:12:

> After this he went down to Capernaum, he, and his mother, and his brethren (ἀδελφοὶ), and his disciples (μαθηταὶ): *and they continued there not many days.* (John 2:12)

Here, "brethren" is not intended to indicate believers, since "disciples" serves that function. Likewise in John 7:3:

> His brethren (ἀδελφοὶ) therefore said unto him, Depart hence, and go into Judaea, that thy disciples (μαθηταί) *also may see the works that thou* doest. (John 7:3)

Here, "brethren" does not refer to believers, for John 7:5 indicates that the "brethren" in this passage did not "believe in him."

In the Gospel of Luke, Jesus distinguishes between "brethren" and more distant "relatives":

> And ye shall be betrayed both by parents, and brethren (ἀδελφῶν), and kinsfolks (συγγενῶν), and friends; and some of you shall they cause to be put to death. (Luke 21:16)

Here, "brethren" refers neither to cousins nor to distant relatives, for "kinsfolks" serves that function. "Brethren" refers rather to siblings of the common parents just mentioned. Otherwise, there would have been no need to distinguish between "brethren" and "kinsfolks." The New Testament writers thus had the means to differentiate between brothers, relatives and disciples when context required it.

The literal use of "brethren"

The New Testament authors also had the means to make clear that "brothers" and "sisters" were to be understood literally as children who have one or two biological parents in common. When the terms "brother" and "sister" and "children" are used in the immediate context of a "mother" and a "father," or "parents," it is clear that the terms "brother" and "sister" and "children" refer to immediate blood relations between family members with common parents. In these cases, the meaning is obviously in the literal sense.

There is no doubt, for example, that the Sadducees intended such a meaning in their reference to the hypothetical "seven brethren" in Matthew 22:25 (c.f. Mark 12:20; Luke 20:29). The Old Testament passage upon which their argument was based assumed that the "brethren" yet unmarried "dwell together" in their father's household. The Levirate obligation of each succeeding brother is described in terms of "a brother-in-law's" duty to his departed brother's wife (Deuteronomy 25:5,7). The Sadducees' question was therefore posed in regard to seven *literal* brothers who had dwelt together under their father's roof. Likewise, in the parable of the rich man and Lazarus, the rich man's reference to his "five brethren" is made in the context of men living together in "my father's house" (Luke 16:27-28). The reference is to actual brethren from a common father.

Just so, Jesus said he came to cause division between son and father, mother and daughter (Matthew 10:35-36; Luke 12:51), resulting in collateral strife between children from those parents: "brother shall deliver up the brother to death" (Matthew 10:21;

c.f. Mark 13:11). Here, the context plainly indicates that "brother" betraying "brother" is to be understood in its literal sense because it is used in the proximate context of "children" who "shall rise up against their parents."

Likewise when Jesus warns against obstacles to discipleship, He says one must hate "his father, and mother, and wife, and children, and brethren, and sisters" (Luke 14:26). The brethren and sisters are to be understood literally in that they are from the same family, from the same parents, as the context plainly indicates. Similarly, when Peter inquires after the rewards of discipleship, Jesus insists that "every one that hath forsaken houses, or brethren, or sisters, or father, or mother, or wife, or children, or lands" will receive a hundred fold in return (Matthew 19:29; Mark 10:29-30). In context of *what is forsaken* to follow Christ, "brethren" and "sisters" are to be understood in their literal sense in light of the proximate reference to "father" and "mother," likewise forsaken. *What is rewarded* a hundredfold, of course, cannot be literal, for one cannot replace literal fathers, mothers, brothers and sisters, but what is *forsaken* most certainly is literal. The "brethren" and "sisters" forsaken to follow Christ are left behind with the parents, the common biological "father" and "mother."

Similar use of "brethren" and "sisters" is employed by Paul when he admonishes Timothy to be pure, respectful and considerate in his relationships:

> Rebuke not an elder, but intreat him as a father; and the younger men as brethren; The elder women as mothers; the younger as sisters, with all purity. (1 Timothy 5:1-2)

In this context, Paul is not instructing Timothy to treat older men and women as uncles and aunts and younger men and women as cousins. Rather, as the context clearly shows by Paul's use of "mother," "father," "brother" and "sister," the nuclear family is the idealized model to which he appeals, and therefore just as elders are to be treated as if they were *literal parents*, younger men and women were to be treated as if they were *literal siblings* from those parents. Paul leaves no doubt as to his meaning.

The particular description of Jesus' "brethren"

In view of this evidence, the words "brethren" and "sisters" ought to be understood in their literal sense when used in the context of "father," "mother" and "parents." It is quite revealing therefore that when Jesus' "brethren" and "sisters" are identified in the Scriptures, *it is always in the context of one or both of their parents.* Of the nine times His brethren and sisters are mentioned, eight of them are explicitly in the company of His father or mother, or both:

> Is not this *the carpenter's* son? is not *his mother* called Mary? *and his brethren*, James, and Joses, and Simon, and Judas? And *his sisters*, are they not all with us? (Matthew 13:55-56; c.f. Mark 6:3)

> After this he went down to Capernaum, he, and *his mother, and his brethren*, and his disciples: and they continued there not many days. (John 2:12)

> While he yet talked to the people, behold, *his mother and his brethren* stood without, desiring to speak with him. Then one said unto him, Behold, *thy mother and thy brethren* stand without, desiring to speak with thee. (Matthew 12:46-47; c.f., Mark 3:31-32; Luke 8:19-20)

> These all continued with one accord in prayer and supplication, with the women, and *Mary the mother of Jesus, and with his brethren.* (Acts 1:14)

In these passages, when Jesus' brethren and sisters are mentioned *it is in the context of His parents*, and always immediately after a conspicuous mention of their common mother, Mary.

Only once are Jesus brethren *not* mentioned in the explicit context of Joseph or Mary. His unbelieving brethren say to Him,

"Depart hence, and go into Judaea, that thy disciples also may see the works that thou doest" (John 7:3,5). Here, the unbelieving brethren are clearly the same family members who heard of His preaching and went out to retrieve Him, saying "He is beside himself" (Mark 3:21), and unsurprisingly, when they arrived on the scene, they arrive as a family, *"his brethren and his mother"* (Mark 3:21).

Thus, as the Biblical data plainly illustrate, it is indeed true that "brethren" and "sisters" can be, and in fact are, used in the New Testament to refer to fellow countrymen, townsfolk and believers. This is done in the allegorical sense of a common "patris" or father, whether it be country, hometown or Jesus' own Father. Nevertheless, when "brother" and "sister" or "brethren" and "sisters" and "children" are used in the same context as a "father" and a "mother," it is clear that a nuclear family comprised of parents and children is intended. Jesus' brethren and sisters are always found in the context of one or both of His parents, and therefore they are to be understood literally as His brothers and sisters.

Traditional Argument

As we noted earlier, Madrid raises a novel objection to Jesus having brothers and sisters by Mary, and we use the word "novel" advisedly. For the first three hundred years of the church, there were essentially two prevalent theories on the brethren of the Lord. On the one hand, it was supposed that such "brethren" were children of Joseph by a previous marriage;[514] on the other hand, other men appealed to the natural meaning of the words, and took His "brethren" to be of "blood-relationship,"[515] "His very nearest relatives."[516] In no case was the matter considered a moral or doctrinal obligation. Men had varying opinions, but in the words of Basil (370 AD), it was not doctrinally relevant to take one side or the other. Had Mary consummated her marriage to Joseph and borne children to him, he wrote, it "would not have affected the

---

514 Origen, *Commentary on Matthew*, Book 10, chapter 17.
515 Tertullian, *Against Marcion*, Book IV.19.
516 Tertullian, *On the Flesh of Christ*, 7.

teaching of our religion at all."[517] But matters took a sudden turn at the end of the fourth century:

> Such was the state of opinion, when towards the close of the fourth century Jerome struck out a novel hypothesis ... in which he put forward his own view. He maintained that the Lord's brethren were his cousins after the flesh, being sons of Mary the wife of Alphaeus and sister of the Virgin. Thus, as he boasted, he asserted the virginity not of Mary only, but of Joseph also.[518]

Setting aside the merits or demerits of his hypothesis, no one can deny that Jerome's hypothesis was late-breaking and new. He was truly striking out on his own, and as a product of his time, he was overwhelmed by a sudden fascination with virginal bodies of women. Much time, ink and papyrus were spent on the exposition and interpretation thereof in the waning years of the fourth century. As David Hunter, formerly Chair of Catholic Studies at Iowa State University, and again at the University of Kentucky, now Chair of Catholic Theology at Boston College, observes, there was a sudden, stepwise collective fascination with virginal female bodies in the closing years of the fourth century:

> In the later years of the fourth century the ascetic and monastic movements led male Christian writers to devote *an extraordinary degree of attention to the bodies of women, especially celibate women.* In the hands of ascetic authors the traditional biblical image of the virgin bride acquired new life. The 'bride of Christ' became the celibate Christian woman. ... In the ascetic controversies of the late fourth century, the identity of the virgin bride—and specifically the question of the relationship between the individual

---

517 Basil, *Homilia in Sanctam Christi Generationem*, 5. (Some apologists claim this Homily is spurious, but esteemed Roman Catholic Mariologist, Juniper B. Carol, O.F.M., held it to be authentic, "without any doubt" (*Mariology* (Milwaukee: The Bruce Publishing Company, 1955), vol. ii)).
518 Lightfoot, J. B. *St. Paul's Epistle to the Galatians, a Revised Text* (Andover: Warren F. Draper, Publisher (1870)), 89.

Christian as virgin and the church as virgin—was clearly a point of contention.[519]

Jerome was not immune to the winds and waves of the changing seas, and was driven upon them like a rudderless ship. He, like many others, became entranced by the very thought of virginity—male and female—proposing that Joseph, too, must have been a virgin,[520] and that Peter was named chief of the apostles according to age, whereas the youthful John, a virgin, would have been a better candidate for the office.[521] As evidence of Jerome's feckless and wavering positions on such things, we simply highlight his perfunctory response to Helvidius on Mary's physical virginity *in partu*. In 383 AD Helvidius had written not only that the Scriptures attributed additional children to Mary, but also what was plainly obvious: *that Jesus' birth had been entirely natural*:

> [A]re we bound to blush at the thought of Mary having a husband after she was delivered? If they find any disgrace in this, they ought not consistently even to believe that God was born of the Virgin by natural delivery. For according to them *there is more dishonour in a virgin giving birth to God by the organs of generation*, than in a virgin being joined to her own husband after she has been delivered.[522]

In response, Jerome was so swift to defend Mary's *post partum* virginity against the Helvidian onslaught that he flew right past the loss of her virginity *in partu*, and conceded it as given:

> Add, if you like, Helvidius, the other humiliations of nature, the womb for nine months growing larger, *the sickness, the delivery, the blood*, the swaddling-clothes.

---

519   Hunter, David G. *The American Society of Church History*, June 2000, 283-84.
520   Jerome, *Against Helvidius*, 21.
521   Jerome, *Against Jovinianus*, Book I.26.
522   Jerome (quoting Helvidius), *Against Helvidius*, 20.

> Picture to yourself *the infant in the enveloping membranes.*
> ... We do not blush, we are not put to silence.[523]

When it came to imagining Jesus' delivery, no *in partu* detail was too graphic, no *in partu* humiliation too severe to be mentioned — for mother or for Child—so long as her *post partum* virginity was left untouched. Yet only ten years later, Jerome succumbed to the times and reversed course, not only insisting on Mary's *in partu* virginity, but so convinced of it that he believed he was under no obligation to defend it! Jesus, he now believed, had passed through Mary's "door" without opening it:

> Let my critics explain to me how Jesus can have entered
> in through closed doors when He allowed His hands and
> His side to be handled, and showed that He had bones and
> flesh, thus proving that His was a true body and no mere
> phantom of one, and I will explain how the holy Mary can
> be at once a mother and a virgin. A mother before she was
> wedded, she remained a virgin after bearing her son.[524]

Such was Jerome's varying position, driven and tossed by the contemporary winds of fashion. Yet that novelty—three centuries removed from the apostles—is the one upon which Madrid lands in order to settle the dispute, claiming with a wave of the hand that he has "Tradition" on his side: "Christian Tradition since the earliest years upheld and affirmed the consistent teaching that Mary was a perpetual virgin." To informed Protestants and honest Roman Catholics, such a claim is laughable. As David Hunter observed, the late-breaking "Marian doctrine (*virginitas in partu*) had only a fragile basis in earlier Christian tradition."[525] For good reason, preeminent Roman Catholic Mariologist Juniper Carol observed that establishing the dogma of Mary's perpetual virginity as an apostolic tradition is "an impossible task with our present

---

523 Jerome (383 AD), *Against Helvidius*, 20.
524 Jerome (393 A.D.) Epistle 48 to Pammachius, 21.
525 Hunter, David G., *Marriage, Celibacy and Heresy in Ancient Christianity* (Oxford University Press, 2007, p. 285).

documentary sources."[526] Yet Madrid rushes in where intelligent scholars fear to tread.

We revisit this history to establish that neither Mary's *in partu* virginity nor her *post partum* virginity were considered settled doctrines even as late as the fourth century, and that the weight of Roman Catholic scholarship is definitively *against* Madrid's claim that the doctrine had been upheld "since the earliest years." As Juniper Carol observed, "even in the middle of the 4th century" we are not surprised to find "persons, sometimes of considerable authority and prestige, who attributed to Jesus a veritable cortege of brothers and sisters."[527] And as evidenced by Jerome's cavalier 383 AD acceptance of the loss of Mary's virginity at Christ's birth, it is clear that there was no definitive dogma on her *in partu* virginity either. It is not until the end of the fourth century that we begin to find serious, polemical and militant opposition to the loss of virginity *in partu* and the idea of Jesus having siblings from Mary. Such a late-breaking novelty as Madrid proposes can hardly be construed as "apostolic," and Madrid's attempt to defend it as such is easily dismissed.

An Abnormal Marriage

As Madrid continues, he addresses the standard objection that it "would not have been normal" for Mary and Joseph to live in marital celibacy. He then walks through several aspects of Mary's life that were not "normal," and concludes that we ought not expect her marriage to be any more "normal" than the rest of her life.

The Annunciation

Here Madrid once again projects his own fanciful narrative onto the Scriptures, and then reads the Scriptures through that lens. He claims that "God's plan for Joseph and Mary was arranged according to what was fitting," and therefore we need to set aside what might otherwise be "normal." "My thoughts are not your

---

526 Carol, J., *Mariology*, vol ii (267).
527 Carol, J., *Mariology*, vol ii (141–142)

thoughts," God says, and therefore Mary must have taken a vow of perpetual virginity:

> The most likely, even certain, reason for Mary not having other children is that she had made a vow of perpetual virginity when she was a girl.[528]

To support this statement, Madrid cites Augustine's claim that Mary would not have responded to Gabriel with surprise "unless she had already vowed her virginity to God."[529] Thus, her question, "How shall this be, seeing I know not a man? (Luke 1:34), must have meant, "How shall this be, seeing that I have already vowed my virginity to God?" To this we respond that like Jerome, Augustine too was a product of his time, equally fascinated with virginity, believing that Mary had taken her vow in order "to be a pattern to holy virgins."[530]

Augustine's fascination with "holy virgins" came when the rite of "consecration of virgins had become a formal practice in the Western church only at the end of the fourth century,"[531] at which time ecclesiastical writers started reading contemporary fads into ancient Scriptural narratives. As David Hunter notes, Pope Siricius had gone so far as to excommunicate a consecrated virgin who stumbled into marriage—an offense as grave as incest and adultery—for which she could not effectually repent until her husband died.[532] Augustine, caught up in the same nonsense, reinterpreted the Scriptures accordingly, as if there could be no other possible explanation for Mary's response than a vow of consecrated virginity. But there is a much simpler explanation. In view of Jewish betrothal customs, the apparent urgency of Gabriel's announcement, and Mary's behavior after his visit, it is clear that Mary was not surprised to find that she would *ever* become

---

528 Madrid, p. 137.
529 Augustine, *Of Holy Virginity* 4.
530 Ibid.
531 Hunter, 288.
532 Hunter, p. 288 (Pope Siricius, *Ad Gallos Episcopus*, Patrologia Latina (P.L.), vol 13, col 1182).

pregnant, but rather to discover that she would become pregnant *before she was taken to wife.*

According to Mishnah *Ketubbot* 5.2, a virgin is given a year from betrothal to prepare herself for marriage, during which time she remains under her father's roof. Gabriel's visit was early in her betrothal, and yet he came bearing imminent news: "behold (ἰδού), thou shalt conceive in thy womb" (Luke 1:31). Such a greeting, "behold," or literally, "Look!" "is an attention grabber appropriate to the context, [and] often introduces something new or unusual, or something that requires special attention."[533] Something very significant was about to happen. Just as Gabriel's "behold (ἰδού)" as spoken to Zacharias a few verses earlier indicated that he would *become immediately mute,* just so the "behold (ἰδού)" to Mary indicated that she would *become immediately pregnant,* and so she interprets it: "Behold the handmaid of the Lord; be it unto me according to thy word" (Luke 1:38). Mary forthwith departed "with haste" (Luke 1:39) to visit her cousin Elizabeth, announcing that she "hath rejoiced" at what the Lord "hath done" (Luke 1:49), spending "about three months" with her, and then "returned to her own house" (Luke 1:56). Although she was *betrothed,* none of her behavior suggests that *the marriage was imminent* at the time of Gabriel's visit. Matthew relates that Mary "was found with child" (Matthew 1:18), indicating that Joseph was not told of the pregnancy, but rather discovered it on his own, something that could have happened no earlier than Mary's return from her visit with Elizabeth, at the beginning of the second trimester (Luke 1:56), when a woman begins to show visibly. Thus, while Mary did not act as if her marriage was imminent, *her pregnancy certainly was.* Her question to Gabriel, therefore, rather than revealing a vow of perpetual virginity, more naturally expresses puzzlement about the proper order of events—to wit, how a pregnancy could take place *immediately* when marriage was still *a distant event.* There is nothing in the text here to suggest the certainty, as Madrid claims, of "a vow of perpetual virginity." Madrid simply followed

---

533 *Revised English Version Bible and Commentary,* Matthew 1:20, https://www.revisedenglishversion.com/Matthew/chapter1/20.

Augustine in his ridiculous *non sequitur*, and Augustine, as we noted, had simply been caught up in the latest fad, interpreting Mary's response through a contemporary late fourth century lens in which consecrated virginity had become fashionable.

Zachariah's Unbelief

Madrid then attempts to prove Mary's vow of "perpetual virginity" by contrasting Gabriel's response to Zachariah in Luke 1:8-22 with his response to Mary in Luke 1:26-38. Zachariah questions Gabriel's announcement that his wife will bear a son, for which he receives a stern rebuke and harsh discipline (Luke 1:19-20). But when Mary questions Gabriel's announcement, he responds much differently, patiently explaining the details of what would soon occur (Luke 1:35). By Madrid's reading, the only possible explanation for the difference between Gabriel's responses is that Mary must have taken a vow:

> Zachariah and Mary both doubted the angel, but notice that only Zachariah was punished for that! … Why? The answer to this points us to Mary's perpetual virginity.[534]

There is of course a simpler explanation. Zachariah, an aged priest, had prayed for the very thing Gabriel came announcing (Luke 1:13), while Mary, a mere child, had not prayed for this. Zachariah responded in unbelief even as his very prayer was being granted so extraordinarily, and was justifiably rebuked for it. Mary, of course, had not prayed for a child, and therefore her question was of a completely different nature. The difference between Gabriel's responses to each is therefore easily understood by the explicit context in which they are related to us. As is typical, however, Madrid introduces a distraction to draw the attention of the reader away from the plain context of the Scriptures, creating the perception that there is a mystery that needs to be solved, and then presenting a fabricated solution to the imagined mystery. But there was no mystery to begin with. Madrid has simply continued his pattern of

---

534 Madrid, p. 140.

assuming something to be true, using that assumption to interpret the Scripture, and then claiming that the Scripture proves his assumption.

The Pilgrimage to Jerusalem

Madrid also believes the pilgrimage to Jerusalem for Passover (Luke 2:41-52) indicates that Mary did not have other children because the narrative appears to suggest that Joseph and Mary had traveled to Jerusalem with Jesus alone. "If Mary had other children after Christ, where are they? None are mentioned."[535] The Scriptures, however, do not mention every member of a household every time the family is present. For example, when Philip is selected as a deacon (Acts 6:5), an office for which godly offspring are a prerequisite (1 Timothy 3:12), no children are mentioned even though "the whole multitude" of the very young church was present at his selection. His several daughters are not mentioned anywhere in the narrative. It is not until Acts 21:9 that we finally hear of his four virgin daughters "which did prophesy." An observant reader will find that the daughters, though they would have been present with their father in the midst of "the whole multitude," were not relevant to the narrative in chapter 6, but were relevant in chapter 21 when the narrative revolves around a gathering of prophets and a prophecy about Paul's plans.

Similarly, when the sons of Zebedee were called as apostles, Luke only mentions two passengers in their boat: the two sons, James and John. By Luke's account, when "they forsook all," they forsook only their ship (Luke 5:11). Where was their father? Matthew, for his part, tells us that Jesus had found James and John "in a ship with Zebedee their father" mending their nets. When they followed Jesus, they left behind "the ship and their father" (Matthew 4:21-22). But where were the hired servants? Mark tells us when James and John followed Jesus, "they left their father Zebedee in the ship with the hired servants" (Mark 1:20). In each narrative, the Holy Spirit has conveyed precisely what He intended to convey, no more and no less. Luke focuses on the

---

535 Madrid, p. 141.

partnership that existed between Peter and the sons of Zebedee. Matthew focuses on James and John working diligently with their father in the boat. Mark's narrative simply conveys the comparative wealth of the household James and John were leaving behind. We are not at liberty, as Madrid supposes, to assume that anyone not mentioned was therefore not present.

Mary and John at the Cross

In His dying moments, seeing Mary and John at the cross, Jesus said to her "Woman, behold, your son!" and to him, "Behold, your mother." The gospel narrative tells us "from that hour that disciple took her unto his own home" (John 19:27). Madrid understands the verse to mean that Mary must have had no other natural children:

> Why would Christ entrust his own mother into the care of a man who was not a member of the family if indeed Mary had other sons and daughters beside Christ? He wouldn't have.[536]

But Jesus had not merely called John the son of Mary. He also called Mary the mother of John. We might well ask why Christ would entrust John to the care of a woman who was not a member of his family if John already had a mother who in fact was standing nearby at the time of this exchange (Matthew 27:56). If the exchange does not prove that John had no other mother, then it cannot possibly prove that Mary had no other children.

What is more, Madrid's argument assumes that Mary was entrusted to the care of John so that her material needs would be met, something that the text simply does not say. Madrid reasons,

> If Mary had actually had other children, she would have gone to live with them. The fact that Christ entrusted his Mother to St. John is a strong indication that Mary had no other children.[537]

---

536 Ibid.
537 Ibid.

This is a common argument based upon an assumption that is nowhere expressed in the text of Scripture. The Gospel does not say *why* He assigned a familial relationship to Mary and John. He did not say to Mary, "Woman, behold thy son who shall henceforth provide for your needs in the absence of your only living relative!" Nor did He say to John, "Behold thy mother for whom it is now your duty to provide in the absence of living relations!" Lacking an explicit reason for His instructions, commentators of every stripe simply supply one of their own, assuming that Jesus meant to provide for Mary's material needs because the now destitute Mary would have nowhere to live and no one to provide for her. Surely if Jesus had brothers and sisters by Mary, they say, He would not have found it necessary to commit her to the care of another. Upon that invalid assumption His dying words are thought to militate against the proposition that Mary had other natural born children.

The argument, however, is constructed upon a single erroneous and easily falsifiable assumption: *that Jesus had up to that moment been providing for His mother who would now be destitute without Him.* What evidence is brought forth from the Scriptures to suggest that His death would require such arrangements to be made for her continued care? Not only is there no evidence of such filial support by Jesus for His mother, but there is a preponderance of evidence that Jesus had neither the means nor the intent to so provide for her. What material support could a homeless, impoverished, itinerant preacher provide for His mother?

Was Mary living in Jesus' home with Him up to then? Of course not. He had no home. "The foxes have holes, and the birds of the air have nests; but the Son of man hath not where to lay his head" (Matthew 8:20; c.f. Luke 9:58). Did Jesus possess money, livestock, buildings and land to sustain her? Of course not. His own apostle Judas was known to help himself to the community treasury (John 12:6 13:29), He had to find money for tribute in the mouth of a fish (Matthew 17:24-27), borrow a colt for his entry into Jerusalem (Matthew 21:1-5), lodge Himself in someone else's furnished guest chamber to celebrate His last meal (Matthew 26:17-19; Luke 22:7-14), and was buried in another man's tomb when He died (Matthew 27:60). From this dearth of material goods Jesus is supposed to have been so abundantly providing for Mary's needs that His death would leave her hungry, naked and homeless, necessitating a plan for her long-term care. If the argument had any merit it all, Jesus would have made such arrangements at the beginning of His public ministry, before He himself had become homeless and impoverished, at the time when He was asking His disciples to forsake everything to follow Him. But He did not.

For his entire public ministry, far from subsidizing the lifestyle of His elderly mother, the women in His entourage *were actually subsidizing Him*. As He was going "throughout every city and village," He subsisted on the generosity of His followers, including "certain women, which had been healed of evil spirits and infirmities, Mary called Magdalene, … Joanna the wife of Chuza Herod's steward, and Susanna, and many others, which ministered unto him of their substance" (Luke 8:2-4). If Mary received any subsistence from Jesus it was of an incidental and extraordinary nature (e.g., wine, fish and loaves). Apart from that, where are we to discover that all this time He had provided so abundantly for Mary that arrangements were necessary for her continued care upon His departure? There simply is no evidence to suggest it. The unspoken assumption upon which Madrid constructs his argument for Jesus being an only child is therefore shown to be flawed, without basis in the Scriptures. It is simply a fanciful assumption, unsupported by the text, which says nothing of *why* Jesus arranged this new relationship. We would no sooner assume by this that John had no other mother than we would that Mary had no other children. It simply is not our prerogative to presume that Jesus intended the arrangement in order to provide for Mary.

Why indeed did Jesus make the arrangement? Any number of possible solutions present themselves, and "caring for Mary's material needs" is the least probable:

- Perhaps John, like the other apostles, had forsaken all to follow Christ, and had nothing (Matthew 19:27), while Mary had joined herself to a company of women of considerable means, and would no longer have Jesus' ministry to subsidize. Did Jesus make the arrangement so that Mary would have an outlet for her generosity, an apostolic ministry to support in His absence?

- John would soon be the first apostle to lose a close family member for the sake of the Gospel (Acts 12:2), something with which Mary alone could truly empathize, having lost both her Son and her nephew to persecution. Did Jesus establish such a maternal relationship so John would be prepared for such a trial, a trial for which his own mother, standing just a few feet away, was not yet equipped to instruct him?

- On the cross, Jesus is forsaken by His Father, stripped both of His dignity and the last of His earthly belongings, naked and hanging on a tree, with only two earthly relationships unbroken at the end: His mother and his beloved disciple, John. Notably, Jesus does not know "that all things were now accomplished" (John 19:28) until He has relieved Himself of these last earthly encumbrances. Did Jesus hand His mother off to John, and John to His mother, so that He could give up the ghost having truly emptied Himself for our sakes (Philippians 2:7), emptied even of the last vestiges of earthly encumbrances?

Any one of these is more likely than Madrid's suggestion that Jesus, having failed to provide for Mary's needs during His entire public ministry, suddenly realized on the cross that someone would need to care for her in His absence. Lacking any Scriptural support for his hypothesis, Madrid has once again succumbed to his besetting temptation, which is to extract from the Scriptures that which he imagines they ought to have said or ought to have meant. To his credit, Madrid at least concedes that the Jesus' message from the cross to Mary and John "certainly does not prove … the Catholic teaching that Mary was a perpetual virgin."[538] On that point we certainly agree with him.

---

538 Ibid.

The Reformers

At this point in his argument, Madrid makes passing reference to some Reformers who believed Mary remained a perpetual virgin, and then asks the reader to "consider just how far modern-day Protestantism has drifted from its 16th century moorings."[539] We are not impressed. Martin Luther adopted Jerome's novel position that "brethren of the Lord" refers to "cousins." We are no more inclined to adopt Luther's regurgitation of Jerome's position than we are inclined to accept Madrid's, and it is no less novel for Luther's regurgitation of it. Luther wrote as well that Mary "is nobility, wisdom, and holiness personified. We can never honor her enough." Superstitious nonsense, all of it. Is Mary holiness personified? If so, then any disciple of Jesus is even more so than she:

> And it came to pass, as he spake these things, a certain woman of the company lifted up her voice, and said unto him, Blessed is the womb that bare thee, and the paps which thou hast sucked. But he said, Yea rather, blessed are they that hear the word of God, and keep it. (Luke 11:27)

Is Mary Jesus' mother? Any believer is as much His mother as Mary is:

> Then one said unto him, Behold, thy mother and thy brethren stand without, desiring to speak with thee. But he answered and said unto him that told him, Who is my mother? and who are my brethren? And he stretched forth his hand toward his disciples, and said, Behold my mother and my brethren! For whosoever shall do the will of my Father which is in heaven, the same is my brother, and sister, and mother. (Matthew 12:47-50)

Madrid produces two quotes from Calvin,[540] who reasons that Elizabeth's salutation, "mother of my Lord" (Luke 1:43) was

---

539 Madrid, p, 142.
540 Ibid.

perfectly appropriate, and that Matthew 1:25 states that Joseph "knew her not till she had brought forth her firstborn son," but does not of necessity imply that he knew her after. These readings are unoffensive to the Protestant mind, but certainly provide no support for Mary's perpetual virginity. Zwingli, for his part, is cited by Madrid[541] for his conviction that Mary "according to the words of the gospel as a pure Virgin brought forth for us the Son of God," with which we find no fault. But then he expressed the extrabiblical position that Mary "in childbirth and after childbirth forever remained a pure, intact Virgin," with which we cannot agree—the Gospels say no such thing, and Zwingli offered no scriptural evidence in support such convictions.

With this question Madrid thinks to prevail upon his Protestant critics by citing Reformers, and so far as the Reformers reason from Scripture, we do not disagree with them. Yet when they spout superstitious nonsense, their arguments are as odious to us as those of Roman Catholics. Luther, Calvin and Zwingli held positions not unlike those of the Roman Catholic religion from which they came. We are not surprised that they brought some of Rome's superstition with them, and Madrid's reliance on them does not convince us that *the Scriptures* teach what he claims.

"Obsession" with Virginity

Madrid then objects to the observation that Roman Catholics are "obsessed" with Mary's perpetual virginity. Catholics are not "obsessed," he responds, but merely hold to the "universal and consistent" belief that prevailed "within Christianity in the fifteen centuries prior to the Protestant Reformation."[542] However, as we have shown in this chapter, the belief was not held universally and consistently at all. The question was so unsettled that even Roman Catholic scholars concede that Mary's *in partu* virginity "had only a fragile basis in earlier Christian tradition" for the first three hundred years of the church.[543] They are as quick to admit that establishing the dogma of

---

541 Ibid,
542 Madrid, p. 144-145.
543 Hunter, David G., *Marriage, Celibacy and Heresy in Ancient Christianity* (Oxford University Press, 2007, p. 285).

Mary's perpetual virginity as an apostolic tradition is "an impossible task with our present documentary sources."[544] Such confessions from Roman Catholic scholars who made a career of studying ancient Mariology would be remarkable if indeed it were true that belief in the perpetual virginity of Mary was held universally and consistently since the apostles as Madrid claims. In reality, the doctrinal obsession with Mary's virginity came about precisely because, as Roman Catholic scholar David Hunter acknowledges, "In the later years of the fourth century ... male Christian writers [began] to devote *an extraordinary degree of attention to the bodies of women, especially celibate women.*"[545] In a word, those proto-medieval male writers became *pathologically obsessed* with virginal female bodies, and began to read the Scriptures in that light, and to impose those obsessions on others with the force of dogma. "Obsessed" is precisely what Roman Catholics are with Mary's alleged perpetual virginity. In striking contrast, the early church was not.

Vain Repetitions

Madrid then takes on Protestant objections to the Rosary, a Marian devotion that to Protestant ears sounds like the "vain repetitions" Jesus forbade in Matthew 6:7. Madrid's response is that Jesus only prohibited *vain* repetitions, not *repetitions*.[546] To Madrid's point, it can be fairly observed that not all repetitions are vain. Psalm 136 repeats the responsorial phrase, "for his mercy endureth for ever" 26 times in a row. Jesus was obviously not prohibiting those repetitions. Jesus also illustrated effective prayer through the parable of an unjust judge who finally relents and answers a widow's continuous plea, "Avenge me of mine adversary." This, Jesus says, is how we ought to pray to our Heavenly Father, who will "avenge his own elect, which cry day and night unto him" (Luke 18:1-8). Likewise, in the garden of Gethsemane Jesus prayed repeatedly, "O my Father, if this cup may not pass away from me, except I drink it, thy will be done" (Matthew 26:42). Jesus obviously was not prohibiting that kind of repetition, either. If the Scriptures contain *repetitions* that

544 Carol, J *Mariology*, vol ii (267).
545 Hunter, David G. The American Society of Church History, June 2000 (283-84).
546 Madrid, p. 146-148.

are not vain, and Jesus encourages praying *repeatedly* for the same thing until the Lord answers, and Jesus Himself actually repeated His prayers, it is clear that Jesus did not prohibit *repetitive praying*. What then did He prohibit? What He prohibited was "much speaking" to ply God's ear:

> But when ye pray, use not vain repetitions, as the heathen do: for they think that they shall be heard for their much speaking. Be not ye therefore like unto them: for your Father knoweth what things ye have need of, before ye ask him. (Matthew 6:7-8)

Based on His words, the *vanity* He prohibits is to think that it is *the much speaking,* rather than *the prayer itself*, that the Lord hears. It is not vain to repeat *the request*. It is vanity to repeat other syllables, words, phrases and sentences as if by speaking *them* the Lord might finally grant *the request that is unspoken.*

If a Christian desires relief from his adversaries, it is not vain to ask every day, or even hundreds of times per day, to be so relieved. It is just such prayers that the Lord hears, "though he bear long with them" (Luke 18:7). Now suppose that same Christian, instead of asking for relief, decided rather to recite John 11:35, "Jesus wept," a thousand times per day hoping that by the repetitions, the Lord might grant relief from his adversaries. And just to make sure he completed the thousand daily recitations, he tied 100 knots in a rope and counted off one knot for each repetition of John 11:35, and progressed through that prayer rope ten times per day hoping that by the repetition of "Jesus wept" he would be granted relief from his adversaries. Far from the legitimate repetition in Jesus' parable and Jesus' prayers in which *it is the request that is repeated*, in this example the *words* "Jesus wept" are repeated, but *the request* is not. That is the difference, and that is what is prohibited. That is what "vain repetitions" are. The Rosary, because it repeats words (*but not the request*) in hopes of gaining *the request*, falls into the category of "vain repetitions." To understand why, one need only understand the purpose of the Rosary.

In the Rosary, the Roman Catholic is asked to repeat the
Hail Mary 50 to 200 times. The Hail Mary prayer is three simple
sentences:

> "Hail Mary, full of grace, the Lord is with thee. Blessed art
> thou among women and blessed is the fruit of thy womb,
> Jesus. Holy Mary, mother of God, pray for us sinners now
> and at the hour of our death. Amen."

Roman Catholics are asked to recite this hundreds of times per
week, sometimes hundreds of times in one sitting, thousands or
tens of thousands of times per year. A single Rosary prayer session
may include 10 Hail Marys recited for each of five Joyful, five
Sorrowful, five Glorious and five Luminous mysteries. That is a
total of two hundred Hail Marys in a single sitting. A person who
does this every day may recite as many as 73,000 Hail Marys per
year, and some repeat it even more than that.

The vanity of such a repetition is evident from the form and
purpose of the Rosary. The Roman Catholic's request is promised
to him if he will only recite the Rosary. Does Bob need a car? Does
Sally desire healing from a chronic disorder? Does Eduardo need
a job? Does Nikita seek godly spouses for her children? If these
merely repeated their requests, there would be no vanity to their
repetition, but instead they are instructed to repeat the Hail Mary
hundreds and thousands of times. In each case, whatever the sup-
plicant may need or desire is to be obtained not by asking *for the
thing itself*, but *by repeating the Hail Mary*. It is the repetition of the
Hail Mary, not the repetition of the request, that is said to gain the
hearing. As John Paul II said,

> The Rosary is both meditation and supplication. Insistent
> prayer to the Mother of God is based on confidence that her
> maternal intercession can obtain all things from the heart
> of her Son.[547]

---

547 John Paul II Apostolic Letter *Rosarium Virginis Mariae* (October 16, 2002), 16.

Repetitive "prayer to the Mother of God" in the form of the Hail Mary is the means by which the Catholic "can obtain all things." Whatever may be desired is to be obtained by the multiplication of words rather than by simply asking for it. That is exactly the vain repetition that Jesus prohibited.

The fact that the Rosary employs vain repetitions "as the heathen do" (Matthew 6:7) is evident from the *Catholic Encyclopedia*'s own brief summary of nonchristian religions that employ it. Muslims, Hindus, Buddhists, to the surprise of the Catholic devotee, also use rosaries:

> [I]t is certain that among the Mohammedans the Tasbih or bead-string, consisting of 33, 66, or 99 beads, and used for counting devotionally the names of Allah, has been in use for many centuries. Marco Polo, visiting the King of Malabar in the thirteenth century, found to his surprise that that monarch employed a rosary of 104 … precious stones to count his prayers. St. Francis Xavier and his companions were equally astonished to see that rosaries were universally familiar to the Buddhists of Japan.[548]

Mariolatry

Madrid next tackles the Protestant objection that Roman Catholics very much appear to worship Mary and the saints. In defense, Madrid cites multiple Bible verses in which people bow down to human beings to show respect. Isaac blessed Jacob, saying, "Let … nations bow down to thee: and let thy mother's sons bow down to thee" (Genesis 27:29). Abraham "bowed himself toward the ground" when his three visitors arrived (Genesis 18:2). Ruth bowed down to Boaz (Ruth 2:10), David bowed to Saul (1 Samuel 24:8), Abigail bowed down to David's servants (1 Samuel 25:41), Bathsheba and Nathan bowed down to David (1 Kings 1:16, 23), the Shunamite woman bowed down to Elisha (2 Kings 4:37), and the assembly bowed their heads to do "obeisance to the king"

---

548 *Catholic Encyclopedia*, Rosary.

(1 Chronicles 29:20). The wicked servant "fell down, and worshipped" the king (Matthew 18:26), and Jesus says the unbelievers will "come and bow down before" the Philadelphians (Revelation 3:9). These are all offered by Madrid as evidence not only that it is acceptable to bow down and worship human beings, but also that Roman Catholics are not "confused about what biblical worship really is."[549]

Protestants in truth find nothing objectionable about public displays of deferential respect to a civil sovereign, and therefore we find nothing objectionable in Bathsheba and Nathan bowing to king David or the sons of Jacob bowing to Joseph. Nor do we find public displays of humility and gratitude objectionable, so we have no problem with Abigail bowing to David's servants or the Shunamite woman bowing to Elisha. None of these are of the nature of bowing before Mary, or more accurately, bowing to images and statues of Mary. Yet Madrid confuses his categories and thinks that because it was acceptable to bow before kings in the Old Testament, it must be acceptable to bow before images today. Having provided evidence that several kings in the Old Testament received homage from their subjects, Madrid poses a question that he thinks will resolve the matter:

> [Jesus] permits mere human kings to receive honor and veneration from their subjects. ... So on what biblical basis do you assert that, once these holy men and women enter into heaven, they are somehow no longer able to receive veneration and honor as they did on earth? ... Or to put it a different way, since the Lord God is not displeased that human beings, such as the monarch ... receive homage and veneration while here on earth, ... what changes once they die?[550]

But that is pure diversion. The real question before us is whether we ought to bow down to statues and images of Mary, the saints and angels. For the answer, we turn to the Roman Catholic Bible,

---

549 Madrid, p. 148-156.
550 Madrid, p. 155.

the Latin Vulgate. According to the Council of Trent,[551] the Latin Vulgate is the official Bible translation of the Roman Catholic Church, and therefore it must be "held as authentic." We will therefore cite Rome's authoritative translation of Romans 1:25 where Pauls says it is wrong to worship (*colere*) the creature:

> English: "who changed the truth of God into a lie and *worshipped* and served the creature rather than the Creator, who is blessed for ever. Amen."

> Latin: "qui commutaverunt veritatem Dei in mendacio et *coluerunt* et servierunt creaturae potius quam creatori qui est benedictus in saecula amen."

Yet *colere* is precisely what Roman Catholics are instructed to offer to Mary, as Pope Pius XII states plainly:

> ...there is nothing 'more sweet, nothing dearer than to worship (*colere*), venerate, invoke and praise with ardent affection the Mother of God conceived without stain of original sin.' ... But where—as is the case in almost all dioceses, there exists a church in which the Virgin Mother of God is worshipped (*colitur*) with more intense devotion, thither on stated days let pilgrims flock together in great numbers and publicly and in the open give glorious expression to their common Faith and their common love toward the Virgin Most Holy. ... But let this holy city of Rome be the first to give the example, this city which from the earliest Christian era worshipped (*coluit*) the heavenly mother, its patroness, with a special devotion.[552]

The Roman Catholic will at once object that the worship Pius XII has in mind for Mary is not the kind of worship that is directed to God. We reply simply that the Latin Vulgate is the authentic Bible

---

version for Roman Catholics, and the kind of worship it prohibits being offered to creatures is exactly the kind that Pius XII requires Catholics to offer to Mary: *colere*.

To understand how difficult it is for Roman Catholics to distinguish between what is offered to Mary and what is offered to God, we must understand their three levels of veneration: *dulia*, *hyperdulia* and *latria*. *Dulia*, a Greek word meaning honor and veneration, is reserved for the saints. *Latria*, the Greek word for worship, is reserved for God. The *Catholic Encyclopedia* insists that "the difference is one of kind and not merely of degree; *dulia* and *latria* being as far apart as are the creature and the Creator." [553] Therein lies the problem: between *dulia* and *latria*, there exists a form of veneration that is reserved for Mary alone, and that veneration is called *hyperdulia*, or literally "hyperveneration." Where exactly *hyperdulia* exists on the spectrum between *dulia* and *latria* is impossible to discern. If *hyperdulia* is offered to the creature just as *dulia* is, then *hyperdulia* ought also to be just as far from *latria* as the creature is from the Creator. But Rome could never separate them so far. To do so would place *hyperdulia* just as far from *latria* as *dulia* is, removing the *dulia-hyperdulia* distinction and reducing Mary to the level of a mere saint. Overcompensating in the opposite direction runs the risk of removing the *hyperdulia-latria* distinction, effectively elevating Mary to the level of God. How then ought Roman Catholics venerate Mary without accidentally slipping downward into the *dulia* reserved for the other saints, or stumbling into the worship that is due to God alone?

There are such indefinite boundaries between *dulia* and *hyperdulia* on the one hand, and between *hyperdulia* and *latria* on the other, that it is truly impossible to determine where one ends and another begins. We seriously doubt the Roman Catholic laity are sufficiently sophisticated to know that the papally prescribed *colere* offered to Mary is the very *colere* Paul prohibited in Romans 1:25. With such a nuanced theology of worship, how can the laity know how much is *too much* to offer to Mary and how little is *too little* to offer to God? Surely God is worthy of more than *hyperdulia*, and one would not want to offer Him *hyperdulia* when He deserves *latria*. But Mary is said to be worthy

---

553 *Catholic Encyclopedia*, dulia.

of more than *dulia*, and one would not want to make the mistake of offering mere *dulia* to one worthy of *hyperdulia*. Similarly, a Roman Catholic ought to want neither to offer *hyperdulia* to saints and angels (for that is reserved for Mary), nor *latria* to Mary (for that is reserved for God). To avoid misdirecting their veneration, they would need to have some objective definition of each so they could know with certainty what they were offering to whom. But such a clear definition does not exist, and Roman Catholicism has been chronically unable to state in clear terms the difference between what is offered to God and what is offered to Mary and the saints. All that can be stated categorically is that if praise, worship and adoration are heaped upon a saint, it must be *dulia*, and if directed to Mary, it must be *hyperdulia*, and if addressed to God, it must be *latria*. The result is that Mary can be worshiped *above God Himself* on the grounds that it is still only *hyperdulia* because it was directed to Mary instead of God. And God can be venerated with adulation that falls well short of *dulia* on the grounds that it was directed at Him, and therefore qualifies as *latria*.

Thomas of Villanova, for example, could not contain himself, assigning to Mary what can only be described as *hyperlatria*, worship that exceeds even that which is owed to God. He wrote that Mary's *fiat* — "be it unto me according to thy word" (Luke 1:38) — was more powerful and efficacious than God's words, "Let there be light" (Genesis 1:3), and should be venerated accordingly, above even that fiat by which God created the heavens and the earth.[554] And St. Bernardine claimed, "At the command of Mary, all obey, even God."[555] This statement magnifies Mary above her Creator, and yet somehow qualifies as *hyperdulia*, since the adulation has Mary as its object. Were Bernardine to inform God of His obligation to obey Mary, such blasphemy would qualify as *latria*, addressed as it is to the Godhead. Small wonder that notorious convert, John Henry Cardinal Newman, gave up trying to figure it out, and distanced himself from the ridiculous *hyperlatria* of some of his Roman Catholic predecessors. Unwilling as he was to imitate

---

554 Alphonsus de Liguori, *The Glories of Mary*, Discourse IV "The Annunciation" Rev. Eugene Grimm (ed.) (Andrew B. Kuhn, C.SS.R., 1931).
555 Liguori, *the Glories of Mary*, Chapter VI.

such idolatrous excesses of *hyperlatria*, he was also unwilling to condemn them.[556]

If Roman Catholic saints, theologians and apologists have such a hard time distinguishing between *hyperdulia* and *latria*, even as they strenuously insist that they are two different things, the laity cannot possibly be expected to do any better. The boundary problem—between *dulia* and *hyperdulia* on the one hand, and between *hyperdulia* and *latria* on the other, and between *latria* and *hyperlatria* in Bernardine and Villanova's cases—is exacerbated by the popes themselves. Offering no plain definition of *dulia*, *hyperdulia* and *latria*—except to state to whom each is directed—they nevertheless insist that Roman Catholics must offer neither too much nor too little to the intended recipients. On the matter of *dulia* offered in "the authentic cult of the saints," Pope Paul VI warned against "any abuses, excesses or defects [that] have crept in here or there," but did not say what those abuses or excesses might be.[557] And on the matter of the *hyperdulia* offered to Mary, Pope Pius XII warned against "unfounded opinions and exaggerated expressions which go beyond the truth," but did not specify what unfounded opinions and exaggerations might sinfully exceed the limits of *hyperdulia*. He also warned the faithful, "on the other hand," to avoid "excessive narrowness of mind in weighing that exceptional, sublime, indeed all but divine dignity of the Mother of God." Such narrow-mindedness, after all, could accidentally cause the devotee to fall sinfully short of the *hyperdulia* to which she is entitled.[558]

And that is the problem with the *dulia-hyperdulia* boundary, and the *hyperdulia-latria* boundary. Roman Catholics are presumed to maintain the proper distinction in their minds—so no idolatry takes place—but that distinction is as imperceptible to the laity as it is to the clergy. The truth is that nobody really knows where *dulia* ends, and *hyperdulia* begins, or where *hyperdulia* ends and *latria* begins. Indeed, Villanova and Bernardine did not know where

---

556 Cardinal Newman, John Henry, *Certain Difficulties Felt by Anglicans in Catholic Teaching*, Volume 2, *A Letter Addressed to the Rev. E. B. Pusey, D.D., on Occasion of His Eirenicon*, §5.4.
557 Pope Paul VI, *Lumen Gentium*, 51 (November 21, 1964).
558 Pope Pius XII, *Ad Cæli Reginam*, 44 (October 11, 1954).

latria ended and *hyperlatria* began! Roman Catholics say things of the saints that, had they been directed to Mary, would have been considered *hyperdulia*, and such things to Mary that, had they been said of God, they would have been construed as *latria*.

For example, consider these statements:

> Joseph, all graces come to us through thee.[559]

> Mary, all graces come to us through thee.[560]

Both statements accurately reflect the veneration expressed by Roman Catholics, but the former is said to be mere *dulia*, in that it is addressed to Joseph, while the latter is said to be *hyperdulia*, addressed as it is to Mary. Or again,

> The world which thou with God didst form from the beginning continues to exist at thy will, O most holy virgin.[561]

> The world which thou with God didst form from the beginning continues to exist at thy will, O most holy Jesus.

The latter is plainly worship, or *latria*, and is based on Hebrews 1:3. The former, however, is ascribed to Mary by St. Bonaventure, and is ostensibly *hyperdulia*. Consider these as well:

> She did not spare her only Son, but gave Him up for all of us.[562]

> He that spared not his own Son, but delivered him up for us all. (Romans 8:32)

---

559 Fr. Domenico, *True Devotion to St. Joseph*, 381, 383, 400.
560 Alphonsus Liguori, *The Glories of Mary*, Discourse II, On the Birth of Mary.
561 Liguori, *The Glories of Mary*, Discourse IV, The Annunciation of Mary.
562 Most, William G., *Mary's Cooperation in Our Redemption*.

Again, the latter is plainly worship, or *latria*, and is quoted directly
from the Scriptures and directed to the Father. The former is said
by Fr. William Most in *Mary's Cooperation in Our Redemption*, and is
alleged to be only *hyperdulia*. Consider these as well:

> Mary is "the gate of heaven, because no one can enter that
> blessed kingdom without passing through her."[563]

> Jesus is the door of heaven, because no one can enter that
> blessed kingdom without passing through Him.

The latter is plainly worship, or *latria*, and is based on John 10:9
and is said of Jesus. The former is ascribed to Mary by St. Bonaventure, and is said to be only *hyperdulia*.

As difficult as it is to distinguish between *hyperdulia* and *latria*,
there are statements, as we have observed, that are said of Mary
that so *exceed* the worship that is due to God that it is impossible
to put them in a lower category than *latria*. When we are asked to
venerate Mary's fiat *even above God's*, and are told that God Himself
is said to venerate Mary's command even higher than His own,
how on earth are we to call it mere *hyperdulia*, when it by definition
it *exceeds* the veneration that is due to God, and God is even said to
venerate her above Himself by His obedience? We thus return to
Madrid's anemic response to the accusation that Roman Catholics
are confused about biblical worship. Indeed they are! Madrid
thinks it can all be resolved by pointing out that people bowed to
kings in the Old Testament. Nonsense. The accusation stands. No
matter how they try to compartmentalize their *hyperdulia* to keep
it distinct and separate from their *latria*, it is clear that the two are
indistinguishable. *Hyperdulia*, as we well know, is just *latria* that is
directed to Mary. And to our point, Roman Catholics indeed *worship*
her, offering *colere* to a mere creature, in violation of their own
"authentic" translation of Romans 1:25.

---

563 Liguori, *The Glories of Mary*, Chapter V.

Praying to Saints

Paul's admonition

Madrid defends the Roman Catholic practice of praying to saints,[564] applying 1 Timothy 2:1-4, in which Paul urges "that supplications, prayers, intercessions, and thanksgivings" be made for all. But Paul says nothing about those prayers being directed to departed saints in heaven. Paul is clear that he means for men to direct their "supplications, prayers, intercessions and thanksgivings" to God through Jesus Christ, for he continues with the simple theological basis for his exhortation:

> For there is one God, and one mediator between God and men, the man Christ Jesus … . I will therefore that men pray every where, lifting up holy hands, without wrath and doubting. (1 Timothy 2:5-8)

In context, Paul would have men make "supplications, prayers, intercessions and thanksgivings" for all men because "there is one God, and one mediator between God and men, the man Christ Jesus." There is nothing in the text about Paul wanting departed saints to pray for the saints on earth. This is just one more example of Madrid expounding what he wishes the text said rather than hearing what it actually says.

The Sub Tuum Præsidium

Madrid also claims that "the early Christians did indeed invoke the intercession of Mary and the saints through prayer."[565] As evidence, he offers the *Sub Tuum Præsidium*, which he claims "dates back to at least the early 200s, perhaps even earlier." In the *Sub Tuum Præsidium*, Egyptian saints are alleged to have prayed to Mary, asking her not to despise their petitions:

---

564 Madrid, p. 157.
565 Madrid, pp. 156-157

Beneath your protection we fly, O Holy Mother of God. In our necessities, despise not our petitions but always deliver us from all dangers, oh glorious blessed Virgin.

The prayer does not prove Madrid's point. *Papyrus* 470 in the John Rylands Library is the fragment upon which the prayer, in Greek, was allegedly written. The fragment is in such tatters that editor C. H. Roberts was only able to extract the following with any confidence:

> "Mother of God (hear) my supplications: suffer us not (to be) in adversity, but deliver us from danger. Thou alone ... "[566]

While it is true that Mr. Lobel, with whom Roberts "frequently consulted on difficulties of interpretation and palæography" would place the fragment no later than the third century, Mr. Roberts is not so confident:

> Lobel would be unwilling to place [papyrus] 470 later than the third century. But such individual hands are hard to date, and it is almost incredible that a prayer addressed directly to the Virgin in these terms could be written in the third century. The Virgin was spoken of as θεοτόκος by Athanasius; but there is no evidence even for private prayer addressed to her before the latter part of the fourth century, and *I find it difficult to think that our text was written earlier than that.*[567]

Yes, some scholars believe the tattered fragment of *Papyrus* 470 is from the third century. Others trace it to the late fourth century, which is where the earliest evidence of such prayers may be found. As if to prove our point rather than his own, Madrid invokes other early church writers as evidence that they often requested that

---

566 Roberts, Colin H., et al. *Catalogue of the Greek Papyri in the John Rylands Library*, Manchester. III, University Press, 1911, 47.
567 Roberts, 47 (emphasis added).

the saints pray for them. He cites two prayers from Ephraim the Syrian (370 AD) and one from Basil the Great (373 AD), both from the latter part of the fourth century. We can add one more: *Oration 24* of Gregory Nazianzus (379 AD) explicitly refers to prayers "beseeching the Virgin Mary to help."[568] The truth is, appealing to the saints in heaven to pray for those still on earth was a practice unknown to the early church, indeed unknown until the end of the fourth century, at which time superstitious prayers like these burst forth upon the scene, which is precisely why the earlier dating of *Papyrus* 470 is controverted. Thus, Madrid's claim that the early church "widely recognized and believed" that "Mary and the saints can and do pray for us" is based entirely upon a fragment that cannot with any confidence be traced any earlier than the end of the fourth century, a full three hundred years too late to be Biblical and apostolic.

The Superhuman Saints

After arguing that the early church prayed to Mary, Madrid turns his attention to the practical matter of how she could hear and answer prayers. Again, Madrid simply assumes that she does, interpreting each verse he cites as if it proved that a glorified Mary is equal to the task of responding to millions of prayers from around the world. Rather than actually finding Bible verses that show Mary answering prayers, Madrid rather focuses on Satan's power and the glorified condition of the resurrected saints, neither of which can possibly prove that Mary hears and answers prayers millions of prayers at once.

"The real difficulty," Madrid writes, "in trying to understand how this could be is that here on earth our abilities are paltry compared to the abilities the blessed in heaven enjoy." Our own shortcomings on earth, he continues, do not mean that the saints in heaven, "with their vastly enhanced, glorified and perfected human natures" are equally constrained.[569] Madrid cites multiple scriptures as if they supported his assertion that Mary and the

---

568 *Select Orations*, Oration 24.11, Saint Gregory of Nazianzus, Helen W Lojek (149).
569 Madrid, pp. 158-159

saints in heaven would be able to hear millions of prayers and dispense grace to all supplicants. As we will show, Madrid repeatedly assumes that the benefits saints will enjoy in their new bodies *at the resurrection* are already available to them in heaven *before the resurrection*, something the text never actually says.

For example, Madrid claims that in Matthew 22:30 and Luke 20:35-36 "Christ says the saints in heaven become 'like angels,'" and "they receive powers and abilities similar to those possessed by the angels."[570] Here he makes two mistakes. First, he assumes that Jesus really means that we become like angels *immediately in heaven* instead of later *at the resurrection as the text plainly says*. Second, he assumes that "like the angels," means saints "receive powers and abilities" currently enjoyed by the angels. But Jesus said neither of those things. First, He said the saints become like angels *at the resurrection*, which is still future, ruling out Madrid's interpretation entirely. Second, the Pharisees had attempted to confound Jesus by asking about a woman who had married seven brothers in succession. "In the resurrection whose wife shall she be?" That is the question He was answering. If we were to accept Madrid's reading, we might imagine that Jesus had responded to them, "Ye do err, not knowing the scriptures, nor the power of God, for *people don't even have to wait for the resurrection* to receive amazing superpowers, because they get them immediately in heaven." What He said, rather, is that *at the resurrection* the saints are like the angels who "*neither marry, nor are given in marriage: Neither can they die any more.*" In context, the way the saints are "like angels" *at the resurrection* is that they are *single* and *immortal*. Therefore, at the resurrection, the woman about whom the Pharisees inquired will not be married to any of her seven husbands—she will be unmarried. Even if Jesus really meant that we take on amazing angelic superpowers *at the resurrection* (and He did not), it would still mean that the saints would not have the remarkable ability to answer millions of prayers *until the resurrection*, a time when nobody would be needing intercessory prayer anyway.

---

570 Madrid, pp. 159, 236.

Madrid makes the same logical leaps in his claim that among their many "vastly enhanced, glorified and perfected" skills is a superpower ability to hear and answer millions of prayers at once.[571] Jesus appeared in the upper room "when the doors were shut" (John 20:19). Madrid takes this to mean that saints in heaven can hear and respond to millions of prayers at once. But the verse merely indicates that Jesus was not physically constrained in His resurrected body. Even if it meant that we, too, would have super-powers *at the resurrection*, it would still rule out saints having such superpowers *until the resurrection*, a time when nobody would be praying to them anyway.

Citing Isaiah 64:4 Paul wrote, "Eye hath not seen, nor ear heard … the things which God hath prepared" for His saints (1 Corinthians 2:9). Madrid takes this to mean nobody knows what the Lord has prepared for us *in heaven*, and therefore we are free to speculate that the saints *in heaven* might be able to hear and respond to millions of prayers at once.[572] But as Paul makes quite clear, the verse is not referring to *saints going up to heaven*, but about *God coming to earth*, as Isaiah makes clear: "Oh … that thou wouldest come down … to make thy name known to thine adversaries" (Isaiah 64:1-2). Paul's application of Isaiah is on the theme of God's revealed wisdom through the incarnation for which His people had waited patiently, and which they had finally received. So much had changed since Isaiah penned those words. The mysteries that were hidden from others, "God hath revealed them unto us by his Spirit: … that we might know the things that are freely given to us of God" (1 Corinthians 2:10-12). Far from marveling at what *we do not know yet about heaven*, Paul was instead reveling in what *we do know of the Gospel* here on earth, for God has revealed it to us. The passage has nothing to do with what it will be like in heaven, and is certainly no help to Madrid.

In death our bodies are "sown in weakness," and at the resur-rection, they are "raised in power" (1 Corinthians 15:43). Madrid takes this to mean that the saints in heaven can hear and respond

---

571 Ibid.
572 Ibid.

to millions of prayers at once.[573] Yet the verse makes mention of no
such power. The fact that our "celestial bodies" are more glorious
and more powerful than our "terrestrial bodies" does not at all
imply that our "celestial bodies" will be equipped to hear and
respond to millions of prayers at once. What is more, the verse
speaks of our bodies being "raised in power" *at the resurrection*, a
time when nobody would be praying to the saints, anyway.

Jesus "shall change our vile body, that it may be fashioned like
unto his glorious body" (Philippians 3:21), which Madrid takes to
mean that the saints in heaven can hear and respond to millions of
prayers at once.[574] Yet the change to which Paul refers is a change
that takes place *at the resurrection*, a time when nobody would be
praying to the saints, anyway.

When Jesus "shall appear, we shall be like him" (1 John 3:2),
which Madrid takes to mean that the saints in heaven can hear
and respond to millions of prayers at once.[575] But in context, John
speaks of Jesus' return, at which time "we shall be like him" *at the
resurrection*, at which time nobody would be praying to the saints,
anyway.

Upon all these flawed arguments, Madrid bases his conclusion
that "while on earth, Mary and the saints couldn't do many of the
amazing things they can now do in heaven." And yet the verses he
cites refer to the gospel preaching *on earth now*, and the general
resurrection *in the future* after the saints return to earth with
Christ. They are not verses about what the saints can do in heaven.
Madrid continues, referring to Hebrews 12:23, which says that we
have come "to the spirits of just men made perfect." Presumably we
are to understand that those "spirits of just men made perfect" are
able to hear and answer millions of prayers at once.[576] Yet that same
passage also says we have come "to Jesus the Mediator of the new
covenant, and to the blood of sprinkling that speaks better things
than that of Abel" (Hebrews 12:24). We suppose Madrid thinks a
martyr's blood might commend him as an intercessor to whom we

---

573 Ibid.
574 Ibid.
575 Ibid.
576 Madrid, p. 160.

might entrust our prayers. But are we really to believe a verse about the *sufficiency* of the blood of Christ and the *inadequacy* of the blood of Abel is to be understood to commend to us the intercessory power of the martyr? Jesus is the "one mediator between God and men" (1 Timothy 2:5), and is "the mediator of the new covenant … that speaketh better things" than the old (Hebrews 12:24). We are at a loss as to how this passage commends additional, lesser mediators to our attention.

Madrid then appeals to Luke 15:7-10, in which Jesus tells the parables of the Lost Sheep and the Lost Coin. Jesus concludes each parable by remarking on the joy in heaven over a repentant sinner:

> I say unto you, that likewise joy shall be in heaven over one sinner that repenteth, more than over ninety and nine just persons, which need no repentance. … Likewise, I say unto you, there is joy in the presence of the angels of God over one sinner that repenteth. (Luke 15:7, 10)

Madrid takes this to mean that Mary, the saints and angels in heaven "can hear our prayers" and "can know about even individual acts of repentance here on earth. This means that they somehow are able to process that information."[577] Yet none of the parables suggest that saints and angels in heaven are immediately aware of and joyfully contemplate "individual acts of repentance" on earth.

Both parables, as well as that of the Lost Son, were in response to the Pharisees criticizing Jesus for receiving sinners and dining with them. In the case of the Lost Sheep, Jesus is signified by the shepherd who goes "after that which is lost" (Luke 15:4) and in the case of the Lost Coin, Jesus is signified by the woman who lights a candle, sweeps the house, and seeks diligently (Luke 15:8). In the case of the Lost Son, Jesus is signified by the father who runs out to greet the returning prodigal (Luke 15:20). In all cases, after the lost item is found, the shepherd, the woman and the father call their friends and neighbors to inform them of that which is found, and a joyful celebration ensues. In the case of the Lost Sheep, the

---

577 Ibid.

shepherd "calleth together his friends and neighbours" to inform them (Luke 15:6). In the case of the Lost Coin, the woman "calleth her friends and her neighbours" to inform them (Luke 15:9). In the case of the Lost Son, the father says to the others, "Let us eat, and be merry. For this my son ... is found" (Luke 15:23-24). In no case do any of the friends invited to the celebration know of the rescue of the sheep, the coin or the son by direct observation. It is always Jesus—the shepherd, the woman, the father—who finds the repentant sinner and informs the others who did not know what had been found, and had not witnessed its finding. According to Jesus, the joy in heaven is like that. There is simply nothing in the parables to suggest in the least that Mary, the saints and angels have a special glorified ability to monitor and respond to individual acts of repentance, as Madrid imagines.

Madrid concludes this section of his arguments on the glorified powers of Mary, the saints and the angels by saying, "in this mortal stage of our lives, our knowledge is imperfect and we can only see 'dimly.' But when we get to heaven, our ability to understand, see, and know will be immeasurably enhanced."[578] His proof for this assumption is 1 Corinthians 15:42-43, but again, Paul states explicitly in that passage that he is referring to what it will be like for us in "the resurrection of the dead," a time when nobody would be in need of a saint to intercede for them.

Madrid's next argument is "that the devil himself has a vast ability to tempt, harass, and even harm the billions of people on this earth." He cites 1 Peter 5:8 which says that the devil "walketh about, seeking whom he may devour," which Madrid takes to mean that "at any given moment, he is able to tempt millions of people in various cultures speaking various languages—hundreds, thousands, even millions, at any given moment." From this Madrid reasons that if Satan can tempt millions of people "at any given moment," then "how much more so can those righteous, grace-filled, spiritually perfected, friends of Christ (Mary and the saints) hear and understand our prayers and petition the Lord on our

---

578 Ibid.

behalf!"[579] But does the Scripture say Satan can tempt millions of people at once? Not at all. Madrid cites John 8:44, but that verse does not say the devil can tempt millions at once. It merely says he is a liar and the father of lies. Madrid cites John 12:31 and 14:30, which identify the devil as "the prince of this world," but they do not say he can tempt millions of people at once. Madrid cites Colossians 1:13 and 2:15, which refer to "the power of darkness" and "principalities and powers," but do not say the devil can tempt millions of people at once. Madrid cites Hebrews 2:14, which says the devil had "the power of death," but does not say he can tempt millions of people at once. Madrid cites 2 Peter 2:4, which refers to "the angels that sinned," but does not say the devil can tempt millions of people at once. Madrid cites Jude 6, which refers to the fallen angels but does not say the devil can tempt millions of people at once. Madrid cites 1 John 3:8, which says that "he that committeth sin is of the devil; for the devil sinneth from the beginning," but does not say the devil can tempt millions of people at once. Madrid's mistake is constantly to read passages about the power of the devil, and the offspring of the devil, and take that to mean that somehow the devil works instrumentally and immediately in those who sin; and since billions of people stumble into sin, the devil must have superpowers. But the scriptures say that when a man sins, "every man is tempted, when he is drawn away of his own lust, and enticed" (James 1:14). The devil need not be personally involved every time someone sins, yet Madrid assumes this to be the case.

Madrid uses a flawed understanding of the scriptures to grant heightened awareness and abilities to the devil, then uses flawed logic to imagine that the righteous saints and angels can do even more than he, concluding that Mary and the saints can hear millions of prayers at once in multiple languages. But it is a false premise serving as a false foundation for a false conclusion—that Satan can be in multiple places at once, tempting individual sinners individually, something he certainly cannot do. The Scripture also says that the "young men" in John's letters had

---

579 Madrid, p. 161.

"overcome the wicked one" (1 John 2:13-14). Well, if the devil could tempt millions of people at once throughout the world, but the young men had overcome such a powerful creature, were those "young men" of the first century able to hear millions of prayers at once from all over the world in many languages while still on earth? Of course not. Just because the saints (even living saints on earth) can overcome the devil does not mean that their powers are superior to his. It just means that they believe the truth of the Gospel. There is no basis for concluding any more than that.

Mother of God

Madrid concludes his chapter on Mary by defending the title "Mother of God." His approach here is two-pronged. First, he claims that rejecting the title *Theotokos*, or as he renders it in English, "Mother of God," is "out of step with two thousand years of historic Christian teaching on this issue." That is not true, and the evidence he provides is both misleading and fraudulent. Second, he claims that we must say that Mary gave birth to God because Mary did not give birth to a nature, but to a Person. However, the early church was quite careful to distinguish between the progenitor of His divine nature and the progenitrix of His human nature. They knew very well the problem with calling Mary *the divine genitrix*, avoiding such foolish language by their carefully selected words.

Theotokos

Θεοτόκος (theotokos) derives from two Greek words, Θεός (Theos), referring to "God," and τόκος (tokos), meaning "bearer." When combined, they form a word that is translated literally as "Godbearer," a title we unashamedly assign to Mary insofar as she bore God in her womb and carried Him about. Wheresoever Mary went while pregnant with Jesus, whether to the hill country to visit Elizabeth, or to Bethlehem for the census, she carried God within her. If Roman Catholics had taken the word only that far, we would have no issue, but they pile much more meaning upon the term than honest etymology can support. We notice immediately that the term lacks the requisite Greek μητέρα (mitéra) for "mother" by which it would be possible to construct the term Madrid seeks, Μητέρα του Θεού, "Mother of God." Lacking the actual term in Greek, Madrid simply renders Θεοτόκος as if it literally meant "Mother of God." It does not, as a cursory review of Madrid's sources will show.

Irenæus

Madrid starts with a 189 AD reference to Mary,[580] whom Irenæus has receiving the glad tidings that she would "portaret Deum" in Latin, which in English is rendered "bear God."[581] Irenæus wrote and spoke in Greek, and for some of his works, we possess the Greek manuscripts, but many of them are lost, his thoughts preserved only in a third century Latin translation. Whatever Irenæus recorded in his original Greek, it is very unlikely that he used the Greek μητέρα του Θεού, which would have been rendered *mater Dei* ("mother of God") in Latin. More likely, he used a term of similar origin as "theotokos," and the translator appears to have taken it for what it plainly means—bearer of God. There is nothing here to suggest that the church in the second century believed Mary was God's mother, or that Irenæus had used the Greek term μητέρα του Θεού to refer to her as such.

"Hippolytus"

Madrid's next exhibit[582] is from Hippolytus' *Discourse on the End of the World*, allegedly from 217 AD. "Hippolytus" allegedly wrote that the prophets foresaw "the advent of God in the flesh to the world, His advent by the spotless and God-bearing Mary (Θεοτόκου Μαρίας)."[583] However, the work is known to be spurious, a late seventh century product of a "pseudo" Hippolytus who had adapted the *real* Hippolytus' *Discourse On Antichrist* as a polemic against the Islamic invasion.[584] By way of illustration, the real

---

580 Madrid, p. 163.
581 Irenæus, *Against Heresies*, 5.19.1, Migne, P.G. VII, 1175.
582 Ibid.
583 Pseudo-Hippolytus, *Discourse on the End of the World*, 1; Migne, P.G. X, 905.
584 Whealey, Alice. "'De Consummatione Mundi' of Pseudo-Hippolytus : Another Byzantine Apocalypse from the Early Islamic Period." *Byzantion*, vol. 66, no. 2, 1996, pp. 461–469. *JSTOR*, www.jstor.org/stable/44172291. Accessed 21 Apr. 2021.

Hippolytus of Rome (202 AD) believed Isaiah 1:7, "Your country is desolate..." referred to the Jews: "Are not the things announced by you fulfilled? Is not their country, Judea, desolate?"[585] The pseudo-Hippolytus, writing centuries later in the document Madrid cites, thought otherwise: "For it is not of the Jews that he spoke this word of old, nor of the city of Zion, but of the Church."[586] The former is known to be the work of Irenæus' disciple, Hippolytus, early in the third century, whereas the latter is known to be a seventh century adaptation, by a different man, for a different time, and certainly no "early" witness of Mary as "Mother of God."

Thaumaturgus

Madrid's next exhibit[587] is ostensibly from Gregory Thaumaturgus' *First Homily* (262 AD) in which he writes, "For Luke, in the inspired Gospel narratives, delivers a testimony not to Joseph only, but also to Mary the mother of God (Θεοτόκω Μαρία)."[588] However, even Roman Catholic scholars acknowledge the homily to be a spurious work. Roman Catholic priest, Thomas Livius, who was attempting to find evidence of early devotion to Mary, conceded that the citation from Gregory was "of doubtful genuineness."[589]

"Methodius"

Madrid's next exhibit[590] is ascribed to Methodius of Olympus (305 AD) from his *Oration on Simeon and Anna*. Of Mary he is alleged to have written, "Hail to you for ever, you virgin mother of God,[591] our unceasing joy, for unto you do I again return."[592] However, the *Oration* as we have it today is obviously a later adaptation of an earlier work, so hopelessly compromised that respected church historian Phillip Schaff acknowledges that it is "obviously

---

585 Hippolytus, *On Antichrist*, 30.
586 Pseudo Hippolytus, *On the End of the World*, 3.
587 Madrid, pp. 163-164
588 Gregory Thaumaturgus, *First Homily*; Migne, P.G. X, 1153.
589 Livius, Thomas, *The Blessed Virgin in the Fathers of the First Six Centuries*, (London: Burns and Oates, 1893), p. 48n.
590 Madrid, p. 164.
591 The Greek original omits any reference to *Theotokos* (Godbearer) or *mitera tou Theou* "Mother of God." (Migne, P.G. XVIII, 381.
592 Methodius, *Oration on Simeon and Anna*, 14.

corrupt,"[593] and Roman Catholic apologist Steve Ray dates it to the ninth century.[594] In the opening paragraph, Methodius rejoices that, *unlike* the Ark of the Old Covenant, which "may not be touched," the New Ark, Jesus Christ invites us to Himself: "'Come unto Me, all you that labour and are heavy laden.' Who, then, will not run to Him?"[595] Then, for some unexplained reason, Methodius completely changes his tune four chapters later, writing that, *like* the Ark of the Old Covenant, the New Ark, Mary, cannot be approached but "with reverence and trembling."[596] Such is the nonsense contained in the *Oration* that was obviously redacted centuries later to accommodate a medieval, superstitious, Mariological mindset. "Tokens of such corruptions are not wanting," Schaff warns, "and there can be little doubt that Methodius the monkish artist and missionary of the ninth century has been often copied into the works of his earlier namesake."[597] Madrid's citation of "Methodius" is hardly credible evidence of an early devotion to the "Mother of God."

Alexander of Alexandria

At last, Madrid finally produces an exhibit with unimagined, unredacted, uncompromised, unforged, unfalsified evidence for the title *theotokos*.[598] As respected Roman Catholic scholar Fr. Michael O'Carroll concedes, this is the "first certain literary use of the title,"[599] and it comes to us from Alexander of Alexandria, the mentor of Athanasius himself, in 324 AD during the Arian controversy.

In his original context, Alexander demonstrated in explicit terms that the early church did not believe, and could not have believed, that *theotokos* was to be understood to mean "Mother of God." In his letter to Alexander of Constantinople, Alexander of

---

593 Schaff, ANF 6, 383.
594 Ray, Steve, *Patristic Sources on Mary as the Ark of the New Covenant*, retrieved June 21, 2015 from the world wide web at http://www.catholic-convert.com/documents/MaryArkPatristics.doc.
595 Methodius, *Oration on Simeon and Anna*, 1.
596 Methodius, *Oration on Simeon and Anna*, 4.
597 Schaff, *General Note on Methodius, AnteNicene Fathers*, Volume 6.
598 Madrid, p, 164.
599 O'Carroll, Michael. *Theotokos: A Theological Encyclopedia of the Blessed Virgin Mary*. United States, Wipf and Stock Publishers, 2000, p. 342.

Alexandria used the term in order to distinguish between Jesus' *incorporeal divine generation* from His Father and His *corporeal generation* from His mother. When speaking of Jesus' eternal generation by the Father, Alexander uses the term Θεογονίας (*Theogonias*), a term used exclusively for the birth or generation of a divine person—Theo referring to God, and *gonias*, the Greek root of "gonads," the organs of generation. Alexander did not believe we could fully understand His *theogonias* by His Father:

> And in one Lord Jesus Christ, the only-begotten Son of God; not begotten of things which are not, but of Him who is the Father; not in a corporeal manner ... but in a certain inexplicable and unspeakable manner .... the nature of rational beings cannot receive the knowledge of His divine generation (Θεογονίας, *Theogonias*) by the Father.[600]

In the same paragraph, Alexander then turns to a discussion on the body Jesus received from Mary. Now speaking of His physical generation, Alexander uses the term Θεοτόκου (*Theotokou*), a term describing the bearing of a physical body received in human gestation:

> ... Jesus Christ, who in very deed, and not in appearance merely, carried (lit. wore) a body, of Mary [the Godbearer] (Θεοτόκου, *Theotokou*) ... [601]

The fact that the "first certain literary use of the title" *Theotokos* is found in an attempt to differentiate between Jesus' human generation from his mother (*Theotokou*) and His divine generation by His Father (*Theogonias*) shows that the term could not have been used to mean "Mother of God." Although it is true that *theotokos* was used early in the fourth century to refer to the fact that Mary carried a divine Person in her womb, the church refrained from

---

600 Alexander of Alexandria, *To Alexander, Bishop of the City of Constantinople*; P.G. XVIII, 565.
601 Alexander of Alexandria, *To Alexander, Bishop of the City of Constantinople*, 12; P.G. XVIII, 568.

using the term Θεογεννήτωρ (*Theogennetor*, divine generator) to refer to Mary, and instead settled on a more appropriate title. Nevertheless, eventually "theotokos" began to be translated into Latin as "Mater Dei" or "Dei Genitrix" at the end of the fourth century, the very construct Alexander of Alexandria had so carefully avoided in his formulations in 324 AD. By the late fourth century, "St. Ambrose first used the title *Mater Dei* in the West" and after the Council of Ephesus in 431 AD, "Dei Genitrix would become widespread" as well. [602] What is missing in church history, however, is any use of *Mater Dei* or *Dei Genitrix* for three hundred years after the apostles, or any indication that *Theotokos* was understood in any way other than Protestants understand it today: God-bearer. That alone is sufficiently damaging to Madrid's claims that the term "Mother of God" dates back two thousand years, but what is far worse for him, the "first certainly literary use" inadvertently proves the exact opposite of what he intended.

Mother of Christ's humanity

Madrid's second point is that "women don't give birth to a nature, they give birth to a person. ... the person born at the Nativity was God himself. Mary is His mother."[603] We are to understand from Madrid that to say otherwise is a rejection of Christ's divinity and the incarnation. Nevertheless, the careful distinction between Mary's generation of His body and His Father's generation of His divinity dates back to the ancient church, as the evidence proves. It was common in the early church to acknowledge that in His divine generation, *Jesus had no Mother*:

> Lactantius (250-325 AD): For in His first nativity, which was spiritual, He was 'motherless,' because He was begotten by God the Father alone, without the office of a mother. But in His second, which was in the flesh, He was born of a virgin's womb without the office of a father ....[604]

---

602 O'Carroll, 127, 258.
603 Madrid, pp. 162-163
604 Lactantius, *Divine Institutes*, Book IV, ch. 13.

Athanasius of Alexandria (c. 356 AD): Now the scope
and character of Holy Scripture, as we have often said, is
this,—it contains a double account of the Saviour; that He
was ever God, and is the Son, being the Father's Word and
Radiance and Wisdom; and that afterwards for us He took
flesh of a Virgin, Mary Bearer of God (θεοτοκου), and was
made man.[605]

Augustine of Hippo (354 – 450 AD): He was in an extraordinary manner begotten of the Father without a mother,
born of a mother without a father; without a mother He
was God, without a father He was man; without a mother
before all time, without a father in the end of times. ...
Our Lord Jesus Christ was both God and man. According
as He was God, He had not a mother; according as He was
man, He had. She was the mother, then, of His flesh, of His
humanity, of the weakness which for our sakes He took
upon Him.[606]

Ambrose of Milan (396 AD): Who in His Divine Generation
had no mother, was in His Birth of the Virgin Mary without
a father; begotten before the ages of the Father alone, born
in this age of the Virgin alone.[607]

Madrid's clumsy statement that "women don't give birth to a
nature" is quite beside the point. The ancient church was comfort-
able enough saying the obvious, and so are we: *according as He was
God, He had no mother*. And therefore, we reject not only the title
"Mother of God," but also Madrid's flawed, misleading, halting, un-
scholarly and anemic attempt to impute apostolicity to it. Madrid
concludes that "those representative quotes from the Fathers
showing the early Church firmly believed in Mary as 'Mother of
God'" should give pause to anyone who denies the title.[608] And

---

605 Athanasius, *Discourse III against the Arians*, 29.
606 Augustine, *Lectures on the Gospel of John*, 8.8-9.
607 Ambrose, Epistle 63.
608 Madrid, p. 166

yet, it is not the title *theotokos* we reject, for we know well what it means (God-bearer), as did the early church, using it to distinguish Jesus' human generation from His divine generation. What gives us pause are the misleading latinizations, *Mater Dei* or *Dei Genitrix*, the very construct the Greek *theotokos* was originally coined to avoid. The early church used the term precisely because God has no mother, and Mary was not God's genitrix. The real problem is not with Protestants who refuse the title "Mother of God," but rather with Roman Catholics who embrace forged, fraudulent, compromised, anachronistic medieval writings to support its apostolicity.

Books of the Bible

———————— (Zins) ————————

Patrick Madrid defends the dramatic inclusion of the Apocryphal books into the canon of Scripture by the Council of Trent
in the sixteenth century. Another name for the seven contested
books that form the Old Testament canon of the Roman Catholic
Bible is Deuterocanonical, meaning "second canon." Madrid wants
his readers to know that in the centuries preceding the Council
of Trent there were other statements made historically about
the extent of the canon. He mentions the Council of Florence and
the Synod of Rome, and councils of Hippo and Carthage. He then
throws in the Council of Laodicea, Pope Innocent I, and the 7th
Ecumenical Council, Nicea II.

He does this in a vain attempt to give the impression that
the end of the fourth century marked the beginning of officially
declaring the Old Testament canon. He wishes to leave the idea that
all other councils and declarations more or less fall in line as to the
exact number of books belonging in the canon. He asserts that the
only thing for the Council of Trent to do was to officially "name"
each book.

However, history tells us quite a different story. A careful
inquiry shows that the Council of Trent did not end up with

the same list of books as Madrid's "African code" of Hippo and Carthage. In fact, the North African councils were nothing more than regional conferences with no authority to bind Christians in other regions.[609] To be clear, there was anything but agreement as to the extent of the Old Testament canon leading up to the Council of Trent. With this assessment even Roman Catholic authorities agree. William Webster quotes from the *New Catholic Encyclopedia*, which explains contra Madrid:

> St. Jerome distinguished between canonical books and ecclesiastical books. The latter he judged were circulated by the Church as good spiritual reading but were not recognized as authoritative Scripture. The situation remained unclear in the ensuing centuries… For example, John of Damascus, Gregory the Great, Walafrid, Nocolas of Lyra and Tostado continued to doubt the canonicity of the deuterocanonical books… According to Catholic doctrine, the proximate criterion of the biblical canon is the infallible history of the Church at the Council of Trent… The Council of Trent definitely settled the matter of the Old Testament Canon. That this had not been done previously is apparent from the uncertainty that persisted up to the time of Trent.[610]

Despite Madrid's efforts to show a lockstep, fall-in-line agreement of the canon of the Old Testament by his Roman Catholic Church, it was only at the Council of Trent where the first infallible and effectually promulgated declaration on the Canon of Scripture was essentially binding on all of Catholicism. The Tridentine list trumped all others and became the standard.

But why the confusion between 400 AD and 1546?

Madrid makes it seem as though the Reformers omitted the Apocryphal books from the Old Testament irreverently and in

---

609 For an excellent analysis of Augustine and the N. African canon see *Holy Scripture: The Ground and Pillar of Our Faith*, Volume II, pp. 345 f.
610 Webster, William, *Holy Scripture: The Ground and Pillar of Our Faith*, Volume II (Christian Resources Inc., Battle Ground, Washington, 2001), p. 349.

defiance of the true canon of the text. However, history tells us another story. There is no conclusive proof that any of these Deuterocanonical writings were a portion of the original Septuagint (LXX).

The LXX is said to have been composed by 70 Jewish writers meeting in Alexandria, Egypt (hence the Septuagint from the Latin *septuaginta* or 70) for the purpose of translating the Hebrew Old Testament into the Greek language. The Septuagint became very popular among the Greek-speaking Jews of north Africa, and it received wide recognition outside of Africa as well. During the time of Jesus Christ early converts to Christianity were Greek-speaking Gentiles who used the Septuagint (LXX) as their Old Testament. The Jewish community that converted to Christianity and spoke Greek was fond of the Septuagint as well. However, the canon of Israel did not accept these disputed books of the Old Testament and refused to recognize them as canonical. Ultimately for Christians, a choice had to be made. Who best knew the God-inspired books of the Old Testament? Following Augustine and many others, the Septuagint with the disputed books was accepted as canonical. However, many were in doubt as to the credibility of adding these books. When Jerome translated the Old Testament into Latin, he refused to include the disputed books as canonical. Hence, a division between Augustine and Jerome ensued on this critical matter. This uncertainty would continue all the way up to the Council of Trent.

At the time of the Reformation research into the Jewish canon led conclusively to the Jewish canon not accepting the Apocryphal books. To some it did not matter. Readily accepting the Jewish exclusion of the Deuterocanonical writings, many prominent Western Church Fathers accepted these books, nonetheless. The Eastern Church was much more suspicious and was not as certain. The testimony of the East was that the original Jewish canon of 22 books was the inspired canon.

It is extremely important to note that the New Testament refers to the fact that the nation of Israel was entrusted with the oracles of God.

Then what advantage has the Jew? Or what is the benefit of circumcision? Great in every respect. First of all, that they were entrusted with the oracles of God. (Romans 3:1-3)

What were the oracles of God? The writers of the New Testament refer to the Old Testament in the threefold division of the law of Moses, the Prophets, and the Psalms.[611] This threefold division is the standard division of the closed Hebrew canon of the Old Testament. The Reformers did not throw out a portion of the inspired text. They merely went back to the oracles of God and dismissed the books not belonging to the canon.

As part of the ongoing Roman Catholic misdirection, Madrid claims that for roughly 300 years after the Reformation virtually all Protestant Bibles contained the Deuterocanonical books. What he does not tell us is that *containing* does not mean *recognizing* them as canonical. The Lutheran Bible, Genevan Bible and the King James version of the Bible all put the Apocrypha in between the Old and New Testaments under special headings. They are not considered as part of the canon of the text. The Westminster Confession of faith of 1646 bans the Apocrypha. Virtually all of the Bibles printed after the Reformation included some of the Apocryphal writings but only under separate categories well-labeled as not part of the canon. Madrid misleads on purpose.

Madrid closes with typical generalities which are designed and arranged to arrive at his conclusions. It is true that some early church Fathers accepted the seven books of the Apocrypha. However, the greater witness is that they erred. The Deuterocanonical books were definitely not a part of the Hebrew canon which constitute the oracles of God. It is true that the Reformers sought to delete these books, but they were not wrong to do so. Contrary to Madrid the Catholic version of the Bible is not the complete version of scripture. It is the fudged version of the Bible. In admitting these non-admissible books Rome sets Herself above history and

---

611 For an excellent discussion on the Hebrew Canon see Webster, *The Ground and Pillar of Our Faith*, Vol. II, Chap. 6 wherein the author mentions among many Philo, Josephus, Aquila, Church Fathers, and Rabbinical Literature which sets the Hebrew Canon as closed and excludes the Apocryphal writings.

scripture. To compound Her error Rome will adduce anti-Christian doctrine from the canon She alone has created.

Calling Priests "Father"

———————— (Zins) ————————

There has been much discussion pertaining to the Roman Catholic custom of referring to their religious leaders by the term "Father." Evidently, many in the Protestant community do not understand why Rome would use the term "Father" when it appears that the Bible forbids Christians from calling anyone their "Father" except God in heaven. The exchange centers upon the meaning of our Lord's words in Matthew 23.

> Then Jesus said to the crowds and to his disciples: "The teachers of the law and the Pharisees sit in Moses' seat. So you must obey them and do everything they tell you. But do not do what they do, for they do not practice what they preach. They tie up heavy loads and put them on men's shoulders, but they themselves are not willing to lift a finger to move them. "Everything they do is done for men to see: They make their phylacteries wide and the tassels on their garments long; they love the place of honor at banquets and the most important seats in the synagogues; they love to be greeted in the marketplaces *and to have men call them 'Rabbi.'* "But you are not to be called 'Rabbi,'

for you have only one Master and you are all brothers. And
do not call anyone on earth 'father,' for you have one Father,
and he is in heaven. Nor are you to be called 'teacher,' for you
have one Teacher, the Christ. The greatest among you will be
your servant. For whoever exalts himself will be humbled,
and whoever humbles himself will be exalted. (Matthew
23:1-12, NIV)

We would certainly agree that Jesus is not forbidding the use of the
term "father" or "teacher" or "master" or "Rabbi" as though these
terms are to be swept from all languages and never used again.
Madrid accurately states that Jesus is not banning these terms from
all use.

However, having recognized that there is no universal ban on
calling fathers father or teachers teacher, etc., we need to ask, "Why
then did Jesus use such strong language in this context?" A closer
look at the contrast Jesus is making suggests that calling Roman
Catholic priests "Fathers" creates the same kind of atmosphere that
Jesus is undoing in this passage.

In this context Jesus assails the hypocritical Pharisees. He calls
them out. They tie up heavy loads on men's shoulders. They do
everything to look good before men. They love the place of honor
at banquets and the most important seats in the synagogues.
Most of all, they love to be recognized in the marketplaces and
to be called Rabbi. In short, they are in love with their positions
and their power. They are prideful and cocky with a suffocating
arrogance about them. They set themselves above their constitu-
ency and expect to be praised by one and all. They are truly self-ex-
alted! They think they are entitled by their title. But their example
proves them to be a sham. A higher authority must prevail in the
minds of the followers of Jesus Christ. There is danger in giving
titles to men and setting them on a pedestal. The New Testament
warns of haughty Elders and the danger of false teachers and
so-called masters. Do not lay hands on anyone too hastily. All
leaders in the New Testament are schooled by the example and the
teaching of the apostles. Hence, it is imperative to understand that

all Christians are to view one another as equally important and saints of the most-high God. All Christians are brothers and sisters in Christ. Heavy-handed authority in the body of Christ is to be resisted. All Christians are to place themselves under the authority of the Word of God.

The Roman Catholic religion has given men authority that is absent from the Bible. Men called priests and informally referred to as "Fathers" have been misled by yet higher authorities in Roman Catholicism. Rome places Her "Fathers" in front of the congregation and anoints them with power to forgive sins, and turn bread wafers into the body, blood, soul, and divinity of Jesus Christ. They are given the power to represent the sacrifice of Jesus on an unbloody altar for forgiveness of sins. This authority is corrupt in a way different from the corruptness of the Pharisees. But they share in the same malady of intoxication via power and stature and an uninterrupted false teaching of the scriptures.

The parallels between the Pharisees of the first century and the religious leaders of the Roman Catholic religion are striking. Both groups dress in finery and strut their positions. Both groups demand absolute obedience to their teachings. Both groups demand that their authority and recourse to history be the final word on truth. Both groups deny the priesthood of all believers and force their religious rituals upon the misled and ignorant. The pomp of Rome matches the arrogance of the Pharisees. The modern exposure of Roman Catholic abuse and cover-up should be a wakeup call to a system that is systemically incapable of reform or true Christianity.

In the light of these observations, the echo of our Lord's words to the Pharisees suit the modern situation as well. You are not to be called Pope, Archbishop or Cardinal. Do not call anyone from earth your 'Father' in the sense of blindly following his instruction without discernment. Do not unthinkingly follow the teaching of men. Rather, consult your Father in heaven and examine all things by the Word of God. Though Rome is guilty on all counts of misleading, false teaching, and "hierarchy hypocrisy," the message of

Matthew is not to be discounted for the real Body of Christ. D. A. Carson sums up the danger:

> ...we must say the risen Christ is as displeased with those in his church who demand unquestioning submission to themselves and their opinions and confuse a reputation for showy piety with godly surrender to his teaching as he ever was with any Pharisee.[612]

---

612 Carson D. A., *The Expositor's Bible Commentary* (Zondervan Publishing House, Grand Rapids Michigan, 1995), p. 475.

Baptism

———————————— (Zins) ————————————

The Roman Catholic religion has emphatically emphasized over and over that water baptism is necessary for salvation. There are only two exceptions to this rule. The first is baptism of blood. The second is baptism of desire. To die as a martyr is the equivalent of gaining the grace offered in baptism. To die due to conditions that prevent the *desire* for baptism is the equivalent of gaining the grace offered in baptism. But in the main all who wish for eternal life must be baptized.

Baptism is one of the seven sacraments in the Roman Catholic system. Each sacrament is said to both signify and make present graces proper to each sacrament. Here is what the New Catholic Catechism has to say about baptism.

> **1213** Holy Baptism is the basis of the whole Christian life, the gateway to life in the Spirit *(vitae spiritualis ianua)*, and the door which gives access to the other sacraments. Through Baptism we are freed from sin and reborn as sons of God; we become members of Christ, are incorporated into the Church and made sharers in her mission: "Baptism

is the sacrament of regeneration through water in the word."

1131 The sacraments are efficacious signs of grace, in-stituted by Christ and entrusted to the Church, by which divine life is dispensed to us. The visible rites by which the sacraments are celebrated signify and make present the graces proper to each sacrament. They bear fruit in those who receive them with the required dispositions.[613]

Patrick Madrid promises us that there is plenty of biblical proof for all the Roman Catholic sacraments. To make his boast come true, Madrid must prove the Bible teaches that water baptism brings about forgiveness of sin, regeneration, and making one a member of the Body of Christ. Let us look at Madrid's defense of Roman Catholic baptism.

He begins by asserting that the water mentioned in John 3:3-7 refers to baptism. But does it? Here is the text:

Now there was a man of the Pharisees, named Nicodemus, a ruler of the Jews; this man came to Him by night, and said to Him, "Rabbi, we know that You have come from God as a teacher; for no one can do these signs that You do unless God is with him." Jesus answered and said to him, *"Truly, truly, I say to you, unless one is born again,* he cannot see the kingdom of God." Nicodemus said to Him, "How can a man be born when he is old? He cannot enter a second time into his mother's womb and be born, can he?" Jesus answered, "Truly, truly, I say to you, *unless one is born of water and the Spirit, he cannot enter into the kingdom of God.* That which is born of the flesh is flesh, and that which is born of the Spirit is spirit. Do not marvel that I said to you, 'You must be born again.' The wind blows where it wishes and you hear the sound of it, but do not know where it comes from

---

613 *Catechism of the Catholic Church, Second Edition* (English Translation for the United States-Libreira Editrice Vaticana, 1994), pp. 312,293.

and where it is going; *so is everyone who is born of the Spirit.*
(John 3:1-9)

We notice here that there is no mention of baptism. The word
baptism is not found in this episode. We also notice that
Nicodemus is being chided by the Lord for not knowing about the
things He is teaching. "Jesus answered and said to him, 'Are you
the teacher of Israel, and do not understand these things?'" (John
3:10). Jesus would hardly chastise Nicodemus for not knowing
about Christian baptism since it had not yet been inaugurated. It is
one thing to claim that the water here refers to baptism. It is quite
another to offer solid biblical proof. Madrid simply declares the
water here is baptism. Many scholars believe that the water here
references the physical birth of a child. The point then would be
that one must be born not just of water (physically) but also of the
spirit (spiritually). Others would translate the passage "unless one
is born of the water *even* the Spirit...". The Greek "and" (*kai)* is used
in an ascensive way, with the water representative of the Spirit.
Still others see the water here as a reference to the Word of God,
picking up the thought of Ephesians 5.

> Husbands, love your wives, just as Christ also loved the
> church and gave Himself up for her; that He might sanctify
> her, having cleansed her by the washing of water with the
> word. (Ephesians 5:25-27)

Perhaps the simple answer to the question may be found in the
background of Nicodemus. He would have been fully aware of the
ceremonial cleansing of Israel. The Lord could very well have said
that the ceremonial washings are not enough (water purification),
but one needs to be born of the Spirit. Others cite the proximity to
John's baptism (see John 1:19-28) and have Jesus expressing the
need of something more than water as a symbol of purification,
even with John the Baptist.

The Bible does not support the allegation that the water in
John 3 is in fact baptism. Simply saying that it is will not pass the

biblical credibility test. Hence the entire platform of water regeneration performed by a Roman Catholic priest certainly cannot be
supported by John chapter 3. Those who are not familiar with the
Bible or serious Bible study must rely on Rome to tell them what
any text really means.

Madrid continues to proclaim support for Roman Catholic
baptismal claims with other assertions. He claims that the Lord's
baptism outlined in John chapter 1 is the "mystical pre-figuration"
of the Sacrament of Baptism. He further contends that Jesus transubstantiated water at the wedding feast of Cana. This too is part of
the so-called pre-figuration of Roman Catholic baptism. Of course,
this is simply Roman Catholic imagination gone wild. There is
nothing in the text of these two incidents that would suggest such
a meaning or significance supplied by Madrid. They are part of a
pattern of wild and dangerous Roman Catholic declarations not
found in the text itself.

Part of Rome's allegations for Her sacraments is that the
physical rites of a particular sacrament not only symbolize what
happens but also make it happen. With this in mind, Madrid
asserts, "The Bible is clear that baptism is more than a mere symbol
of our initiation into the Body of Christ. It really does what it signifies."[614] His proof text is found in Acts 2:38.

> And Peter said to them, "Repent, and let each of you be
> baptized in the name of Jesus Christ for the forgiveness of
> your sins; and you shall receive the gift of the Holy Spirit."
> (Acts 2:38)

As an addendum Madrid adds after citing this verse, "It doesn't get
much clearer than that."[615]

By saying it cannot get any clearer than this, Madrid suggests
that Acts 2:38 establishes baptismal regeneration/salvation and
reception of the Holy Spirit. This, of course, is wishful thinking and
selective verse quoting to convince the inexperienced. Madrid is

---

614 Madrid, Patrick, *Answer Me This!* (Our Sunday Visitor Publishing Division Huntington,
Indiana, 2003), p. 183.
615 Ibid.

merely stating and not proving or providing any in-depth analysis of the text. We concur with Polhill in his concise and penetrating treatment of Acts 2:38 as he canvasses the rest of Luke-Acts and shows forth from the rest of the Bible the fallacy of ascribing regeneration/salvation to baptism:

> The connection of baptism with the forgiveness of sins in v. 38 has often been a matter of controversy. A literal rendering of the verse runs: "Repent and let each of you be baptized in the name of Jesus Christ *for/on the basis* of the forgiveness of your sins." The disputed word is the preposition *eis*, which could indicate purpose and thus be taken to mean that baptism is the prerequisite for the forgiveness of sins. There is ample evidence in the New Testament, however, that *eis* can also mean on the ground of, on the basis of, which would indicate the opposite relationship— that the forgiveness of sins in Luke-Acts is with repentance and not with baptism at all (cf. Luke 24:47; Acts 3:19; 5:31). In fact, in no other passage of Acts is baptism presented as bringing about the forgiveness of sins. If not linked with repentance, forgiveness is connected with faith (cf. 10:43; 13:38f.; 26:18). The dominant idea in 2:38 thus seems to be repentance, with the other elements following. Repentance leads to baptism, the forgiveness of sins, and the gift of the Spirit. The essential response Peter called [for] from the Jewish crowd is the complete turnabout that comprises true repentance, to turn away from their rejection of the Messiah and to call upon his name, receive baptism into his community, and share the gift of the Spirit they had just witnessed so powerfully at work in the Christians at Pentecost.[616]

We would add that the connection of the reception of the Holy Spirit and baptism is depicted in various sequences in Acts. In 2:38

---

616 Polhill, John B. *The New American Commentary, Acts,* Volume 26 (B&H Publishing Nashville, 1992), p. 117.

the Spirit is said to come on the basis of or on the ground of forgiveness of sins. However, in Acts 10:44-48 the Spirit is given before
baptism. The Spirit has no set pattern and is not tied down to water
in the New Testament.

As we move forward into Madrid's defense of Roman Catholic
baptism we again are faced with more declarations, assertions, and
proclamations with virtually no biblical analysis or evaluation.
As with John 3, Madrid simply says that it is so by throwing out a
verse. This is indoctrination by declaration! But this is not how one
ought to arrive at biblical teaching.

Madrid summons Romans 6 as his next proof text. He does not
attempt to explain this text. He simply sees the word "baptized"
and assumes it is Roman Catholic baptism.

> Or do you not know that all of us *who have been baptized*
> *into Christ Jesus have been baptized into His death?*
> Therefore, *we have been buried with Him through baptism*
> *into death,* in order that as Christ was raised from the dead
> through the glory of the Father, so we too might walk in
> newness of life. (Romans 6:3-5)

There is much written about the lack of water in this passage. The
Roman Catholic must assume two vital things from this passage.
The first is that baptism here references water baptism. Second,
that the ceremony of actual water baptism brings about union
with Christ in His death and burial.

The apostle Paul can talk about the Christian experience in
several ways. The promise of the Holy Spirit is given to those who
by faith are *baptized* with the Holy Spirit. It is by one Spirit that we
are all *baptized* into the Body of Christ. The prerequisite for being in
union with Christ in His death and burial is faith alone. Only those
who have believed are baptized into Christ.

> But before faith came, we were kept in custody under
> the law, being shut up to the faith which was later to be
> revealed. Therefore, the Law has become our tutor to lead

us to Christ, that we may be *justified by faith*. But now that
faith has come, we are no longer under a tutor. *For you are
all sons of God through faith in Christ Jesus. For all of you
who were baptized into Christ have clothed yourselves with
Christ.* There is neither Jew nor Greek, there is neither slave
nor free man, there is neither male nor female; for you are
all one in Christ Jesus. And if you belong to Christ, then
you are Abraham's offspring, heirs according to promise.
(Galatians 3:23-29)

Even if Romans 6 refers to water baptism (and that assumption is
precarious) there is no biblical hint that water baptism does what
Rome says it does. Water baptism cannot bring about being buried
with Jesus Christ into His death. The claim of Madrid that water
baptism does what it signifies is false. To be sure, water baptism
signifies the death, burial, and resurrection of Jesus Christ but it
does not put us into it. Faith alone puts us into it. Only those of
faith enter the waters of baptism to signify their faith by union
with the death and burial of Jesus Christ. Water comes after the
Holy Spirit falls and faith is given in every occasion of conversion to
Christ in the New Testament.

While Peter was still speaking these words, *the Holy Spirit
fell upon all those who were listening to the message.* And
all the circumcised believers who had come with Peter
were amazed, because *the gift of the Holy Spirit had been
poured out upon the Gentiles* also. For they were hearing
them speaking with tongues and exalting God. Then Peter
answered, "Surely no one can refuse the water for these to
be baptized *who have received the Holy Spirit just as we did,
can he?*" And he ordered them to be baptized in the name of
Jesus Christ. Then they asked him to stay on for a few days.
(Acts 10:44-48)

But *when they believed Philip* preaching the good news
about the kingdom of God and the name of Jesus Christ,

they were being baptized, men and women alike. (Acts
8:11-12)

After citing 5 other passages that touch upon baptism Madrid
makes this extraordinary claim on behalf of Roman Catholicism. "If
the common Anabaptist theory that baptism is an ordinance that
does not actually do what it signifies [is correct], the passages above
would be rendered meaningless."[617]

Yet the passages quoted above do not come close to teaching
Rome's claims. After a careful analysis, the passages teach the
opposite. Also, what the baptism passages really teach is of
immense comfort and encouragement for Christians. Wayne
Grudem summarizes in his systematic theology:

> The Greek word *baptizo* means "to plunge, dip, immerse
> something in water." This is the commonly recognized and
> standard meaning of the term in ancient Greek literature
> both inside and outside of the Bible.[618]

> The Roman Catholic argument that baptism is necessary
> for salvation is very similar to the argument of Paul's
> opponents in Galatia who said that circumcision was
> necessary for salvation. Paul's response is that those who
> require circumcision are preaching "a different gospel"
> (Gal. 1:6). He says that "all who rely on works of the law are
> under a curse" (Gal. 3:10) and speaks very severely to those
> who attempt to add any form of obedience as a require-
> ment for justification: "You are severed from Christ, you
> who would be justified by the law; you have fallen away
> from grace" (Gal. 5:4). Therefore, we must conclude that

---

617 Ibid., p. 183.
618 *Systematic Theology: An Introduction To Biblical Doctrine* (Zondervan 1994), p. 967.
Grudem lists in his footnote on *baptizo* the following: So LSJ, p.305: "plunge"; passive, to be
drowned." Similarly, BAGD, p.131; "dip, immerse", and middle, "dip oneself, wash (in non-
Christian literature also 'plunge, sink, drench, overwhelm). In TDNT, 1:530: to immerse...to
sink the ship"; passive, 'to sink...to suffer shipwreck, to drown...

no *work* is necessary for salvation. And therefore *baptism* is not necessary for salvation.[619]

Madrid closes his section on baptism bringing about salvation by comparing it to marriage. Consistent with Roman Catholic indoctrination by proclamation, Madrid believes that joining of hands, exchanging vows, and exchanging rings actually brings about a real inward change. Obviously, there is not a shred of biblical truth to this. Does not common sense teach us that the inward change precedes the ceremony? Do not love and willingness to be one precede the ceremony? Evidently not in Rome, where the ceremony brings about the inward change. Ceremonies cannot make two people become "one flesh," any more than a ribbon cutting can create a building.

Infant Baptism

Roman Catholics are taught to baptize their infants. Interestingly, Madrid admits that there is no explicit statement concerning *children* baptism to be found in the Bible. He uses the word children and not infant.

> As far as any explicit statement goes, the Bible is silent on whether *children* should be baptized or not.[620]

The fact is that Rome teaches Her adherents to baptize their *infants.* So if there is no biblical proof for this practice by way of clear command or statement, then why do it? Madrid thinks there is ample *implicit* evidence.

His first proof once again is indoctrination by proclamation. Without any biblical proof or investigation, he boldly proclaims, "First, recall that the New Testament Sacrament of Baptism replaced the Old Testament ordinance of circumcision."[621] Nowhere does the New Testament teach us that male circumcision, as the covenant sign of national identity for Israel, is replaced

---

619 Ibid., p. 973.
620 Madrid, p. 185. Emphasis mine.
621 Ibid.

by Christian baptism in the New Testament. In the first place
they are two radically different covenants. They signify totally
different realities. Also, the recipients of the two covenant signs
are different. In the Old Covenant only infant males are circumcised. There is no regenerating grace or sins forgiven related to the
Old Covenant sign of circumcision. In the New Testament only
believers in Christ are baptized. In the New Testament baptism
does not make one a part of a national identity. It is important
to note that whereas Rome claims that regenerating grace and
adoption into the spiritual family of God magically take place with
male and female infant baptism, they claim no such significance
for Old Testament circumcision. So to say that one replaces the
other is pure fantasy.

Madrid believes that the passive rite of circumcision opens the
door for the passive rite of infant regeneration, justification, redemption, salvation, and reconciliation with God through infant
baptism. In so doing, Madrid gives the power of eternal life and
forgiveness of sin to Roman Catholic sacraments in the hands
of Roman Catholic priests. He believes this without an ounce of
biblical validation.

Madrid believes that God grants grace through the efforts of
third parties, the point being that the faith of the church or the
parents can stand in for the lack of ability to believe of the infant
in their passive infant baptism. He points to Mark 2:1-12, where
friends carry a paralytic to Jesus. Madrid thinks that because of the
friends' faith, Jesus healed the paralytic. But the text nowhere eliminates the faith of the paralytic himself.

Madrid moves on to 1 Peter 3:18-21 and selectively quotes a
small section of the passage. He glibly says that St. Peter declared,
"Baptism…now saves you."[622] Madrid does not want to get into
the entire verse because it has nothing to do with infant baptism.
There are no infant baptisms in the entire New Testament. We
should take a moment to reflect on the big picture in Rome. Madrid
would have to say that this verse teaches way too much. If baptism
actually saves, then what need is there of the other sacraments?

---

622 Madrid, p. 186.

The answer in Rome reveals their entire system. There is no true salvation in Rome. To believe that you are really saved eternally is the sin of presumption in Roman Catholicism. Hence, baptism does not save. Madrid simply throws out a quarter of a verse with no elucidation. The reality is that baptism in Rome is merely the beginning of a long and lengthy attachment to the Roman Catholic system of sacraments, sacramentals, meriting grace, and Romish religious rituals.

Grasping at more straws, Madrid argues that the command to repent that precedes the command to be baptized in Acts 2:38 must not prevent infants from being regenerated and "saved" in infant baptism. In Rome, the fact that infants cannot repent is no obstacle to being baptized. His logic is that Paul commands anyone who does not work should not eat. Madrid asks, "Since infants cannot work so should they not eat?" Likewise, if infants cannot repent, should they not be baptized? However, Madrid misreads the text of 2 Thessalonians 3:10. The text says, "If any one does not *wish* to work, neither let him eat." Paul's command is only to those who wish not to work and has nothing to do with babies. Likewise, Peter's command is to those who can repent and has nothing to do with babies or inability.

Madrid presses forward to prove infant baptismal regeneration. He maintains that because John the Baptist was filled with the Holy Spirit while yet in his mother's womb that the Christian argument against infant baptism is invalid. How so? Madrid explains the passage about John the Baptist would make no sense since as a fetus, unable to repent, John received the gift of God's grace. Yes, John was filled with the Holy Spirit prior to being physically born. But this is an extreme exception. No other person other than perhaps the Lord Jesus Christ is afforded this gift. Also, this gift did not come about through the waters of infant baptism. Madrid defeats his own religion. John the Baptist is not baptized as an infant!

Finally, in a bewildering non sequitur Madrid summons Luke 18:15-17.

> And they were bringing even their babies to Him so that
> He might touch them, but when the disciples saw it, they
> began rebuking them. But Jesus called for them, saying,
> "Permit the children to come to Me, and do not hinder
> them, for the kingdom of God belongs to such as these.
> Truly I say to you, whoever does not receive the kingdom of
> God like a child shall not enter it at all." (Luke 18:15-17)

He then follows this with the question, "How do we come to Christ and become members of His mystical Body? Through baptism."[623] Yet there is no baptism in this text, much less infant baptism.

Madrid closes out his declarations on baptism with yet one more pretentious indoctrination by proclamation. "And finally, don't forget that the practice of infant baptism was universal in the early Church. The early Church Fathers are unanimous and emphatic that the historic Christian teaching on infant baptism comes directly from the apostles themselves."[624] Madrid then cites Irenaeus of Lyons, Hippolytus, and Augustine in his end notes without quoting them directly. In so doing Madrid ignores the avalanche of research into the Church Fathers that directly contradicts his claim of unanimity among the early Church Fathers.[625]

It is much better and to be on much safer ground to remember that the early Church Fathers were vague and difficult to understand when mentioning baptism, much less infant baptism, which is not cited at all in the earliest handbook for baptism, the *Didache* (AD 100-110). This is the most ancient handbook on baptism and contains no reference to baptizing infants. It is pure fiction to suggest that they were unanimous in their acclaim for infant baptism. Of all the early Church Fathers both east and west, the earliest and most complete statement concerning the baptism of infants comes from Tertullian (AD 200). He emphatically states that it is better to wait until children know what they are doing and

---

623 Madrid , p. 188.
624 Ibid.
625 See Jewett, Paul K., *Infant Baptism and the Covenant of Grace* (William B. Eerdmans Publishing, Grand Rapids, Michigan, 1978) for an excellent summary correction of the supposed early church mandate and practice of infant baptism.

really believing. "Let them 'come' then, while they are growing up; while they are learning, while they are learning whither to come; let them become Christians when they have become able to know Christ."[626] Tertullian ends his section on baptism with these words: "They that understand the weight of baptism will rather dread the receiving of it, than the delaying of it. An entire faith is secure of salvation!"[627]

Contrary to Madrid, it is much better to not forget that the New Testament teaches emphatically a believer's baptism. Grudem sums it up precisely:

> But how does one become a member of the church? The means of entrance into the church is *voluntary, spiritual, and internal*. One becomes a member of the true church by being born again and by having *saving faith*, not by physical birth. It comes about not by an external act, but by internal faith in one's heart. It is certainly true that baptism is the sign of entrance into the church, but this means that it should only be given to those who *give evidence* of membership in the church, only to those who profess faith in Christ.[628]

626 *The Ante-Nicene Fathers*, Volume 3 (Wm. B. Eerdmans Publishing); Tertullian, *On Baptism* Chapter xviii, p. 678.
627 Ibid.
628 Ibid., p. 977.

Confession of Sins

―――――――――― (Zins) ――――――――――

Within the rigors of Roman Catholic religious duties is confession to a priest. This is sometimes called "the second plank" of salvation after the shipwreck which is the loss of grace due to post-baptism sins. It is thus called because confession to a priest is part of the sacrament of penance. Penance is the performance of suitable satisfactions for the attainment of forgiveness of sins. While Rome readily admits that only God can forgive sins, She also believes that God works through Her priests to do so. The Catholic Catechism explains:

> **1456** Confession to a priest is an essential part of the sacrament of Penance: "All mortal sins of which penitents after a diligent self-examination are conscious must be recounted by them in confession, even if they are most secret and have been committed against the last two precepts of the Decalogue; for these sins sometimes wound the soul more grievously and are more dangerous than those which are committed openly."[629]

―――――――――

629 *Catechism of the Catholic Church*, p. 365.

Madrid wishes to respond to what he considers the three main objections to the practice of confessing sins to a priest. The first is the biblical teaching that there is only one mediator between God and man. The second is that priests are sinners like all men. The third is that confessing one's sins to a priest is un-biblical.

We shall take Madrid's defense as he presents it in his own order. While recognizing that Christ alone is uniquely qualified to bridge the gap between God and man, Madrid nevertheless believes that man has what he calls a *subordinate participatory share* in the ministry of Christ. Armed with this reasoning Madrid defends the idea that man shares in the mediation of Christ. We must keep in mind that the text says that there is only one mediator between God and men.

> For there is one God, and one mediator also between God and men, the man Christ Jesus, who gave Himself as a ransom for all, the testimony borne at the proper time. (1 Timothy 2:4-7)

It is the one man, Jesus Christ, who carries the title of one mediator. Just as there is only one God, there is only one man mediator. The burden of proof is on Madrid to show where the Bible teaches that several classes of men have a subordinate share in Christ's mediation.

Madrid seizes upon the fact that Jesus is the perfect and complete sacrifice for redemption, but Christ shares the redemptive mission with man who has a limited subordinate share in the mystery of the Lord's suffering. To prove this, he quotes the Bible.

> Now I rejoice in my sufferings for your sake, and in my flesh I do my share on behalf of His body (which is the church) in filling up that which is lacking in Christ's afflictions. (Colossians 1:24-25)

But does this verse teach that man somehow has a subordinate role in Christ's atonement? We notice the words atonement, satisfaction, propitiation, reconciliation, and redemption are not in this text. There is not a single thing missing in Christ's perfect sacrifice. Paul is referring here to his willingness to suffer the afflictions associated with serving the Body of Christ. There is a filling up of the afflictions of Christ in the sense that the Body of Christ on earth must suffer until the return of Christ. Paul does his share in filling up that which is absent in an eschatological sense. What remains to be filled (not lacking in the atonement) is the continued suffering for and in the Body of Christ until He returns. This suffering is predetermined and represents not what is lacking in the atonement but what is missing until fulfilled.[630]

The next proof for Madrid is an odd assortment of evidence based upon the same faulty reasoning and premise. Madrid reasons that Jesus is the supreme judge, shepherd, creator, high priest, divine healer and king of kings. Thus, every time a man judges, shepherds, partners in producing a baby, sits on a throne in heaven and participates in healing he shares in Christ's ministry. The key word is *share*. What does Madrid mean by *share*? What becomes clear for Madrid is that this make-believe idea, that Christ *shares* His one and only unique ministry and role, is indispensable to bring to pass His ministry. In other words, the way Christ gets things done, like forgiveness of sins, is dependent upon a *shared* ministry with men. The fly in Madrid's ointment is that there simply is no proof that Jesus Christ established a *shared* ministry of redemption, justification, satisfaction, reconciliation, mediation, and forgiveness of sins. Rome thinks that He has because this is what She claims and does. But there is no biblical foundation for Her assertions.

The strongest biblical evidence for a derived authority to forgive sins is found in John 20:21-23. Madrid makes full use of this passage to substantiate the Roman Catholic claim that her Bishops

---

630 For an excellent discussion of this centuries-old controversy over this one verse, see Peter O'Brien in the *Word Biblical Commentary* pages 75 f. Drawing our attention to the first person singular pronouns of Paul, "*I* rejoice in *my* sufferings for your sake, and in *my* flesh *I* do *my* share..", O'Brien shares this valuable insight: "His (Paul's) contribution to the sum total of the messianic afflictions, through his service and suffering bound up with his calling as an apostle or minister to the Gentiles, is on behalf of Christ's body." *Word Biblical Commentary* Volume 44, p. 80.

and Priests have the power and authority invested in themselves to forgive sins. Here is the passage.

> Jesus therefore said to them again, "Peace be with you; as the Father has sent Me, I also send you." And when He had said this, He breathed on them, and said to them, "Receive the Holy Spirit. If you forgive the sins of any, their sins have been forgiven them; if you retain the sins of any, they have been retained." (John 20:20-23)

From these verses Madrid assumes that Jesus is bestowing inherent power to forgive sins on a select few. He then assumes that this select few can bestow this same power on others as they pass into death. He then assumes that the way these select few actually forgive sin is through the penitent whispering into their ears the sins they have committed via a confessional box. He then assumes the retaining and forgiveness of sins is dependent upon the confessor doing penance prescribed by these same Roman Catholic priests.

However, the New Testament teaches none of this. We find that the forgiveness of sins is based upon simple faith in the finished work of Jesus Christ and all Christians are invested with the authority to announce just such forgiveness established through faith alone. Jesus Christ gave his disciples authority to announce full pardon and full forgiveness founded upon His atonement.

This is exactly what they were to do as faithful messengers of the gospel. Notice Luke 24:

> Then He opened their minds to understand the Scriptures, and He said to them, "Thus it is written, that the Christ should suffer and rise again from the dead the third day; and that repentance for forgiveness of sins should be proclaimed in His name to all the nations, beginning from Jerusalem. You are witnesses of these things." (Luke 24:45-49)

There are no confessional boxes in the New Testament. Peter
and Paul do not hear confessions. The message of the gospel is to
repent (change your mind) not do penance (satisfy God with your
own suffering). Madrid perpetuates the Roman Catholic severe
twisting of scripture by declaring that the ministry of reconciliation is dependent upon a new priesthood with supreme authority
to forgive sins and dish out penance. On the contrary, the New
Testament reveals that the ministry of reconciliation is that God
was in Christ reconciling a world of sinners unto Himself through
the atonement of Jesus Christ. The benefit of eternal life and
complete pardon for sins is gained by faith alone apart from works
of the law and personal penance.

> Now all these things are from God, who reconciled us to
> Himself through Christ, and gave us the ministry of rec-
> onciliation, namely, that God was in Christ reconciling the
> world to Himself, not counting their trespasses against
> them, and He has committed to us the word of reconcilia-
> tion. (2 Corinthians 5:18-19)

The word of reconciliation has nothing to do with Roman Catholic
confession to a priest.

Finally, knowing that the straightforward teaching of scripture
is that a person can go directly to Christ and confess his/her sins
without any need for a confession to a priest, Madrid makes up a
bewildering story. Yet the Bible is emphatic that we can go directly
to the Lord and confess our sins.

> If we say that we have fellowship with Him and yet walk
> in the darkness, we lie and do not practice the truth; but if
> we walk in the light as He Himself is in the light, we have
> fellowship with one another, and the blood of Jesus His
> Son cleanses us from all sin. If we say that we have no sin,
> we are deceiving ourselves, and the truth is not in us. If we
> confess our sins, He is faithful and righteous to forgive us
> our sins and to cleanse us from all unrighteousness. If we

say that we have not sinned, we make Him a liar, and His word is not in us. (1 John 1:6-10)

To get around the finality of this biblical promise Rome adds that one must confess to Jesus first and then go to a Roman Catholic priest and make confession to the priest. This second confession gains the priest's forgiveness, which allows the sinner to rejoin the community of saints. So where does Madrid get this nonsense? His proof is that a leper came to Jesus and asked Jesus first to heal him. After getting healed by Jesus he was told to go to the Jewish priest and make an offering according to Jewish law as testimony to them. From this Madrid adduces that the healed leper would then be free to rejoin the community. In a somewhat bizarre statement Madrid says that the townspeople would not know the leper was actually healed until he first went to the priest. It is hard to imagine the lengths to which Rome will go to defend the indefensible. A leper healed by Jesus somehow becomes a Roman Catholic confessing his sins to Jesus and then confessing his sins in a confessional box to a priest. Of course, there is no correlation between the two and scripture does not attempt to draw one. Madrid compounds error upon error in a bid for biblical credibility that vanishes as soon as he seeks it. Faced with the impossible task of defending Rome's nonbiblical doctrine of penance and confession to a priest Madrid amazingly concludes:

> This (the leper healing) parallels the Sacrament of Con-
> fession, in which the repentant sinner goes before the
> priest of the New Covenant, "shows himself" by making a
> complete and sincere confession of the sins he has already
> confessed directly to God. The priest acts in the name of
> Jesus Christ, and with the power of forgiveness that Christ
> imparted to His apostles to pronounce the words of ab-
> solution, forgiving the sinner. This enables the sinner to
> re-enter the "community" of the Body of Christ.[631]

---

631 Madrid, pp. 194-195.

All of this is pure fiction, as we have labored to point out. The scripture twisting, false analogies, and general fantasy of Roman Catholic doctrines come to an end with an honest reading of the Bible in context. Madrid champions Rome and seduces the unwary with his utter gobbledygook.

The Eucharist

———————— (Kauffman) ————————

In his arguments regarding the Lord's Supper, Madrid again assumes that which it is his duty to prove. His first focus here is on the institution narratives in the Gospels, i.e., "this is my body" and "this is my blood," and secondly on Paul's admonition that partaking of the bread and cup unworthily makes the recipient "guilty of the body and blood of the Lord" (1 Corinthians 11:27). Claiming to have two thousand years of history on his side, Madrid states as fact that, until the Protestant Reformation, the passages had always been understood literally to mean that the bread and wine are really, substantially, the body, blood, soul and divinity of Christ. He is wrong on all counts.

Symbolic vs. Literal understanding in the Early Church

Madrid claims that the Protestant symbolic, memorial view of the Lord's Supper is "at odds with two thousand years of historic Christianity," and that the "Real Presence" of Christ in the consecrated bread and wine "has been the constant teaching of the Catholic Church since the time of the Apostles." "The fact is," Madrid continues, "the early Church was consistent and unanimous in its belief that Christ was truly present in the Eucharistic Sacrifice."[632] By "Real Presence," Madrid means Jesus Christ is really present, "Body, Blood, Soul, and Divinity," in the consecrated bread and wine of the Supper. As usual, Madrid's approach is to assert as fact what he wishes were true but cannot substantiate, and then to declare victory on the basis of his wishful thinking.

With Madrid's sweeping claims of "two thousand years" of "constant," "consistent and unanimous" teaching on the literal view, *actual liturgical scholars* may be forgiven for wondering what Madrid knows that they do not! If an honest apologist and an earnest reader would know whether the early church held to a symbolic memorial view, he need only read what scholars themselves tacitly admit: The ancient evidence for a symbolic, figurative, memorial view of the Lord's Supper is so abundant that generations of liturgists have gone to great lengths to say that the early writers cannot possibly have meant or even understood what they were plainly saying! We are assured, on their scholarly authority, that the symbolic, memorial language from the ancient writers ought to be construed opposite its known meaning. Consider this sampling of expositors from the previous centuries:

> *Adolph Harnack (1896):* What we now-a-days understand by "symbol" is a thing which is not that which it represents; at that time "symbol" denoted a thing which, in some kind of way, really is what it signifies.[633]

> *Darwell Stone (1909):* [On] The question of the meaning of such [figurative] words in connection with the Eucharist … . It may be sufficient here to express the warning that to suppose that "symbol" in Clement of Alexandria or "figure" in Tertullian must mean the same as in modern speech would be to assent to a line of thought which is gravely misleading.[634]

---

632 Madrid, p. 196.
633 Harnack, Adolph, *History of Dogma*, vol ii, translated from the 3rd German edition, Neil Buchanan, trans (London: Williams & Norgate, 1896), p. 144.
634 Stone, Darwell, *A History of the Doctrine of the Holy Eucharist*, vol 1 (London: Longmans,

Joseph Pohle (1917): For want of a more accurate terminology, they often refer to the sacramental species as "signs," "types," "symbols," or "figures."[635]

Burton Scott Easton (1934): None of this language, however, is "symbolic" in the modern sense; ... in the earlier Patristic period the deeper nature of this connection was left unexplored.[636]

J. N. D. Kelly (1977): Yet we should be cautious about interpreting such expressions in a modern fashion. According to ancient modes of thought a mysterious relationship existed between the thing symbolized and its symbol, figure or type; the symbol in some sense *was* the thing symbolized.[637]

Indeed, these strident and dismissive cautions by the scholars show that the early writers so freely attached a symbolic, figurative, memorial meaning to the consecrated elements of the Supper that the scholars have gone to great lengths to explain that they must not have meant, or even understood, their own words! What did the early church writers believe that so exercised these scholars? A survey of their symbolic, figurative, metaphorical, allegorical, memorial language will show how pervasive the *Protestant* view was in the early church:

Irenæus of Lyons (190 AD)
Irenæus refers to the consecrated elements—"the bread the body of Christ, and the cup the blood of Christ"—as "these antitypes (ἀντίτυπον)."[638]

Green and Co., 1909), p. 31.

635 Pohle, Joseph, S.J., *Dogmatic Theology*, vol ix, "The Sacraments: a Dogmatic Treatment" vol ii, "The Holy Eucharist" 2nd edition (London: B. Herder Book Co., 1917), p. 75.

636 *The Apostolic Tradition of Hippolytus*, Easton, Burton Scott, trans. (Cambridge University Press, 1934), 94.

637 Kelly, J. N. D., *Early Christian Doctrines*, 5th ed. (London: A&C Black, 2000), p. 212. Emphasis in original.

638 Irenæus of Lyons, *Fragment 37*. Migne, *PG*, vii, 1253. N.B.: Fragment 38 in Migne.

Clement of Alexandria (202 AD)

In his exposition of the gospels and the Supper, Clement observes: "Elsewhere the Lord, in the Gospel according to John, brought this out by symbols (συμβόλων), when He said: 'Eat my flesh, and drink my blood;' describing distinctly by metaphor (*lit.* allegory, ἀλληγορῶν) the drinkable properties of faith ..."[639]

Tertullian of Carthage (208 AD)

In his argument against the Gnostics, Tertullian explained the meaning of "this is my body": "Then, having taken the bread and given it to His disciples, He made it His own body, by saying, 'This is my body,' that is, the figure (*figura*) of my body."[640]

Hippolytus of Rome (215 AD)

The Greek original of Hippolytus' instructions on the thank offerings and the Supper is no longer extant, but the Verona Latin fragments helpfully preserve both the Latin translation and a Latin transliteration of the Greek. At the thank offering, prior to the blessing, the bread is called an example, "*exemplum*," of the body of Christ, or in Greek "*antitypum*." The wine is called an antitype, "*antitypum*," of the blood of Christ, or in Greek, "*similitudinem*."[641] Yet, even after the consecration, the communicant is instructed to receive "the image (*antitypum*)[642] of the blood of Christ."[643]

Origen of Alexandria (248 AD)

In his commentary on *Matthew*, Origen insisted, "...it is not the material of the bread but the word which is said over it which is of advantage to him who eats it not unworthily

---

639 Clement of Alexandria, *Pædagogus* 1 6. Migne, *PG*, viii, 296.
640 Tertullian of Carthage, *Adversus Marcionem* 4 40. Migne *PL*, ii, 460.
641 *Didascaliae Apostolorum Fragmenta Veronensia Latina*, Hauler, D., trans. (Lipsiae: in Aedibus B. G. Teubneri (1900), 112.
642 *Hauler*, 117.
643 Hippolytus of Rome, *Anaphora*, 32. Easton, 60.

of the Lord. And these things indeed are said of the typical (τυπικοῦ) and symbolic (συμβολικοῦ) body."[644]

Adamantius (c. 300 AD)

Arguing against the Gnostic error, Adamantius asked, "If, as these say, He was fleshless and bloodless, of what flesh or of what blood was it that He gave the images (εἰκόνας)[645] in the bread and the cup, when He commanded the disciples to make the memorial of Him by means of these?"[646]

Eusebius of Cæsarea (325 AD)

Explaining the origin of the Supper, Eusebius recorded, "Yea, and perfect services were conducted by the prelates, the sacred rites being solemnized, ... and the mysterious symbols (σύμβολα) of the Saviour's passion were dispensed."[647]

"...we have received a memorial of this offering which we celebrate on a table by means of symbols (σύμβολων) of His Body and saving Blood."[648]

"...the wine which was indeed the symbol (σύμβολον) of His blood ... He gave Himself the symbols (σύμβολα) of His divine dispensation to His disciples, when He bade them make the likeness (εἰκόνα) of His own Body. ... bread to use as the symbol (σύμβολω) of His Body."[649]

Cyril of Jerusalem (350 AD)

In his instruction to catechumens, Cyril insisted that they understand the consecrated bread and wine figuratively: "Wherefore with full assurance let us partake as of the

---

644 Origen of Alexandria, *Commentary on Matthew*, 11-14. Migne *PG*, xiii, 952.
645 Migne *PG*, xi, 1840.
646 Adamantius, *Dialogue* 5, 6. English translation by Stone, 62.
647 Eusebius of Cæsarea, *Historia Ecclesiastica* 10, 3.3. Migne *PG*, xx, 848.
648 Eusebius of Cæsarea, *Demonstratio Evangelica* 1, 10. *Translations of Christian Literature*, Series I Greek Texts "Demonstratio Evangelica of Eusebius of Caesarea" Ferrar, W. J., trans (New York: The Macmillan Company, 1920), p. 60. Migne *PG*, xxii, 89.
649 Eusebius of Cæsarea, *Demonstratio Evangelica* 8, 1. Ferrar, 114-115. Migne *PG*, xxii, 593, 596.

body and blood of Christ: for in the figure (τύπῳ) of bread is given to you His body, and in the figure (τύπῳ) of wine His blood."[650]

"Trust not the judgment to your bodily palate, no, but to faith unfaltering; for they who taste are bidden to taste, not bread and wine, but the *anti-typical* (ἀντίτυπου) body and blood of Christ."[651]

Sarapion of Thmuis (353 AD)

"This bread is the likeness (ὁμοίωμα) of the holy Body, ... the cup, the likeness of the Blood, for the Lord Jesus Christ, taking a cup after supper, said to his own disciples, 'Take, drink, this is the new covenant, which is my Blood'... "[652]

Gregory of Nazianzen (361-381 AD)

In his preparation for the Supper, Gregory refers to the unconsecrated elements using the language of symbolism, calling them "the antitype (ἀντίτυπον) of the great mysteries,"[653] but also uses figurative language even after the consecration: "Now we will partake of a Passover which is still typical (τυπικῶς); though it is plainer than the old one ..."[654]

Apostolic Constitutions (380 AD)

In the communion prayer, the celebrant acknowledges that the bread and cup are a *representation* of Christ's body and blood, "We also, our Father, thank Thee for the precious blood of Jesus Christ, which was shed for us and for His precious body, whereof we celebrate this representation (ἀντίτυπα), as Himself appointed us, 'to show forth His death.' [1 Corinthians 11:26]"[655]

---

650 Cyril of Jerusalem, *Catechetical Lecture* 22.3. Migne *PG*, xxxiii, 1100.
651 Cyril of Jerusalem, *Catechetical Lecture* 23, 20. Migne *PG*, xxxiii, 1124.
652 Sarapion of Thmuis, *Eucharistic Anaphora. Bishop Sarapion's Prayerbook: An Egyptian Pontifical Dated Probably about A.D. 350 – 356* Wordsworth, J., D.D., ed (London: Society for Promoting Christian Knowledge, 1899), pp. 62-63.
653 Gregory of Nazianzen, *Oration* 2.95. Migne, *PG*, xxxv, 497.
654 Gregory of Nazianzen, *Oration* 45.23. Migne, *PG*, xxxvi, 656.
655 *Apostolic Constitutions* 7, 25. Migne, *PG*, i, 1017.

Macarius the Egyptian (390 AD)
The consecrated bread and wine are "the symbol (ἀντίτυπον) of His flesh and blood," Macarius wrote, and "those who partake of the visible bread eat spiritually the flesh of the Lord..."[656]

There are other early writers who testify of the symbolic, figurative, memorial nature of the consecrated elements and the meal itself, but these are more than adequate to disprove Madrid's fallacious claim of "two thousand years" of "consistent and unanimous" teaching. These same ancient writers argued against the unbelief of the Jews on the one hand, and the idolatry of the pagans on the other, all while deconstructing the complex worldviews of the Gnostics and Philosophers. It is unconscionable to lay at their feet (as scholars have often done) the charge of an insufficient vocabulary, or that they had left "unexplored" the mysterious connection between the symbol and what it symbolized. They knew very well what these words meant and knew exactly why they were using them. The bread and wine were symbolic representations of Jesus' incarnation, remembrances of His sufferings for our sins, typical, figurative, sensory objects intended to stimulate our senses and bring to mind the reality of His incarnation. If these men had truly understood that the bread and wine were *literally, really, truly* changed into the body and blood of Christ, their sophisticated vocabularies were more than equal to the task of explaining and defending that belief to us in the original languages. Instead, they used *figure, antitype, example, similitude* in Latin, and *antitype, symbol, allegory, icon, likeness* and *type* in Greek. None of them would have denied that the bread and wine were *spiritually* the body and blood of Christ to the recipient by faith, nor do Protestants today. In fact they insisted upon it, just as Protestants do. What is lacking in the ancient church, however, is a confession from any of them that the consecrated elements were *literally, truly* His body and blood. Even Bishop Gelasius of Rome *(496 AD)*, one

---

656 Macarius the Egyptian, *Homily 27*, 17. *Fifty Spiritual Homilies of St. Macarius the Egyptian*, Mason, A. J. trans. (London: Society for Promoting Christian Knowledge, 1921), p. 209. Migne, *PG*, xxxiv, 705.

of Madrid's own popes, acknowledged that the consecrated bread and wine *remain* bread and wine *in both nature and substance* after the consecration: "By the Sacraments we are made partakers of the divine nature, *and yet the substance and nature of bread and wine do not cease to be in them.*"[657]

Paul's Admonition to the Corinthians

Part of Madrid's argument for the "Real Presence" of Christ in the Eucharist is Paul's admonition, "whosoever shall eat this bread, and drink this cup of the Lord, unworthily, shall be guilty of the body and blood of the Lord" (1 Corinthians 11:27). "This harrowing statement," Madrid says, "points to the truth that, if one is in the state of serious sin, he should not receive the Lord's body and blood."[658] We certainly affirm the verse, but cannot affirm Madrid's interpretation of it, for he has simply assumed that it means the cup contains Jesus' literal blood. The verse no more proves the "Real Presence" of Christ's blood in the cup than 2 Samuel 23:17 proves the "Real Presence" of the blood of the "mighty men" in the vessel they brought to David from Jerusalem. David would not drink of it for to do so would make him guilty of their blood: "Is not this the blood of the men that went in jeopardy of their lives?" It is a metaphor for disrespecting what the cup *signifies*, not proof that its contents are literal.

What is more, according to the *Catechism of the Catholic Church*, the bread and wine of the Supper are not consecrated until Jesus' words are spoken over them: "This is my body which will be given up for you ... This is the cup of my blood."[659] At the uttering of those words, the bread and wine are alleged to become the literal body and blood of Christ. Thus, according to Madrid, it is drinking unworthily from a *consecrated cup* that is so "harrowing." But in the Gospel accounts of the Lord's Supper, the cup is not consecrated until after it has already been distributed and consumed. Matthew says, "And he took the cup, and gave thanks, and gave it to them,

---

657 *Pope Gelasius of Rome, De duabus naturis in Christo, adversus Eutychen et Nestorium, 496 AD.*
658 Madrid, p. 198.
659 *Catechism of the Catholic Church*, paragraph 1412.

saying, Drink ye all of it" (Matthew 26:27). According to Luke, Jesus did not say, "This cup is the new testament in my blood" (Luke 22:20) until after the cup had already been distributed (Luke 22:17), and Mark indicates that they partook of the cup before the consecration, for "they all drank of it" before Jesus said, "This is my blood of the new testament" (Mark 14:23-24). Paul's account of the Supper in 1 Corinthians 11:23-26 cannot be otherwise, and thus Paul's warning cannot be about drinking unworthily *from a consecrated cup* as Madrid suggests. There must be a meaning other than that which Madrid has interpolated.

Paul indeed chided the Corinthians for their cavalier attitude during the Supper, saying

> ...whosoever shall eat this bread, and drink this cup of the Lord, unworthily, shall be guilty of the body and blood of the Lord. ... For he that eateth and drinketh unworthily, eateth and drinketh damnation to himself, not discerning the Lord's body. (1 Corinthians 11:27,29)

Paul's explicit intent is no mystery. At the Last Supper the disciples had returned to their strife and posturing about "which of them should be accounted the greatest," whereupon they were all reminded that they ought rather defer to one another (Luke 22:24). We are not surprised that similar strife arose in the early church, and the Corinthians were no exception, for "every one taketh before" his brother (1 Corinthians 11:21). Paul responds to them just as Christ responded to the disciples at the Supper, warning the Corinthians to be mindful of, and to wait for, their brethren and sisters before partaking. "He that is greatest," Jesus said, let him be as a servant (Luke 22:26). On account of that same carnal behavior, Paul reminded the Corinthians of the manner in which Jesus had instituted the Supper, and taught them the same lesson. As he had also instructed the Philippians, Christians are to look after the interests of others, as Christ had done, becoming "obedient unto death" (Philippians 2:3-8).

What therefore were the Corinthians to make of Paul's rebuke of their carnality? Had he demanded more respect for Christ's "Real Presence," or that they adore the bread and wine before consuming, or perhaps that they should understand the institution narrative according to Madrid's anachronism and treat the unconsecrated cup as if it were already consecrated, or perhaps that they must eat the soul and divinity of Christ in addition to His flesh and blood? Nay, none of these. Rather, the institution narrative lays upon each believer the obligation to consider the interests of his brethren, that they may come together without divisions, and therefore, without condemnation:

> Wherefore, my brethren, when ye come together to eat, tarry one for another. And if any man hunger, let him eat at home; that ye come not together unto condemnation. (1 Corinthians 11:33-34)

Here Paul continues on a theme of correct behavior in church "when ye come together," completing the thought he had begun in the previous chapter, namely that the reception of the bread and cup is a communal activity, and therefore ought to be done mindfully of the brethren:

> The cup of blessing which we bless, is it not the communion of the blood of Christ? The bread which we break, is it not the communion of the body of Christ? For we being many are one bread, and one body: for we are all partakers of that one bread. (1 Corinthians 10:16-17)

Paul's elegant solution to the Corinthian problem is not that the offending parties be mindful of the "Real Presence" of Christ in the bread and wine, but that the offending parties ought to be mindful of the "communion of the blood of Christ" and the "communion of the body of Christ," either waiting for their brethren at church, or eating somewhere else beforehand. It was a simple correction to a carnal problem, and Paul both identified the cause and prescribed the solution, just as Jesus had done at the Last Supper.

Madrid's interpretation, on the other hand, is simply a wishful catalogue of things Paul *ought to have said*. Madrid might have a point if Christ had consecrated the cup before administering it, or if Paul had warned that partaking unworthily makes one "guilty of blasphemy." But they did not. Madrid might have a point if Paul had prescribed, "when ye come together to eat, *be sure to kneel before the body, blood, soul and divinity of Christ*" or "if any man *deny the Real Presence, let him contemplate the literal meaning of the institution narrative*, that ye come not together unto condemnation." But he did not. He said rather, "When ye come together to eat, *tarry one for another*." Hardly an appeal to the "Real Presence" of Christ in the Eucharist, but rather an earnest appeal to the real presence of Christ among His people.

The Symbolic View does not Nullify 1 Corinthians 11:27-29

As to Madrid's conviction that 1 Corinthians 11:27-29, on its face, proves "the necessity for believing in the Real Presence of Christ in the Eucharist,"[660] we simply respond that the early church did not agree. The *Apostolic Constitutions* (380 AD) invoke 1 Corinthians 11:29 to explain why the uninitiated ought not receive the Supper, but the author tacitly rejects Madrid's interpretation, insisting that the uninitiated "eats eternal damnation" by receiving a *symbolic* "representation" of Christ's body and blood:

> We also, our Father, thank Thee for the precious blood of Jesus Christ, which was shed for us and for His precious body, *whereof we celebrate this representation (ἀντίτυπα)*, as Himself appointed us, 'to show forth His death.' ... But if any one that is not initiated conceal himself, and partake of the same, 'he eats eternal damnation;'[661]

---

660 Madrid, p. 198.
661 *Apostolic Constitutions*, 7, 25.

We recall as well that Origen, appealing to the same passage, warned against eating "the typical (τυπικοῦ) and symbolic (συμβολικοῦ) body" unworthily.[662] These were written only centuries after the Institution Narrative, and the authors did not believe Paul's "harrowing statement" was an acknowledgement of the "Real Presence" in the bread and wine.

The ancient rejection of the "Real Presence" doctrine

Although Madrid does not raise the issue of Eucharistic Adoration, it is important that Protestants understand the implication of the Roman Catholic belief in the "Real Presence" of Christ in the bread and wine. If Jesus is really, truly, substantially present, body, blood, soul and divinity, in the consecrated bread, then the consecrated bread is to be worshiped. According to the *Catechism of the Catholic Church*, Roman Catholics "express our faith in the real presence of Christ under the species of bread and wine by, among other ways, genuflecting or bowing deeply as a sign of adoration of the Lord."[663] That is, during the Supper they bow or genuflect to adore the bread. So deeply held is this conviction that Josef Ratzinger, before he became pope Benedict XVI, wrote in 2000 that "[a] liturgy no longer familiar with kneeling would be sick at the core."[664] With this high emphasis on kneeling to worship the Eucharist in a healthy liturgy, one would think that for two thousand years, the church would have required kneeling during the liturgy.

And yet the ancient and medieval eucharistic liturgy not only omitted kneeling from the Sunday liturgy for more than a thousand years, *but actually prohibited it*. Canon 20 of the Council of Niceæa (325 AD) prohibited kneeling on Sunday and on any day from Easter to Pentecost, and as late as the 4th Council of Constantinople (870 AD), the assembled bishops declared "that we are preserving and maintaining" the canons of Niceæa. The *Catholic Encyclopedia* even acknowledges that the "practice of kneeling during the Consecration [of the bread] was introduced during the Middle

---

662 Origen of Alexandria, *Commentary on Matthew*, 11-14. Migne *PG*, xiii, 952.
663 CCC, 1378.
664 Ratzinger, Joseph, *The Spirit of the Liturgy*, p. 194 (2000).

Ages," originating "in the same period" as the elevation of the host,[665] which "is not known to have existed earlier than the close of the twelfth century."[666] It is for this reason that "most scholars trace … the practice of Eucharistic adoration … back at least to the early thirteenth century" and possibly even "to the eleventh century." It is difficult to discover proof of eucharistic adoration manifesting any earlier than that.[667]

All of these historical facts raise an important question for Madrid: If the early church believed in the real presence of Christ in the Eucharist, and kneeling is the way Roman Catholics "express our faith in the real presence," and a liturgy that omits kneeling is "sick at the core," how on earth did the church go twelve hundred years with a liturgy that was so "sick" at its "core" that it rejected liturgical kneeling to "the source and summit"[668] of his faith? How could the ancient and medieval church *forbid kneeling* on the one day of the week all Christians gathered to partake of bread and wine? Why is it so difficult to find evidence for this "apostolic practice" of Eucharistic Adoration before the eleventh century? And yet Madrid is convinced not only that the "Real Presence" of Christ in the consecrated bread "has been the constant teaching of the Catholic Church since the time of the Apostles," but also that a symbolic view is "at odds with two thousand years of historic Christianity."[669] Quite wrong. Not only did the early church understand the consecrated elements of the Supper to be *symbolic* of Christ's body and blood, but their understanding of their symbolic nature was so indelibly etched in their minds that it did not occur to them for more a thousand years to kneel before it or worship it as Roman Catholics do today!

---

665 *Catholic Encyclopedia*, "Genuflexion."
666 *Catholic Encyclopedia*, "Elevation."
667 Reynolds, Roger E. "Eucharistic Adoration in the Carolingian Era?" *Journal of Medieval Art and Architecture* (2013), vol. iv, iss. 2, pp. 77-78.
668 *Catechism of the Catholic Church*, 1324.
669 Madrid, p. 196.

Scriptural Proof for the Symbolic Interpretation

Although Madrid does not appeal to John 6 in his chapter on the Eucharist, he appeals to it in his earlier chapter on Catholicism, claiming that Jesus taught us to "eat My flesh and drink My blood in the Eucharist." Yet in John 6, the apostle illustrates clearly why we must take Jesus figuratively when He says "he that eateth me, even he shall live by me" (John 6:57).

To Believe the Doctrine of the Father

In His preamble to the conversation on His flesh and blood in John 6, Jesus drew from Isaiah to admonish the Jews to "[l]abour not for the meat which perisheth, but for that meat which endureth unto everlasting life" (John 6:27). That is the language of the prophet: "Wherefore do ye spend money for that which is not bread? and your labour for that which satisfieth not?" (Isaiah 55:2). Isaiah made it quite clear that our hunger and thirst could only be satisfied by believing God's word: "hearken diligently unto me, and eat ye that which is good … . Incline your ear, and come unto me: hear, and your soul shall live" (Isaiah 55:2-3). Having laid down that construct from the Old Testament, Jesus uses "eat" and "drink" thenceforth to refer to hearkening to, listening to and hearing the words that He spoke. It is about *believing words*, not about *eating food*. That is the construct Isaiah established, and that is how Jesus applied it. To "eat" Jesus is to hear and believe His words that we may live, precisely as Isaiah had said: "Hear, and your soul shall live" (Isaiah 55:2-3). Throughout John 6, Jesus never once departed from that construct:

> Moses gave you not that bread from heaven; but *my Father giveth you the true bread from heaven*. (John 6:32)

> Verily, verily, I say unto you, *He that believeth on me hath everlasting life*. (John 6:47)

This is the bread which cometh down from heaven, *that a man may eat thereof, and not die.* … if any man eat of this bread, he shall live for ever" (John 6:50, 51)

This is that bread which came down from heaven: not as your fathers did eat manna, and are dead: *he that eateth of this bread shall live for ever.* (John 6:58)

… the words that I speak unto you, they are spirit, and they are life. But there are some of you that believe not. (John 6:63-64)

As with Isaiah, so with John 6: To be satisfied with true food *is to believe the words that His Father had commanded Jesus to speak.* To eat the "true bread from heaven" was *to believe* what Jesus was saying. From the death of John the Baptist until Peter's confession at Cæsarea Philippi, Jesus had been traveling about performing miracles, healing the sick, feeding the hungry and preaching the gospel of the kingdom. After two miracles of loaves and fishes, and multiple confrontations with the Jews, Jesus warned His apostles of "the leaven of the Pharisees and of the Sadducees," a food metaphor that referred to their "doctrine" (Matthew 16:12). His reference to "true bread from heaven" and the warnings about the "leaven" of the Pharisees had taken place concurrently, in which it is abundantly clear that by "bread" and "leaven" He meant "doctrines," the former of His Father, the latter of His detractors. To "eat" either "bread" or "leaven" was to "believe" either true doctrines or false doctrines, respectively.

To Believe the Doctrine of the Resurrection

Whence therefore Jesus' words about eating "the flesh of the Son of man" and drinking "his blood" (John 6:53)? Had Jesus departed from the opening Isaiaic construct of John 6:27 in which "to eat" and "to drink" is "to believe" and "to hearken diligently"? Had Jesus diverged from "eating" His Father's doctrine and struck out on a new path about *literally* eating His flesh and drinking His blood?

Madrid would have us believe Jesus had changed from figurative to literal, from believing "words" to eating "flesh," but a simple harmonization of the Gospel accounts tells us otherwise.

Hidden within the loaves narratives of the synoptic gospels is an intentionally cryptic reference to His death and resurrection. After two miracles of multiplication, the Pharisees and Sadducees demanded that He "shew them a sign from heaven" (Matthew 16:1; Mark 8:11), but Jesus refused: "There shall no sign be given … but the sign of the prophet Jonas" (Matthew 16:4), a cloaked reference to His death and resurrection (Matthew 12:39-40; Luke 11:29-30). An inspection of the Johannine account reveals the same demand made by the Jews, and the same cryptic response from Jesus.

When the witnesses to the first miracle of the loaves sought more bread for their bellies, Jesus drew on Isaiah to challenge them to believe (Isaiah 55:1-3; John 6:26-29). The Jews then arrived on the scene after the Passover, and they, too wanted a "sign from heaven" after the pattern of Moses who "gave them bread from heaven" (John 6:28-31), but as in Matthew, Jesus refused. Just as Isaiah had said, Jesus repeated that they should seek after the "true bread from heaven" (John 6:32). In the same fashion of the cryptic allusion to His death and Resurrection in Matthew 16, Isaiah 55 alludes to it as well, for He promises them "the sure mercies of David" (Isaiah 55:3b), a cloaked reference to Jesus' death and resurrection (Acts 13:34). Corruptible "flesh and blood cannot inherit the kingdom of God," but incorruptible flesh and blood can (1 Corinthians 15:50). The "sure mercies of David" mean Jesus would rise "no more to return to corruption" (Acts 13:34), and instead of seeking after perishable food, they should have sought after food that endures to eternal life: "He that believeth on me hath everlasting life … if any man eat of this bread, he shall live for ever" (John 6:47,51).

The unfolding conversation in John 6 is therefore the very same conversation Matthew and Mark recorded, in which the Jews ask for a sign, and in all three accounts, Jesus refuses. As in Matthew, Jesus' response in John 6 is a cloaked reference to His death and resurrection, in which His followers are called to partake (Romans 6:5). It is not an invitation literally to eat His flesh and drink His blood. It is an invitation to believe in the resurrection.

It is in this simple harmonization of Matthew and John that we understand Jesus' references to eating His flesh and drinking His blood. Jesus had not wavered from His initial construct in which "to eat" and "to drink" refers to hearing and believing the doctrines of His Father. His answer to their desire for a sign in John 6 cannot be different than His answer in Matthew 16 or Isaiah 55. The Jews demanded a sign from heaven, and the only sign they would be given is that of His death and resurrection. "The bread that I will give is my flesh, which I will give for the life of the world" (John 6:51) can mean nothing else, and Jesus proceeds accordingly. He repeatedly refers to the resurrection from the dead (John 6:39, 40, 44, 54) even though not one of His hearers yet understood that Jesus must die (Matthew 16:21; Mark 8:31; Luke 9:22) or even what it might mean to rise from the dead (Mark 9:10, John 20:9, Luke 18:34). And yet that remained the focus of His exchange with them. In the Scriptures, to eat the flesh or drink the blood of another person is a figure for participating or sharing either literally or symbolically in his death (2 Samuel 23:17; 1 Chronicles 11:19; Isaiah 49:26; Ezekiel 39:17-19, Matthew 20:22-23, Mark 10:38-39 (Cf., John 18:11), 1 Corinthians 10:16-21 (Cf. 1 Corinthians 11:26), precisely what Jesus' followers are asked to do (Romans 6:5, 8:17; Philippians 3:10). Jesus had not implored His listeners literally "to eat" or "to drink" anything, but to believe in the doctrine of His resurrection. He hid that meaning from the hearers in John 6, just as He had done in the same conversation in Matthew 16, but the appeal to His listeners to "eat my flesh" in John 6 was just as allegorical as "the sure mercies of David" had been in Isaiah 55.

The Chronic Roman Catholic Misunderstanding

The Roman Catholic error in John 6 is to take Jesus literally and perspicuously at the very moment He is being deliberately figurative and evasive. In Isaiah, in the Synoptics and in John, the Lord conveyed something to His audience in a form that was intentionally obscure, oblique and mysterious. Only by additional revelation (e.g., Acts 13:34, Luke 11:29-30) can Isaiah and Matthew be understood to refer to His resurrection. Similarly, Jesus' meaning in John 6 is intentionally obscure but is revealed to us when John is understood in the context of Isaiah and harmonized with the Synoptic accounts.

Madrid's failure is that he has misunderstood Jesus in the same way His audience often misunderstood Him. From the beginning, John focused on the propensity of Jesus' hearers to take him *literally* at the precise moment that they ought to have taken Him *figuratively*. John opened His gospel stating that "the light shineth in darkness; and the darkness comprehended it not" (John 1:5). From that point forward, Jesus' *figurative* teachings are chronically and incorrectly taken *literally* by His listeners.

- Jesus promises to raise up the temple "in three days," only for his hearers to assume He meant the *literal* temple. He had been referring *figuratively* to His body. (John 2:19-21)
- Jesus says that a man must be *figuratively* reborn in a spiritual way, only for Nicodemus to take him to mean *literally* that a man must return to his mother's womb. (John 3:3-4)
- Jesus offers *figurative* "living water" of everlasting life, and the Samaritan woman assumes He is offering her *literal* water. (John 4:10-15)
- Jesus offers *figuratively* "the true bread from heaven" for the life of the world, and His hearers assume He is talking about *literal* bread. (John 6:32-34)
- Jesus proclaims that if anyone believes in Him, "out of his belly shall flow rivers of living water," and John quickly points out that He had been speaking not *literally* of rivers, but *figuratively* "of the Spirit." (John 7:38-39)

It is in the middle of this unrelenting volley of *figurative* language that Jesus also insists that "if any man eat of this bread, he shall live for ever: the bread that I will give is my flesh" (John 6:51). His confused listeners, again, immediately take His figure literally, asking "How can this man give us his flesh to eat?" As with the Jews in the temple, Nicodemus by night, the woman at the well and the people at Capernaum, His figurative statements confound those who can only conceive of a literal meaning.

We therefore add Madrid to the long list of Jesus' confounded hearers, for again, just when Jesus is speaking *figuratively*, Madrid casts his lot with the dull of mind and heart, demanding that we understand Him *literally*—something even His apostles did not do. When Jesus turned to them to ask, "Will ye also go away?" (John 6:67), Peter did not respond, "Lord, to whom shall we go? thou hast the *flesh* of eternal life," but rather "thou hast the *words* of eternal life" (John 6:68), indicating that Peter and the others had understood Him well enough even if they did not immediately understand His reference to the resurrection.

To eat the true bread from heaven is to believe the words His Father had commanded Him to say (John 5:24, 14:29), for "the words that I speak unto you, they are spirit, and they are life" (John 6:63). To believe His words is to believe in the Resurrection for "this," too, is a "commandment have I received of my Father" (John 10:18). In the Supper, when Christians eat Christ's flesh and drink His blood under the sensible symbols of bread and wine, we confess that we believe with the apostles that Jesus "hast the words of eternal life." We confess this not because we believe we must eat His literal flesh but rather because we believe in "the sure mercies of David" and the sign of Jonah, which is to say, we believe He was crucified and was raised from the dead. With Paul, we understand our need figuratively to be "planted together in the likeness of his death" (Romans 6:5) and "made conformable unto his death" (Philippians 3:10), that we might partake of His death and resurrection by faith. To eat His flesh and drink His blood means nothing other than that, and it is symbolic and figurative, not literal. Clement of Alexandria encapsulated this Scriptural truth succinctly when he said, "the Lord ... brought this out by symbols, when He said: 'Eat my flesh, and drink my blood;' describing distinctly by metaphor the drinkable properties of faith ... ."[670] So with Tertullian of

---

670 Clement of Alexandria, *Pædagogus* 1, 6.

Carthage: "He likewise called His flesh [life-giving]; because, too, the Word had become flesh, we ought ... to devour Him with the ear, and to ruminate on Him with the understanding, and to digest Him by faith."[671] So with John Chrysostom — "Wherefore with full assurance let us partake as of the body and blood of Christ: for in the figure of bread is given to you His body, and in the figure of wine His blood."[672] And with Augustine of Hippo— "'the words that I have spoken unto you, they are spirit, and they are life.' Understand spiritually what I have said; ye are not to eat this body which ye see; nor to drink that blood which they who will crucify Me shall pour forth."[673] The early writers abundantly attested to the figurative reading of John 6.

On that note, we conclude this chapter on the Eucharist by repeating Madrid's own questions back to him:

> How can you be so sure that your interpretation of the eucharistic Bible verses is correct and all the early Christians (many of whom lived very close to the time of the apostles and who spoke and read Greek, the language of the New Testament) were wrong?

> On what basis do you assert your interpretation as being correct over the way they interpreted the Bible? After all, you are living some two thousand years after the time of Christ.

> Doesn't it seem reasonable to you that if anyone would know what the Lord meant when He said 'This is my body" and "this is my blood," the early Christians would know?

Indeed. Madrid would do well to ask these questions of himself.

---

671 Tertullian, *On the Resurrection of the Flesh* 37
672 Cyril of Jerusalem, *Catechetical Lecture 22.3.* Migne *PG*, xxxiii, 1100.
673 Augustine, *Exposition on Psalm 99* 8

Purgatory

──────── (Zins) ────────

It is important that Christians counter the Roman Catholic doctrinal claims with correct biblical responses. Roman Catholic defenders often cite well-meaning Evangelicals who are not careful in their response to Rome, and they are easily refuted because the Bible passages marshaled against Rome do not hit the mark. Evidently many Evangelicals reason from 2 Corinthians 5:6, 7 and Philippians 1:20-24 proof that there cannot be a Purgatory.

Sometimes Evangelicals are fond of compressing and interpreting 2 Corinthians 5:6,7 to say, "To be absent from the body *is to be present with the Lord.*" Madrid is quick to point out that the verse does not make this statement. Here is the passage:

> Therefore, being always of good courage, and knowing that while we are at home in the body we are absent from the Lord for we walk by faith, not by sight, we are of good courage, *I say, and prefer rather to be absent from the body and to be at home with the Lord.* (2 Corinthians 5:5-8)

Madrid is correct in pointing out that Paul is not asserting to be absent from the body *is* to be immediately with the Lord. Paul is saying that he would *prefer* to be absent from the body and to be at home with the Lord. There is no time frame other than after death mentioned. We agree with Madrid that there could be an intermediate state between *absent from the body* and *home with the Lord* if this were the only passage in the Bible used to refute Purgatory. But it is not, as we shall see.

One other passage that is said to deny the possibility of Purgatory is Philippians 1:20-24.

> … according to my earnest expectation and hope, that I shall not be put to shame in anything, but that with all boldness, Christ shall even now, as always, be exalted in my body, whether by life or by death. For to me, to live is Christ, and to die is gain. But if I am to live on in the flesh, this will mean fruitful labor for me; and I do not know which to choose. *But I am hard-pressed from both directions, having the desire to depart and be with Christ,* for that is very much better; yet to remain on in the flesh is more necessary for your sake. (Philippians 1:20-24)

Once again Madrid is correct. This verse also speaks of Paul's desire to depart and be with Christ but does not make the claim that to depart *is* to immediately be with Christ. Purgatory is not ruled out by this verse. If these two passages do not eliminate the possibility of Purgatory as a stop-off on the way to heaven, then what does? According to Madrid nothing in the Bible prevents Purgatory. And, according to Madrid, the Bible teaches Purgatory. Madrid boldly proclaims, "I think you'll see that it's not at all the unbiblical teaching you've been led to believe."[674] We shall examine this assertion and see if it is indeed a biblical teaching.

As a first line of defense, Madrid begins by making general comments on biblical terminology and interpretive standards. We agree that the word Trinity is not a biblical term. But the Bible still teaches the Trinity. Hence, it is possible for the Bible to teach Purgatory without using the word Purgatory. We will not quibble

---

674 Madrid, p. 201.

over this. However, Madrid immediately runs afoul of his own religion when he writes of the sacrifice of Jesus. Madrid affirms, "We also agree that His *perfect sacrifice* was *infinitely sufficient* to satisfy God's justice and *atone for the sins of humanity*."[675]

This statement seems to contradict the clear teaching of the Council of Trent, which declares in the 14th Session Chapter 9 the following:

> The council teaches the liberality of Divine generosity
> is so great that *we are able* through Jesus Christ to *make*
> *satisfaction* to God the Father not only by punishments
> voluntarily undertaken by ourselves *to atone for sins*, or by
> those imposed by the judgment of the priest according to
> the measure of the offense, but also, and this is the greatest
> proof of love, by the *temporal afflictions imposed by God* and
> borne patiently by us.[676]

Whereas Madrid declares that Jesus made a *perfect sacrifice to satisfy God's justice and atone for the sins of humanity, Trent affirms personal punishments satisfy God and atone for sins.* Madrid cannot have it both ways. This theme of inherent contradiction within the Roman Catholic system will continue as we unpack the Roman Catholic defense. Certainly, the sacrifice of Jesus cannot be perfect and infinitely sufficient to satisfy the justice of God and atone for the sins of humanity if we are able through our own punishments to make satisfactions and atone for our own sins. Rome will try to make this obvious contradiction vanish by introducing her own understanding of the results of the atonement of Jesus. Rome will claim that the death of Jesus accomplished a safeguard against the eternal punishment of Hell for all who are within the Roman Catholic religion. But the application of the blood of Jesus stops with the elimination of eternal Hell. The second accomplishment of the sacrifice of Jesus is the establishment of a door of opportunity for Roman Catholics to pay the punishment for their sins here

---

675 Ibid. Emphasis mine.
676 Council of Trent Session 14, Chapter 9. Emphasis mine.

on earth through the Roman Catholic sacrament of Penance. They then pay a final punishment for unpaid earthly sins after death in Purgatory. In essence Jesus died to end the possibility of eternal Hell for Roman Catholics and to *allow* Roman Catholics to pay the punishment for their sins as well.

> Those who die in God's grace and friendship imperfectly purified, although they are assured of their eternal salvation, undergo a purification after death, so as to achieve the holiness necessary to enter the joy of God.[677]

The problem with all of this is that the Bible nowhere teaches that personal punishments for sin alleviate the guilt of sin or can pay the price demanded by God's justice for forgiveness of sin. The idea that personal punishment pays off the justice of God for sin undercuts and terminates the necessity of the entire Christian gospel. If man can pay the penalty for his own sins, then there is no reason for the Son of God to die. However, the Bible teaches that the atonement of Jesus Christ is the only perfect penalty that has infinite value. It is precisely why the perfect God/man Jesus Christ was given to the world. No amount of law keeping, personal sacrificing, personal punishments, or meritorious works can satisfy the wrath of God against sin. Rome invents a new gospel by insisting that the blood of Christ was limited to escaping eternal Hell. There is no such sentiment in all of Scripture. In fact, personal works of satisfaction or punishments that supposedly merit forgiveness of sin are strictly forbidden by the Bible.

The Bible is extremely clear that Jesus Christ died for the eternal penalty of sins as well as the temporal sins committed prior to death.

> And when you were dead in your transgressions and the uncircumcision of your flesh, He made you alive together with Him, *having forgiven us all our transgressions*, having *canceled out the certificate of debt* consisting of decrees

---

677 New Catholic Catechism, paragraph 1054.

against us and which was hostile to us; and *He has taken it out of the way, having nailed it to the cross* (Colossians 2:13-15).

The apostle tells those in Christ that all transgressions and decrees against them have been forgiven. Jesus has taken the debt owed sin and decrees against Christians out of the way, having nailed them to the cross. The Bible throughout proclaims the wonderful news that blessed are those whose lawless deeds are forgiven and whose sins are covered.

Just as David also speaks of the blessing upon the man to whom God reckons righteousness apart from works: "Blessed are those whose lawless deeds have been forgiven, And whose sins have been covered. Blessed is the man whose sin the Lord will not take into account." (Romans 4:6-8)

Rome would introduce a different gospel limiting the forgiveness at the cross of Jesus to something called "eternal penalty due to sin" and enslaving her members to paying a penalty now (Penance) and in Purgatory (then) for their own sins. The idea of it constitutes a different gospel. Nowhere are the penal consequences and punishments resulting from temporal sin said to be sufficient to satisfy the wrath of God and obtain forgiveness. As we have seen in the above verse the New Testament cites David as one whose sin is not reckoned to his account much less satisfied by David's punishment. Thus, it is for all Christians who trust that Jesus paid it all.

> For by one offering He has perfected for all time those who are sanctified. And the Holy Spirit also bears witness to us; for after saying, "This is the covenant that I will make with them After those days, says the Lord: I will put My laws upon their heart, And upon their mind I will write them," He then says, "And their sins and their lawless deeds I will remember no more." Now where there is forgiveness of these things, there is no longer *any offering for sin.* (Hebrews 10:14-18)

An Appeal to Places

Madrid continues to build a case for the *possibility* of Purgatory by referencing places that exist between heaven and hell. He argues that these places are proof that a middle ground Purgatory *might exist*. However, a careful consideration of the places mentioned does not suggest a middle ground, let alone the fantastic idea of Roman Catholic Purgatory. The places set forth by Madrid are sheol, hades, the netherworld and paradise. Of these places Madrid says that they are neither heaven nor hell. However, these places in and of themselves do not prove that Purgatory exists. Sheol and hades refer to the place of the dead or the grave, depending on context (Acts 2:27,31). The term "netherworld" is a rare translation (Ezekiel 32:18) and refers to going down to the lowest part of the earth. In the ancient Near East it is the place of the dead. Paradise is another word for heavenly splendor used only three times in the Bible. This word was employed by Jesus when he made promise to the thief on the cross that he would be with Jesus in paradise (Luke 23:43).

An Appeal to Verses

While stopping short of insisting that Jesus went and preached to those in Purgatory from such passages as 1 Peter 3:18-20 and 1 Peter 4:6, Madrid finds in them the idea that Purgatory *could* exist. Such is the logic. However, a closer look at the 1 Peter passages does not yield the conclusion that Jesus went and preached to those held in a kind of holding tank prison. More likely it was the spirit of Jesus Christ in the preaching of Noah, prior to the construction of the ark, that sealed the eternal destiny of the unbelievers of Noah's day. 1 Peter 4:6 indicates that the gospel has been preached even to those who are dead. It does not teach that Jesus went and preached to dead people. It should be added that even if Evangelicals disagree on the difficult interpretations of 1 Peter 3 and 4 some things are important to remember. The Bible does not teach a second opportunity to gain heaven after death (Hebrews 9:27). Also, there is no room for Purgatory in these biblical scenarios. Purgatory is not presented as a field of evangelism by Rome. It is a place of cleansing through personal punishments, patiently borne by those in Purgatory, making them ready to move up to heaven. All those in Purgatory eventually get out according to Rome. This concept is not even remotely supported by any kind of interpretation of 1 Peter 3 and 4.

Rome is absolutely committed to the proposition that the temporal effects of sin (the consequences of sin) serve to propitiate (satisfy) the wrath of God. Madrid cites the consequences of Adam's sin and David's sin as proof that punishment imposed by God was a payment of satisfaction to God. The idea is that all temporal sins must be cleansed with temporal punishments. If they are not, then the only thing hoped for in the Roman Catholic religion is a place in Purgatory where the punishment follows the death of all the imperfectly purified.

For Christians, who are by faith alone in the New Covenant in Christ, God will not remember their lawless deeds. And where there is forgiveness of these things there is no longer any offering for sin. We cannot express more strongly that this so-called two-tiered effect of the atonement of Christ is anti-Christ to the core. We notice in the verse above that the author sums things up by boldly saying where God's forgiveness is given there is no longer any offering for sin. Yet Rome would contradict and interject her entire system of offerings, penalties, and religious rituals as a satisfaction not only for the sins of the living but for those suffering in Purgatory.

The apostle Paul in his letter to the Corinthians sets matters in order. He wishes it to be absolutely clear that Christ died for our sins *according to the Scriptures* (1 Corinthians 15:3). Certainly not according to the dictates of the Roman Catholic religion.

Madrid tries in vain to find a biblical passage that teaches the doctrine of Purgatory. He appeals to 1 Corinthians 3:10-15. However, before examining this passage we should note the "soft sell" of Madrid on the nature of Purgatory.

> Purgatory is a place, or process, or state (however you'd like to think of it), in which the fire of God's love purifies us from the temporal effects due to sin.[678]

The Council of Trent calls Purgatory a place where the debt of temporal punishment is discharged. Modern Roman Catholics like Madrid would hasten to run away from the word *punishment* and substitute *purification* to make Purgatory more palatable. But make no mistake, the discharge of temporal sin is temporal punishment which involves pain. Now let us turn our attention to what Madrid calls a passage of Scripture that is *an excellent presentation of the Catholic teaching on Purgatory.*

> According to the grace of God which was given to me, as a wise master builder I laid a foundation, and another is building upon it. But let each man be careful how he builds upon it. For no man can lay a foundation other than the one which is laid, which is Jesus Christ. Now if any man builds upon the foundation with gold, silver, precious stones, wood, hay, straw, each man's work will become evident; for the day will show it, because it is to be revealed with fire; and the fire itself will test the quality of each man's work. If any man's work which he has built upon it remains, he shall receive a reward. If any man's work is burned up, he shall suffer loss; but he himself shall be saved, yet so as through fire. (1 Corinthians 3:10-15)

Since this passage is the formative passage of biblical proof for Purgatory let us scrutinize Madrid's argument one step at a time, with full refutation following each of his points.

Madrid brings five points of proof to the question.

---

678 Ibid., p. 204.

First, the person being described here died in the state of friendship with Christ. He had "built" his life on the "foundation that is Jesus Christ."[679]

We notice right from the start that there is no biblical category called "friendship with Christ." Paul wrote this letter to those who were professing Christians. He is writing

> … to the church of God, which is at Corinth, to those who have been sanctified in Christ Jesus, saints by calling, with all who in every place call upon the name of our Lord Jesus Christ, their Lord and ours. (1 Corinthians 1:1-3)

These are hardly just in friendship with Christ. In chapter six Paul identifies them as those who were washed, justified, and sanctified in the name of the Lord Jesus Christ. There is no need of purgatorial cleansing, as they are already sanctified. Also, the text is not teaching about a dead man who "built his life on the foundation of Jesus Christ." The text is concerned with what kind of works are built on the foundation of Jesus Christ. It is the quality of each man's work that is in question. Madrid starts wildly off base.

> Second, the "day" on which the deeds of this person's life are disclosed takes place after his death. "[I]t is appointed for men to die once, and after that comes judgment" (Heb. 9:27). He is now standing before God giving an account of his life.[680]

The "day" referenced here is indeed a day of judgment. However, it is not a day to examine the deeds of a person's life. The person mentioned here by Paul shall see whether he has built well on the foundation laid by the apostle. Will his works endure or be burned up? If his work is built using the figure of gold, silver, and precious stones he will receive a reward. The apostle has laid a foundation of

679 Ibid., p. 205.
680 Ibid.

faith alone in Christ alone as the establishment of the gospel. Some at Corinth have shown signs of immaturity and inclined toward the wisdom of the world. Deviation from the foundation Paul laid comes in many ways and forms. Hence, Paul warns them to build rightly on the foundation he has laid. In this sense all Christians must examine *what* they are building upon the foundation of Jesus Christ and His gospel. But much more so for those involved in leadership and evangelism/teaching. Will their building withstand the light and heat of God's inspection? Contrary to Madrid, Paul envisions a standing before God that will reveal what he has built on the one and only true underpinning. This has nothing to do with Rome's Purgatory.

In his third point Madrid claims that the figures of gold, silver, and precious stones, along with wood, hay, and stubble, refer to man's virtues or lack of virtues. Madrid states that the "ignoble (immoral) aspects of this man's life" must be purified.

As we can see from our above rebuttal, the question of the passage is not the moral life of the man. It is the value, duration, and quality of each man's work that he has done on the foundation of the gospel. Paul has already addressed his audience as those who are saints, justified, sanctified, and cleansed. We are reminded that Peter stood up and corrected those who wished to add a ceremony of purification alongside the gospel that had been received by the Gentiles. Some thought the Gentiles to be impure without circumcision. Peter's rebuke is relevant to us now.

> And God, who knows the heart, bore witness to them, giving them the Holy Spirit, just as He also did to us; and He made no distinction between us and them, *cleansing their hearts by faith.* Now therefore why do you put God to the test by placing upon the neck of the disciples a yoke which neither our fathers nor we have been able to bear? But we believe that we are saved through the grace of the Lord Jesus, in the same way as they also are. (Acts 15:7-11)

All Christians already have their hearts purified and are saved by the grace of our Lord Jesus Christ. It is pure fantasy to invent a place of so-called purification where temporal sins are paid for by temporal punishments of pain.

> Fourth, St. Paul says this process involves suffering, and he uses the metaphorical language of passing through fire to describe the pain of this purification.[681]

Madrid is now far afield from the Bible as he misquotes the text. This Bible passage does not teach that the man suffers pain by passing through the fire for the purpose of purification. On the contrary, it is the work a man has built upon the foundation of the gospel that will be revealed. Let us re-read verses 13-14 of this context:

> ...each man's work will become evident; for the day will show it, because it is to be revealed with fire; and the fire itself will test the quality of each man's work. If any man's work which he has built upon it remains, he shall receive a reward. (1 Corinthians 3:13-14)

Notice the text says, "*Each man's work* will become evident; for the day will show it (his work). It (his work) is to be revealed with fire; and the fire will itself test the quality *of each man's work.* If *any man's work* which he has built upon it remains, he shall receive a reward." There simply is no purification of the man by passing through a painful fire to satisfy God's wrath for temporal sins. The entire foundation of Purgatory is inserted into this passage. It is Roman Catholic fiction. We would add that the entire caution by the apostle Paul could very well be zeroed in on "all who labor" and have nothing to do with all individual Christians. Either way, it is Rome's fabrication and not biblical legitimacy.

At this point we have dispensed with the most common Roman Catholic biblical proof for Her Purgatory. However, we need to understand that Roman Catholic defenders like to bombard our minds

---

681 Ibid.

with snippets of Bible verses from the Old and New Testament that
might mention fire but have zero reference to Rome's Purgatory.
If we bring Rome's understanding of Purgatory to any of these
scattered verses containing the words fire or purification, they
present no proof. Madrid throws out the vision of Isaiah in chapter
six, the salted by fire statement of Jesus in Mark 9, the Seraphim
(burning ones) of the Old Testament, the presence of God as a pillar
of fire guiding the Nation of Israel to the promised land, and the
fact that the New Testament tells us that our God is a burning fire.
However, not one of these passages teaches, even remotely, the
doctrine of Roman Catholic Purgatory. Remarkably, Madrid bases
his entire argument, along with 1 Corinthians 3, on an accumula-
tion of passages that have nothing to do with Purgatory. Here is his
conclusion:

> So you see, even though St. Paul didn't use the term
> "purgatory" to describe this process of purification
> that some, perhaps many, will undergo before entering
> heaven, the principle of that purification is very clear. It's
> a temporary process of passive purification performed by
> God as a way to cleans [sic] and completely wash a sinner in
> the blood of the Lamb.[682]

Indeed, the apostle Paul does not use the term Purgatory because it
is a Roman Catholic invention. The apostle knows that Christians
are already washed in the blood of Jesus. He knows that all Christians are sanctified already. He knows that by one offering God has
perfected for all time those who are sanctified (Hebrews 10:14).
The apostle knows that of Him all the prophets bear witness that
through His name everyone who believes in Him receives forgiveness of sins (Acts 10:43).

We take notice that the modern defender of Rome shies away
from the force of true Roman Catholic Purgatory. He calls it a
temporary process of passive purification to cleanse and wash a
sinner. However, since the New Catholic Catechism in paragraph

---

682 Ibid., p. 207.

1031 defers to the Council of Florence (1438) for the formulation of her doctrine on Purgatory, we shall compare Florence with Madrid.

> The Council has likewise defined that if those truly penitent have departed in the love of God, before they have made satisfaction by the worthy fruits of penance for sins of commission and omission, *the souls of these are cleansed after death by purgatorial punishments; and so that they may be released from punishments of this kind, the suffrages of the living faithful* are of advantage to them, namely, the sacrifices of Masses, prayers, and almsgiving, and other works of piety, which are customarily performed by the faithful for other faithful according to the institutions of the Church.[683]

The official Roman Catholic teaching on Purgatory is "purgatorial punishment" in which those in Purgatory can be released from such *punishment* by the "suffrages" of the living faithful. This language is altogether different from the soft sell of Madrid's "process of passive purification." Simply put, Purgatory is a painful punishment for sins committed. Therefore, it is an anti-Christ cultic denial of the true gospel. The purification of sins has been accomplished fully by the cross of Christ for all temporal sins.

> And He is the radiance of His glory and the exact representation of His nature, and upholds all things by the word of His power. When *He had made purification of sins*, He sat down at the right hand of the Majesty on high. (Hebrews 1:3)

> But He, having offered *one sacrifice for sins for all time*, sat down at the right hand of God, waiting from that time onward until His enemies be made a footstool for His feet. For by *one offering He has perfected for all time those who are sanctified*. And the Holy Spirit also bears witness to us; for after saying... (Hebrews 10:12-15)

---

683 Council of Florence. Emphasis mine.

In closing we notice that Madrid makes use of Hebrews 12:22-23, wherein the writer mentions what Christians have come to in stark contrast to "the mountain that could not be touched" in the days of Moses. Christians come to the city of God, to the church of the first born, to God the judge of all men, to spirits of just men having been made perfect, and to Jesus the mediator of the New Covenant. Madrid thinks that Purgatory was the place where the just men had been made perfect or complete. However, Purgatory is never mentioned as a place where just men are made perfect. On the contrary, by Madrid's own admission and Roman Catholic doctrine, it is a place where unjust men are punished. Also, Hebrews 10:1 makes it clear that no amount of sacrificing can make perfect anyone who wishes to draw near to worship. It is the application of the righteousness of Jesus and His shed blood that makes one holy and perfect, not punishments endured in a fictitious Purgatory.

> Therefore, when He comes into the world, He says, "Sacrifice and offering Thou hast not desired, but a body Thou hast prepared for Me. *In whole burnt offerings and sacrifices for sin Thou hast taken no pleasure.* Then I said, 'Behold, I have come (In the roll of the book it is written of Me) To do Thy will, O God'. After saying above, "Sacrifices and offerings and whole burnt offerings and sacrifices for sin Thou hast not desired, nor hast Thou taken pleasure in them (which are offered according to the Law) then He said, "Behold, I have come to do Thy will." He takes away the first in order to establish the second. *By this will we have been sanctified through the offering of the body of Jesus Christ <u>once for all</u>.* (Hebrews 10:4-10)

At the end of the day the Bible teaches that all those in Christ are forgiven all of their sins past, present, and future on the sole basis of the penalty that Jesus Christ paid on His cross alone. There is no double jeopardy taught in the Bible. Nor is there a hint or suggestion that a man can pay the price due God's justice by suffering for his own sins.

Conclusion

Patrick Madrid published *Answer Me This!* "to provide factual, convincing answers to people's questions about Catholicism."[684] He has failed to do so, as his answers are neither factual nor convincing. What Madrid has demonstrated for us in his apologetic work, rather, is the typical approach of a Roman Catholic apologist, which is to overwhelm the ignorant and the naïve with sweeping claims, historical glosses and logical leaps that crumble under even modest scrutiny. When subjected to sober investigation, the Roman religion is exposed as the novelty it clearly is, and her defenders as the propagandists they clearly are. The Sacred Congregation of Propaganda was originally constituted by Pope Gregory XV in 1622 to shore up the Roman Catholic religion against the onslaught of Protestant evangelism. It is no surprise that "propaganda" eventually came to refer to the distribution of biased or misleading information. In this, at least, we can say Mr. Madrid has succeeded. His efforts to honor the longstanding tradition of Roman Catholic propaganda through his biased and misleading approach are worthy of the best Prefect of that Sacred Congregation.

We need not revisit Mr. Madrid's every argument, but it will be profitable to conclude with a modest sampling of his methodology. To allege early Roman primacy, Madrid cited Corinth's request for advice from Rome, ignoring Philippi's request to Smyrna and Rome's appeal to Carthage. To support Petrine primacy, Madrid claimed that Paul had not begun his public teaching ministry until first checking with Peter, but the Scriptures indicate Paul began teaching publicly "straightway" (Acts 9:20). To bolster his

---

684 Madrid, p. 9

argument for an infallible Magisterium, he claimed that Jesus had said "He that heareth you heareth me" (Luke 10:16) to the apostles, when in fact Jesus said that not to the Twelve but *to the Seventy*. To support the apostolicity of Mary's *post partum* virginity, he invoked Jerome's novel late fourth century argument, three hundred years removed from the apostles, omitting Basil's concession that it was neither apostolic nor even significant to the Christian faith. To allege ancient reverence of the eastern bishops for *the Pope*, Madrid cited John Chrysostom's reverence *for Peter*—hoping the reader would not know that Chrysostom had nothing to say "in favor of the primacy of the Pope."[685] To prove the intercessory powers of the saints in heaven *now*, Madrid cited Bible verses about the bodily glory of the saints *at the resurrection*. To justify confession to a priest as a prerequisite to reconciliation with God,[686] Madrid appealed to the case of the leper who was reconciled to God *before* showing himself to a priest (Matthew 8:2-4, Mark 1:40-44, Luke 5:12-14; c.f. Luke 17:19). Throughout his arguments, Madrid criticizes the inquirer for not being familiar with Scripture and history. Yet as we have shown, it is Madrid who is ignorant—misreading and misunderstanding the source material, overplaying his hand and outrunning his coverage at every turn.

Had Madrid limited his arguments to history and tradition, we could let him lie in the bed of error that he has made. But Madrid's arguments have a theological and soteriological end in mind, with eternal consequences. While the Scriptures commend sinners to the Gospel of reconciliation to the Father by the death of His Son, Madrid's religion would substitute "Catholicity" for the Gospel, and the Roman Church for the Son. Thus, Madrid concludes that Jesus wants all men to be reconciled to the Father "in and through this one Church He established."[687] In this, Madrid is consistent with his religion which states that "reconciliation with the Church is inseparable from reconciliation with God,"[688] and forgiveness of sins

---

685 *Catholic Encyclopedia*, volume 8:457A.
686 *Catechism of the Catholic Church*, 1445
687 Madrid, p. 31
688 *Catechism of the Catholic Church*, 1445

rests ultimately upon "faith in the Church."[689] In the end, Madrid must convince his readers to *believe in Roman Catholicism*.

Books like Madrid's must be answered in order to contrast starkly the false Gospel of Romanism with the glorious Gospel of Christ. Madrid would exhort his readers to study history, scriptures and traditions, perchance to discover the church Jesus founded, and by that church to gain access to the Father. To enter in and be born again through baptism, one must first discover Roman Catholicism, and place his trust in it, drinking continually from the font of her grace. And even then, Rome cannot guarantee that the believer who drinks thereof will be saved.

But Jesus' says we cannot find His Church unless we are first born again by the Spirit (John 3:3,8), and being born again, we are saved by belief in the Gospel He preached: "He that heareth my word, and believeth on him that sent me, hath everlasting life, and shall not come into condemnation; but is passed from death unto life" (John 5:24). Come to Me, and drink, and you shall never thirst again, He promises: "whosoever drinketh of the water that I shall give him shall never thirst; but the water that I shall give him shall be in him a well of water springing up into everlasting life" (John 4:14). Such faith, *such confidence*, is forbidden in Rome, for it is anathema to believe one "hath everlasting life" and believing, that one "shall not come into condemnation." In Madrid's religion, it is considered the height of arrogance to believe one already possesses eternal life, and the apex of humility to deny it. Rome is therefore a religion that requires *unbelief* in Jesus' Gospel as a condition of entrance! So different are these two religions, the one Jesus established and the one Madrid has offered to us!

Paul warned "If anyone is preaching to you a gospel contrary to the one you received, let him be accursed" (Galatians 1:9). Madrid is such a man and would have us all join him in his error. But unless his eyes are opened to the truth, he is accursed, and his whole religion with him. He has taught a gospel contrary!

---

689 *Catechism of the Catholic Church*, 976

Greek Words

Index

Made in the USA
Las Vegas, NV
30 September 2023

78361289R00188